RECOLLECTIONS OF FRANCE

Contemporary France
General Editor: Jolyon Howorth, University of Bath

Volume 1
Humanity's Soldier: France and International Security, 1919–2001
David Chuter

Volume 2
The Road to War: France and Vietnam, 1944–1947
Martin Shipway

Volume 3
France at War in the Twentieth Century: Propaganda, Myth and Metaphor
Edited by Valerie Holman and Deborah Kelly

Volume 4
Recollections of France: Memories, Identities and Heritage in Contemporary France
Edited by Sarah Blowen, Marion Demossier and Jeanine Picard

To Come
The Extreme Right Wing in France: From Boulanger to Le Pen
Edited by Edward Arnold

Party, Society and Government: Republican Democracy in France
David Hanley

The Shaping of French Environmental Policy
Joseph Szarka

RECOLLECTIONS OF FRANCE

Memories, Identities and Heritage in Contemporary France

Edited by
**Sarah Blowen, Marion Demossier
and Jeanine Picard**

Berghahn Books
New York • Oxford

First published in 2000 by **Berghahn Books**

www.BerghahnBooks.com

©2000 Sarah Blowen, Marion Demossier
and Jeanine Picard

Library of Congress Cataloging-in-Publication Data
Recollections of France : memories, identities and heritage in contemporary France / edited by Sarah Blowen, Marion Demossier and Jeanine Picard.
    p. cm. -- (Contemporary France : 4)
Based on papers from a one-day conference, Recollections of France:
the past, heritage and memories, held Dec. 15, 1997, London.
    Includes biliographical references and index.
    ISBN 1-57181-728-X (alk, paper) -- ISBN 1-57181-499-X (alk. paper)
        1. France--History--20th century--Congresses. I. Blowen, Sarah,
1966- II. Demossier, Marion. III. Picard, Jeanine. IV. Contemporary
France (Providence, R.I.) : v. 4.

DC361.R43 2001
944.083--dc21

2001025284

British Library Cataloguing in Publication Data

A catalogue record for this book is available
from the British Library.

Printed in the United States on acid-free paper

ISBN 1-57181-728-X hardback
ISBN 1-57181-499-X paperback

CONTENTS

ACKNOWLEDGEMENTS

The editors wish to thank the *Service Culturel* of the French Embassy, the *Institut Français*, the British Academy, the University of Bath, the University of the West of England and the ASMCF (Association for the Study of Modern and Contemporary France) for their support of the one-day conference, 'Recollections of France: the past, heritage and memories', which was held in London on 15 December 1997, and which forms the basis of this book.

They would also like to express their gratitude to Ted Freeman. Jolyon Howorth and Julian Swann for their assistance and support throughout this project.

Sarah Blowen, Marion Demossier and Jeanine Picard

Editorial Note

Chapters 3, 5, 7 and 12 have been translated from the French original by the editors. Chapters 10 and 11 have been translated from French with the assistance of Ivan Dufour.

INTRODUCTION

Sarah Blowen, Marion Demossier and Jeanine Picard

Memories, identities and heritage have become the new holy trinity for contemporary academic research. In France, this fascination is borne out by a wide variety of sacred texts, be they Pierre Nora's *Les Lieux de mémoire* (1984–1993) or the more recent *Patrimoine et passions identitaires*, edited by Jacques Le Goff in 1998.[1]

The purpose of the present volume is to explore the relationship between this surge in academic interest and a demonstrable shift in public consciousness and public passions; the contributors exemplify the many and varied forms that these passions take. Its originality resides in the fact that it brings together university scholars and French professionals working in sectors where this shift is particularly in evidence. The combination of a theoretical gaze and practical experience affords a unique insight into France as a cultural construct, highlighting the role played by memory, identity and heritage as manifestations of change at every level of French society.

Change has indeed been profound and has had far reaching consequences. The shift from a rural to an urban society has now been more or less completed in France: the most recent census of 1999 indicates that nearly 80 per cent of the population have adopted an urban way of life. Social problems such as the growth in inequalities and lack of opportunities are therefore increasingly delineated within an urban framework, except when beleaguered French farmers, faced with insurmountable financial problems, make their desperate voice heard. Following the convergence of urban and rural societies, a large consumption of *ruralité* on the

1. For details of these and other texts mentioned in this introduction, see the general bibliography at the end of this volume.

part of town and city dwellers has also taken place, motivated by a nostalgic quest for roots and identity.

Changes have been particularly evident in the country's cultural infrastructure and these specific changes are analysed in the pages that follow. France has responded to global standardisation in a unique way in the shape of support for *exception culturelle* (protectionist measures to exclude the cultural domain from free trade agreements) and the promotion of cultural diversity. Cultural institutions of all kinds have also been used as channels for socio-economic transformation in an attempt to address the social conflicts and economic problems caused by serious decline in traditional industrial and agricultural activities. As one might expect in France, this transformation of cultural practices has almost invariably been institutionalised, with the remit of the French Ministry of Culture encompassing an ever-widening range of activities. Some have been more controversial than others – the support given to graffiti artists was one of the first to come to the attention of the public. As the work of Susan Wright and other commentators has demonstrated, culture has been transformed into a powerful political tool. It has become the object of intense negotiations between the state, its representatives and a whole variety of social groups, be they young followers of hip-hop culture or war veterans, lovers of traditional sailing boats or good food.

Culture is one of the fields of activity in which the highly centralised model of French society has been most overtly challenged. In some cases, the impetus has come from civil society, but in general the decentralisation of cultural decision-making has been the most significant catalyst for change. The opportunities this has presented – as much for crystallising debate at local and regional level as for leading to concrete actions and results – form the background to most of the examples explored in this book.

At the core of the repositioning of cultural activities, the past has become a prime commodity, reworked in a variety of ways. Some of the greatest changes can be observed in the extension of the field of heritage and several sections of the book will address this directly. The authors raise the following questions: how does France's relationship with her past have a direct impact on the cultural practices of her citizens? What are the complex processes by which the various sectors of contemporary French society reinvent the past for their own consumption? What contradictions and conflicts arise when those in charge of cultural institutions come up against those who played a role in the events and actions they wish to recreate? Other chapters will explore how a wide range of cultural activities are instrumental in creating values, which themselves are shaped by the values held by different social groups. It is not only the past, however, that finds itself repackaged: the present itself can be open to the same reinterpretation, as will be argued in the final section of this book.

Memory holds a central position in the shaping of values. The process by which 'recollections' are constructed and the uses to which these constructs are put must be part of any analysis of how individual, professional and local memories express themselves and how they relate to the problematic notion of 'collective memory'. The concept of collective memory has become the subject of intense debate amongst historians and social scientists. According to Maurice Halbwachs, 'collective memory' is defined as an act of remembering which is always social, because what is recalled has to be socially acceptable and the individual actors who construct this memory are not themselves fully aware of the process. The purpose of this book is to argue for a more pragmatic approach, reconciling the part played by individuals within the process of creating shared – albeit fragmented – memories. Memory is thus seen as a constantly regenerative process whereby people learn through their experience. It is by this process that identities emerge in society. Society has become the arena of multiple voices, values and meanings, where the past, the present and the future coexist.

Underpinning both the fascination with the past and the desire to remember is a tacit search for identity. The basic unit for understanding social processes has shifted to the local level as it is at that level that current modes of belonging are re-imagined or reactivated. The days have long passed when one model dominated society as a whole and when some sense could be made of it. French society, like so many others, has become increasingly fragmented and differentiated. Stable identities have thus given way to more transient sets of values. Culture, defined as a set of practical, meaningful, everyday social practices, taking place in regularly used locations within a framework of familiar institutions all adding up to form a specific and complex identity, has followed a similar pattern of fragmentation. This atomisation of society has altered the link between people and their 'imagined' communities. Traditional community values and a sense of the desirability to conform to them have been eroded; conversely, new complex networks of relationships have been created outside the traditional channels, offering new opportunities for self-expression.

These networks find a concrete manifestation in the multifaceted explosion of cultural and festive activities or in the growth of the voluntary sector. On the whole, despite some strong reactionary responses fighting a rearguard action in an attempt to forge inward-looking identities which find their expression in nationalism and religious intolerance, the peaceful defence of a fragmented identity is in tune with the sensibility prevalent in France at the beginning of the new millennium.

In this book, the authors examine the role played by culture in the expression of local and national identity, offering insights into the construction of these identities through new cultural activities. They consider how people living in the present engage with the past and build their future through the consumption of a wide range of cultural artefacts. By taking four different examples – war museums, maritime heritage, culinary heritage and urban cultures – they have attempted to deconstruct some of the micro-narratives and identities which have shaped France since the end of the 1970s.

In the first section 'Making sense of the present', Brian Jenkins and Siân Reynolds help to contextualise the whole and suggest two very different ways in which these examples might be construed by the reader. Brian Jenkins argues that, at an institutional level, the political and socio-economic environment has shaped and is continuing to shape the way in which French cultural identities are expressed. He stresses that the changes analysed in this book take place against a background of rapid social transformation dominated by the crisis of the nation-state. By contrast, Siân Reynolds reflects on the process by which the individual can appropriate objects invested with cultural significance. Taking the works of Marcel Proust and Pierre Nora as a starting point, she elaborates on the way that memory and history, the object and the narrative are interlocked in a complex relationship. She wonders whether the preoccupation with memory is a particular form of displacement activity and what the relationship between the real and the fictive or reconstructed should be.

In the second section 'Memories of War', we begin our exploration of our first thematic example. The museum sector is of particular interest as it is often condemned as a 'dead' cultural institution which has failed to move with the times, its venerable age setting it apart from contemporary concerns. Yet this picture is highly misleading because many museums recognise that they have a duty to reflect the populations they serve and have moved on accordingly. The authors trace the response of museum professionals in particular to the growing demand for sites dedicated to the experience of war in twentieth century France. In many cases, the commemorative zeal has been linked to the anniversaries of key events, such as the fortieth and fiftieth anniversaries of D-Day. In Chapter Three, Marie-Hélène Joly presents an overview of the development of war museums in France since 1945, underlining the way in which successive generations remember war differently and therefore demand different presentations. Her chapter highlights the shift towards the use of museums for the transmission of memories of war and raises questions as to the consequences of this relationship for the field of public history and for the social role of the museum in contemporary France.

The following two chapters draw out the wider implications of recent historical events entering the museum space. Jay Winter continues the debate on public history, focusing his remarks on the creation of the *Historial*, the museum of the First World War situated in Péronne on the Somme. Here, international perspectives meet in a space which began as the vision of one man profoundly affected by his family's experience of war. The Historial owes its present form to a battle between creative and bureaucratic forces which are symbolic of the struggles in the whole cultural sector. Professor Winter's thought-provoking remarks question the role of the historical profession at a time when the private purchase on the past challenges its 'authorial voice'.

Sarah Blowen then explores the development of the Musée de la Résistance et de la Déportation in Grenoble and the central role played by war veterans themselves in its inception. When those who lived the events on display become their guardian fifty years on, certain challenges arise which call into question the function of the museum narrative and the museum object. The chapter examines whether museums anchored to a local past can transcend this to have a global resonance. The author demonstrates that, in refusing to call itself a *musée d'histoire*, the Grenoble museum has been central to the debate as to whether museums should be repositories of memory as opposed to history and whether the past should be used for the transmission of collective values.

In the third section 'Maritime Heritage', the maritime context has been chosen to illustrate how the decline in traditional naval and fishing activities, which shaped an original cultural identity, forced communities to find new ways of exploiting their natural resources. A similar analysis could equally have been applied to rural or industrial areas suffering from the same economic fate;

however, the passion for all things maritime is particularly fascinating as it is relatively new in France.

After years of neglect, during which French specialists envied the British their rather better record of conserving their historic ships and paying tribute to their naval heroes and ordinary seafaring folk, a renewal of interest in maritime heritage has been much in evidence in the last thirty years. One of the side effects is that coastal communities are facing the growing risk of seeing the maritime way of life which is central to their identity relegated to the status of things past, fit only to feed the needs of the local tourist industry. The popularity of cultural tourism makes maritime heritage an increasingly attractive replacement for economically threatened activities such as fishing and ship-building. Life for seafaring communities was inherently perilous but the new dependency on tourism is equally problematic, as exemplified by the havoc wrought by the Erika oil spill on the western coast of France in December 1999.

In Chapter Six, Françoise Péron reflects on the way that the Breton maritime heritage was constructed from the nineteenth century onwards. She examines the scale and success of various heritage activities and ponders on the manner in which this heritage was repackaged to suit modern urban aspirations, in particular the need to find substitute physical and human environments after the loss of a distinctive identity in urban areas.

In the following chapter, the historian François Chappé warns us of some of the dangers inherent in the heritage process, particularly that of rewriting or ignoring social history. He also seeks to arrive at a satisfactory definition of heritage and carries out a challenging analysis of the relationship between heritage and history.

The failure of the Douarnenez venture, where a floating museum was set up at the beginning of the 1990s, is described in Chapter Eight by Jeanine Picard and justifies some of the misgivings expressed in the two previous chapters. The repackaging of maritime heritage can also give rise to tensions between the different parties involved in the creation of a heritage venture. The case study illustrates what is at stake in the future development of maritime heritage, caught between the limited objectives of museum specialists whose priorities may be excessively academic for the tastes of a wider public, and those of private developers with 'theme park' type activities in mind.

In the fourth section 'Culinary Heritage', we move on to an important element of French national identity which is highly instrumental in the way the country is perceived abroad. The introduction into the French diet of standardised and processed 'fast' food for the mass market, has provoked a strong reaction in some quarters. The desire for authenticity and contact with nature, tradition and the past has become a complement to urban living. An exploration of the concept of culinary heritage and *produits de terroir* (traditional food or agricultural produce of specific geographical and historical origin) shows how rural France has adapted to the restructuring of French agriculture since the 1960s. It also illustrates the changing patterns of French food consumption which have led to the emergence of what has been termed *vagabondage alimentaire* (culinary 'pick and mix'). At another level, the French state, farming associations and culinary experts have supported the inclusion of culinary heritage and *produits de terroir* as part of broader policies designed to promote tourism and economic development.

In Chapter Nine, Marion Demossier charts the progress of culinary heritage from its emergence as a literary genre to its modern guise as a political and economic tool. She examines the relationship between economic changes and territorial construction, leading to the recomposition of social identities. Finally, she discusses how these changes have interacted with new patterns of consumption and the urbanisation of French society, highlighting the role of the tourist in giving a new lease of life to certain foodstuffs.

Culinary heritage has taken on a European dimension. In Chapter Ten, Laurence Bérard and Philippe Marchenay discuss the role of anthropologists who are called upon to research and define this phenomenon. The European legislative context is explored together with the debates provoked by the creation of regional culinary inventories. They argue for a critical, comparative and pragmatic approach to the study of *produits de terroir* and examine the nature of their role as 'experts' in the fabrication of values.

In the following chapter, François Portet offers a detailed case study of the Burgundy region. Based on his professional experience as regional adviser on ethnology, he recalls the different steps in the composition of a culinary heritage at regional level and describes some of the principal research undertaken since the 1960s. Although reputed internationally for its wines, Burgundy is also home to other emblematic products, notably Charolais beef and Bresse poultry. By looking at these two examples, Portet examines the evolution of food consumption in rural Burgundy and the way in which it can be defined by sets of structural oppositions: rural versus urban, ordinary versus festive, lean versus fat.

Finally, the last section of the book 'Urban Cultures and new expressions' deals with French cities, as young and growing cultural spaces, and the way they look to the past or subscribe to present trends in order to construct their future. They have been confronted with new cultural, social and economic challenges, particularly that of integrating an increasing plurality of recollections, many from beyond the boundaries of metropolitan France. As a place of conflictual expressions, the city offers an example of social identities that are both condensed by its specific and delineated space and encouraged to intertwine and create new social forms.

In Chapter Twelve, Susan Milner provides a comprehensive survey of the heady rise of cultural policy as a central tenet of local development, against the backdrop of the decentralisation of political decision-making. She discusses the concept of urban identities in the context of post-industrial France and highlights recent trends, such as new contractual relationships between councils, service providers and associations that have consolidated the increasing role of cultural policies as agents of change.

François Ménard then looks at the use of cultural projects in districts where integration and social cohesion are not possible through normal economic channels. Focusing on programmes related to hip-hop culture, he argues that the relationship between the target public and the institutions involved is an uneasy one: the 'top-down' approach is abandoned in favour of genuine partnerships only with great difficulty. He reflects on the fact that new urban cultural practices, notably those developed around hip-hop, are only assimilated once they have lost their radical edge.

In the last chapter, the urban landscape and its culture are explored by Chris Warne. In an in-depth study of hip-hop culture, the street is presented as the main stage of social discontent and the focal point for negotiating social identities. He explores the various cultural functions of the street and the wider meaning of urban culture in contemporary France. The street is seen as a guarantor of personal and social authenticity, a space invested by those who do not find their needs met in any institutionalised form.

Despite the variety of approaches and themes developed in these five sections, the reader is invited to adopt a cross-thematic exploration of four common preoccupations running through all the contributions: the heritage industry and the museum sector as agents of change; history and memories as conflictual voices; time and space as cultural markers; and finally the negotiation between the individual and society in the process of cultural construction.

All the authors show that genuine attempts are being made to channel public interest in cultural projects and heritage in order to create new dynamics, especially at local and regional community levels. However, this path is recognised to be a perilous one: the creation of a *lien social* is often hostage to outside economic factors or power struggles. It can only exist if common values emerge as representative of a collective identity. In that process, recollections are constructed and often find themselves put to uses for which they were never intended, or they are appropriated by groups who transform their meaning. With every generational change, new ways of remembering and identifying are developed and the notion of what can constitute a legitimate *lieu de mémoire* is extended. This is of course a positive development, but the process, which finds its academic corollary in the work of Pierre Nora for example, is itself challenged on two counts: firstly, for creating a hierarchy of what is worthy of remembrance, promotion, protection or celebration. Secondly, by extension, this hierarchy itself engenders imitation and an element of falsification – new myths – when it is seen that such labels can create public demand.

It could be argued that *appellation contrôlée* is a notion that has spread to the whole fabric of France. This has far-reaching consequences in the search for an identity fixed in a historical continuum which would dispel the fears of coping with rapid social change. For ironically, the process of *labélisation* serves only to distance the past: as a consequence, heritage becomes a fixed institutionalised fact and any organic relationship with the past is lost.

PART I

MAKING SENSE OF
THE PRESENT

1

RECONSTRUCTING THE PAST:

In Search of New 'National Identities'?

Brian Jenkins

For a long time the writing of French history was profoundly influenced by what are now referred to as 'grand narratives', which structured our perceptions of the national past. The concern to tell a convincing and coherent story, to make history intelligible and relevant to the present, led historians from a variety of schools and disciplines to focus on the *longue durée*, to seek out the underlying processes of change, often linked to notions of social progress, and to invest history with an inherent and unfolding logic.

These narratives have since lost some of their persuasive power. They are now often viewed with suspicion, as ideologically driven in an age mistrustful of all ideologies and as the product of a particular historical mindset, imposing preconceived patterns on the complexities of lived historical experience. The current vogue is to deconstruct such narratives, to reveal their historical relativism, and to uncover aspects of the past which they were seen to have misrepresented or ignored. The enlargement of the historian's territory, a recognition of the complexity of reality, a new sensitivity to the nature of historical discourse, are all features of this historiographical sea change. The range and diversity of themes covered in this collection of essays, their conceptualisation in terms of heritage, memory, identity and reconstruction of the past, is symptomatic of such developments.

This shift of perspective inevitably raises questions about the concept of national identity. France is one of the oldest established states in the world, and her self-image as a unique and exemplary nation has drawn more on universalist discourses than on narrow definitions of common ethnicity. Whether as the romanticised *France éternelle* with a privileged historical destiny, or as the incarnation of civilising Enlightenment values, or as the progenitor of revolutionary ideas, France has a past whose enduring immanence in the present has sustained this albeit ambiguous and sometimes conflictual national identity.

However, nations are relatively recent artefacts, socially and ideologically constructed. They are not impervious to processes of historical change, nor indeed to reinterpretations of the past. And the post-modernist vogue for the deconstruction of historical 'meta-narratives' cannot simply be dismissed as an intellectual fad. It reflects the genuine novelty of historical conditions in the late twentieth century, and a real 'crisis of credibility' for at least some of these explanatory orthodoxies. In as far as these traditional narratives have underpinned the construction of French national identity, their crisis might be expected to have weakened the edifice of nationhood itself.

So what happens when the complex fabric of national identity begins to unravel, when historical myths, symbols and practices lose their discursive power? For Ernest Renan (1882), 'the common possession of a rich legacy of memories' is one of the two elements that constitute the 'soul' of a nation, the other being 'the actual consent, the desire to live together, the will to continue to value the heritage that has been received in common'.[1] Is that *desire*, that *will* at risk now that historical certainties are being challenged and historical continuities are being severed? Or will the re-examination of the past uncover new sources of solidarity and collective pride which are more relevant to contemporary realities and a more solid basis for future cohesion?

French national identity has traditionally been highly politicised, for at least three major reasons. First, because of the key historical role of the state in building national consciousness; a process which began under the absolute monarchy, was accelerated by the Revolution and Napoleon, and 'completed' under successive Republics since 1870 through the gradual integration of different regions, social classes and ethnic minorities into the national community, not to mention women, the history of whose relationship to the nation has

---

1. E. Renan, 'Qu'est-ce qu'une nation?' (Paris, 1882) republished in J. Hutchinson and A. D. Smith, *Nationalism*, Oxford, Oxford University Press, 1994, p.17.

yet to be fully explored. Second, because this deep interdependence of state and nation has ever since the Revolution made national identity a politically divisive concept; rival ideological movements seeking to control the state have claimed to be the true representatives of authentic 'national' traditions and aspirations.[2] Finally, ever since the Revolution, the French state, especially in its democratic form as *la République,* has promoted the idea of France as an exemplary nation with a universal vocation, a world power with a *mission civilisatrice,* a country whose values were those to which the rest of humanity aspired, and whose duty it was to disseminate these values, not least in the colonial territories where it had direct influence.

The mobilising myths of French national identity – echoed in flags, anthems, public holidays, mottoes, school textbooks, anniversaries, monuments and street names – testify to these strongly political overtones, which though far from unique are more pronounced than in many other countries. Furthermore, these myths have been mediated largely through institutional agencies, some more consensual – the 'assimilationist' Republican state, *l'Ecole laïque, le service militaire,* the *francophonie* of former Empire, *le Code de la nationalité* – others more partisan, such as the revolutionary legacy through the organised socialist and labour movement, *la France éternelle* through the Catholic Church and the Army officer corps.

These longer historical traditions were supplemented by new ones born in the Occupation and Liberation era. The socio-economic reforms of the post-war period built a thirty-year social-democratic consensus in Western Europe which bound state and nation together more completely than before, and in France *l'Etat-Providence* (welfare state) and the notion of public service still retain the capacity to mobilise popular support. The dominant mass political movements of the 1950s and 1960s, Gaullism and Communism, both drew on their patriotic credentials as the main organisers of resistance to the Nazi occupation and the fiercest defenders of national sovereignty against post-war American domination. Indeed, in one author's view the common ground for the 1970s *Union de la Gauche* (the Socialist-Communist alliance) and Mitterrand's 1981 election victory was a revival of the essentially nationalist 'Left resistance-liberation discourse' of 1944–5.[3]

2. B. Jenkins, *Nationalism in France: Class and Nation since 1789,* London, Routledge, 1990.

3. G. Ross, 'Adieu vieilles idées: the middle strata and the decline of resistance-liberation left discourse in France' in J. Howorth and G. Ross (eds), *Contemporary France: A Review of Interdisciplinary Studies, Vol. 1,* London, Frances Pinter, 1987, pp.57–83.

The Gaullist regime of the 1960s appeared to have successfully synthesised some of the conflictual elements in this complex national mythology, and to have laid the bases for a more consensual and self-confident national identity. Empire was finally abandoned and the Army was neutralised as a political force. Economic modernisation was vigorously promoted by state-led industrial policy within the liberalising framework of the European Economic Community (EEC). Secularisation in a mass consumer society reduced the political significance of religious belief. The presidential structures of the Fifth Republic were consolidated on the basis of strong majority coalitions, and the anti-constitutional opposition that had bedevilled all previous regimes virtually disappeared. De Gaulle's foreign policy exploited the 'space' between the power blocs – adopting a critical and 'semi-detached' position inside the Western Alliance, and a distinctive vision of the future of Europe inside the institutions of the EEC – thereby contriving to create an image of independence and world status. At least until the events of May 1968, these formulae appeared to have re-established national optimism and self-belief on a broad basis, extending well into the electoral constituency of the Left.

However, what remained intact in Gaullist nationalism was the republican view of the state as the focus of national identity, both internally as the incarnation of the 'general will' and externally as the sovereign agent of the national interest. Indeed, this image of the state was reinforced by its new depoliticised, technocratic managerialism and by the overblown rhetoric of *grandeur*. When, in the 1970s and 1980s, the capacity of national governments to 'deliver the goods' was seriously called into question, what has been called 'the crisis of political representation' (electoral volatility, abstentionism, protest votes, reduced support for mainstream parties) was accompanied by growing introspection about the nature of national identity itself. This may be conceptualised as an increasing separation between state and nation, a particularly problematic development in France because of the historical symbiosis between the two ideas. In as far as it has become detached from the state, the nation is an increasingly uncertain entity, open to redefinition.

Globalisation and the nation-state

It has now become commonplace to argue that even relatively large and formerly powerful nation-states like France have lost leverage over a range of domestic policies as a result of their integration into an increasingly globalised market economy. While their sovereignty remains intact in the sense that the nation-state is still the main framework for the ratification of decisions and the organisation of consent, their autonomy is diminished in the sense that external constraints prevent them from developing indigenous solutions to internal problems. Sovereignty without autonomy or responsibility without power may weaken 'legitimacy' (e.g.'the crisis of political representation'), unless popular expectations about what the nation-state can deliver are significantly reduced. This may be more difficult to achieve in countries like France with a legacy of great-power status, than in those that have never nurtured such pretensions.

However, globalisation is not some bland descriptive term which simply records the deepening interdependence of national economies. It is an ideologically charged concept which reflects the political victory of a particular model of socio-economic organisation, i.e.market liberalism, and the defeat of its main rivals, the post-war social-democratic consensus in Western Europe and the communist command economies in the former Soviet bloc. Here is not the place to debate whether this political outcome should be seen as the inevitable and irreversible result of global economic processes, or rather as a decisive victory for one side in the 'class struggle'. It is worth remembering however that globalisation was previously described by the radical Left as 'international capitalism', and that behind its pretended neutrality the new term celebrates the prospect of the capitalist restructuring of the globe in the image of the unfettered free market.

Traditional socialism, as an ideology and discourse underpinning the state as an agent of social transformation, is thus in crisis. Arguably, so is the ideology and discourse of liberalism, in its broad sense as an Enlightenment philosophy based on the freedom of the individual. The notion that the economic liberalism of the free market goes hand in hand with liberal democracy, human rights and social tolerance is increasingly exposed as a myth, as its eager recipients in Eastern Europe have quickly discovered. Its perpetrators in the West, who should have known better, are now having to come to terms with the social and political costs of this crude equation between deregulated economic individualism and the free exercise of civil and democratic liberties. Fukuyama's suggestion that history itself has come to an end, because liberal capitalism and liberal democracy together provide the best attainable model of social organisation, is based on the illusion that these two elements are in fact compatible. In reality the tensions between the two have been the source of many of the conflicts that have driven history along over the last two hundred years, and there are few signs that these tensions have been resolved.[4]

The reinvention of the public domain, and of the state as an enabler, regulator and coordinator rather than as an interventionist centralised bureaucracy, is thus very much on the agenda. In the case of France, where national identity has been so closely bound up with the image of the state as the incarnation of the 'general will', the restitution of the state's credibility is vital for the maintenance of collective solidarities. However, this will require public recognition of the French state's reduced autonomy on the world stage – the collapse of the bloc system makes the Gaullist strategy for limited national self-assertion obsolete – and its reduced capacity to engineer domestic change. The continued aspiration to play a leading role in the construction of Europe is one potential source of renewed legitimacy. Another is the process of devolved responsibility which began with the decentralisation reforms of the early 1980s, and which brings France in line with general trends across the European Union. Both developments, however, reflect a new situation whereby 'authority is scattered and sovereignty shared'[5] and where 'government' is being replaced by 'multi-level governance'. In this context, there is no longer any room for the concept of the 'heroic' nation-state, either as a world actor or as the sole legitimate representative of an undifferentiated citizenry.

Multicultural France: state and civil society

Two inherent features of the French state have been so widely noted and analysed that they have become proverbial. The first is its centralisation and tentacular reach, the supposed corollary of which is that intermediate institutions between state and citizen have remained relatively weak, and that the growth of 'civil soci-

---

4. F. Fukuyama, *The End of History and the Last Man*, London, Hamish Hamilton, 1992.

5. U.Bullman, 'The politics of the Third Level' in C. Jeffery (ed.), *The Regional Dimension of the European Union: Towards a Third Level in Europe?* London, Frank Cass, 1997, p.9.

ety' has been stunted.[6] Critics point not only to the fetters on economic freedom and individual enterprise, but also to the lack of
local government autonomy, the low membership of political parties and trade unions, the weakness of all those forms of collective
self-organisation and associational activity (*vie associative*) which
sustain political and cultural pluralism. The second related feature
is its assimilationist ethos, which has made it intolerant of diversity in its efforts to create a homogeneous culture based on undifferentiated citizenship. This formula once proved relatively
effective in diluting indigenous regional identities and integrating
foreigners of largely European origin, though it was far less successful in assimilating the colonial subjects of the French Empire.
The post-war migratory flows from these former colonies, and
especially from North Africa, have further exposed the limitations
of the French political and cultural 'melting-pot'.[7]

With the benefit of hindsight we can now recognise that these
traditional features of the French state were becoming increasingly
anachronistic throughout the post-war period. The economic modernisation which has transformed France's socio-occupational
structure was already underway in the 1950s, gradually undermin-
ing social identities based on class and religion, and weakening the
organisations and institutions which reflected and articulated these
identities.[8] The disappearance of the traditional peasantry; the
emergence of the new 'middle strata' of salaried executives, technicians and professionals; the fragmentation of the working class
under the impact of new technologies, changed working environments, feminisation, immigration and mass consumerism (the
alleged *embourgeoisement* of better-paid workers); all combined to
produce a more pluralistic society based on a diversity of life-styles
and increasingly individualistic, rather than collective, social aspirations. Despite resistance in the 1950s from Communists, Gaullists
and Poujadists alike to what was often perceived as 'americanisation', the emergence of an advanced capitalist and later a post-
industrial society was irresistible and would inevitably erode some
of the distinctive characteristics of French 'exceptionalism'.

6. See, for example, M. Crozier, *La société bloquée*, Paris, Seuil, 1970 and S. Hoff-
mann, *Decline or Renewal? France since the 1930s*, New York, Viking, 1974.

7. See M. Silverman, *Deconstructing the Nation: Immigration, Racism and Citizenship in Modern France*, London, Routledge, 1992. See also P. Fysh and J. Wolfreys,
The Politics of Racism in France, London, Macmillan, 1998.

8. See H. Mendras and A. Cole, *Social Change in Modern France*, Cambridge,
Cambridge University Press, 1991.

In this respect the movement of May 1968 was emblematic. It harnessed the aspirations of new occupational categories and of a self-confident post-war generation impatient with the authoritarianism and paternalism of traditional elites, as exemplified politically by the bureaucratic structures of the Gaullist regime on the one hand and the French Communist Party on the other. At one level the movement expressed a cultural individualism which would all too easily be converted into the market consumerism of the neo-liberal economic model, atomistic and corrosive of collective values. At another level, however, it reflected the revolt of 'civil society' against an overbearing state, and would lay the foundations for new solidarities, new patterns of sociability and new forms of collective organisation.

The broad 'social movements' of the 1970s – regionalism, feminism, ecology, workplace democracy – have not all maintained their momentum, but they remain a focus for collective action in *la vie associative* and have since been supplemented by new themes, especially those concerned with poverty, anti-racism and 'social exclusion'. The overall effect has been to widen the gap between an increasingly diverse, pluralistic and multicultural French society on the one hand; and on the other a French state which still aspires to represent a culturally homogeneous nation.

Today it is, of course, the multi-ethnic composition of French society that dramatises this multiculturalism. In this context, the mobilising national myths of *la République une et indivisible* (not to mention *nos ancêtres les gaulois*) appear at best irrelevant and at worst insulting. *Liberté, égalité, fraternité* has a hollow ring for the descendants of French colonialism. The mythology of the Resistance has little resonance for those more likely to remember the Algerian War. The secular convictions of the Republican Left look more like ethnocentric intolerance when used to forbid Muslim headscarves in state schools. When the *Front National* can hide its racist nationalism in the respectable cloak of assimilationist Republicanism, arguing that Muslim communities are culturally incapable of being assimilated, it is surely time to abandon monolithic views of Frenchness and to acknowledge the rich multicultural texture of French identity.

Conclusion

When the final whistle blew in the football World Cup Final in Paris on 12 July 1998, one of the French television commentators saluted the victory of *la France plurielle*. France's multi-ethnic national team is a convenient symbol for the constituent elements of contemporary national identity. In their unity, they reflect their common citizenship of a state that has always proclaimed itself to be in the vanguard of human rights and civil liberties. The will to make this ideal a reality provides the kind of common purpose which, for Renan, secures nationhood. In their diversity, they reflect a multicultural France which not only has a present, but also a past – a 'rich legacy of memories' in Renan's words again, a legacy that has all too often been neglected in a historiography constrained by state ideologies.

The weakening of these constraints is at one level liberating. It awakens our historical consciousness to hitherto unacknowledged contradictions and anomalies. It opens up new fields of enquiry and reveals the complex fabric of social and cultural life in cities and regions; the submerged identities of hitherto neglected communities; activities and practices that have previously been confined to the margins of historical scholarship. At the same time this liberation is disquieting. It may uncover unpalatable truths which disturb comfortable prejudices and conventional assumptions. We cannot escape the need to make sense of what is uncovered, to reconstruct what has been 'deconstructed', to develop new narratives, more tentative perhaps than those that they seek to replace, but no less interpretive in their drive to understand rather than just to know. One of the novelties of this collection of essays is the acknowledgement that this quest is not only the business of academic historians, but of all those professions engaged in exploring the complexities of the past, and in mediating its presentation in the form of heritage and sites of remembrance.

In such reappraisals and revelations, however, lie the foundations of a reinvented national identity. One which draws more on the lived experience of civil society and less on inflated political discourses. One which promotes the ideal of equal citizenship at every level, but simultaneously celebrates cultural diversity. This new sense of nationhood would perhaps be less heroic and less assertive than before, but more attuned to the challenges facing contemporary democratic societies, and therefore no less exemplary, and no less distinctively French.

2

RECALLING THE PAST AND RECREATING IT:

'Museums Actual and Possible'

Siân Reynolds

Is it true, as Pierre Nora claimed in 1984, that memory becomes precious just when it vanishes? 'On ne parle tant de mémoire que parce qu'il n'y en a plus'. What he seems to mean is not that individuals have forgotten their own past, but that collective repositories of memory – such as the French *paysans* – have been destroyed or scattered by devastating and rapid change in recent times. Memory as something magical, often tied to physical objects, rituals or sensations, can be contrasted as it is by Nora, with history, which implies critical reflection: memory is poetry, history is prose. Or as Antoine Prost has strikingly put it, memory is in the shell-holes and dugouts, history in the educational museums about the First World War which show how the battles were fought.[1] In fact it can sometimes seem as if memory and history, authentic object and superimposed narrative, are still fighting it out in today's museums.

The late twentieth century has certainly been a time of unprecedented memorialisation, with even the recent past already being seen as a world we have lost. Centenaries govern public events and the arts, costume dramas dominate cinema and television sched-

---

1. P. Nora, 'La fin de l'histoire-mémoire' in P. Nora (ed.), *Les Lieux de mémoire*, Vol. I, La République, Paris, Gallimard, 1984, p. 23: 'People talk so much about memory [today], because it no longer exists'. The whole collection has now been published in paperback (Paris, Gallimard Quarto, 1997) and a selection is available in English. Cf. Antoine Prost, *Douze leçons sur l'histoire*, Paris, Seuil, 1996, p. 300.

ules. Anyone over the age of forty can today see the toys and house-hold goods of his or her infancy carefully preserved in museums of childhood or everyday life. How different these museums are from those of fifty years ago! The old glass cases, showing real but mys-terious objects (fossils, spoons, stuffed animals or clocks), unmedi-ated fragments of the past, have been replaced by reconstructed front parlours, kitchens or coalmines, accompanied by explana-tions, spoken and written. Coherence of interpretation (based on history) has largely replaced an arrangement of objects which may have carried an implicit world-view, but which seemed to the visi-tor – especially the child – an arbitrary but magical collection.

'Museums of childhood' did not exist in Proust's day (for which his readers will be thankful: but it is a sign of our times that 'Tante Léonie's bedroom', a fictional *lieu de mémoire*, has been reconstructed in the house in Illiers where the novelist stayed as a child). However, it was in his day, the late nineteenth century, that many national museums were founded, often in celebration of an imagined national past. Pierre Nora suggests that a critical turning-point occurred at very much the same time, at the turn of the century, when memory became, as he puts it, 'central to philosophy with Bergson, central to the personality with Freud, and central to auto-biographical literature with Proust'.[2] Nora argues that this moment marks the shift of memory from the collective (unreflective, sacred) to the individual (conscious, historical). Proust does indeed provide suggestive illustration of the shift. It takes place almost before our eyes in the pages devoted to the church of Saint-Hilaire at Combray, for example. For the child Marcel, the church had possessed magical qualities, which the older narrator recognises have nothing to do either with aesthetic beauty nor even with religious faith: 'L'abside de l'église de Combray, peut-on vraiment en parler? Elle était si grossière, si dénuée de beauté artistique et même d'élan religieux'.[3] The inhabitants of Combray did not attend church for spiritual inspi-ration so much as for social and collective confirmation of their iden-tity – in a word for the gossip that Eulalie reports to Tante Léonie. The age of faith might have passed, but the church was still the cen-tre of communal life, the vanishing point of every perspective in Combray, as the child realised: 'C'était le clocher de Saint-Hilaire qui donnait à toutes les occupations, à toutes les heures, à tous les points

2. P. Nora, *Les Lieux de mémoire*, I, p.35.
3. M. Proust, *A la recherche du temps perdu*, Vol. I, 'Du côté de chez Swann', Paris, Pléiade edition, 1962, p. 62: 'What is there to say about the apse in the church at Com-bray? It was so crude, so lacking in artistic beauty and even in religious inspiration'.

de vue de la ville, leur figure, leur couronnement, leur consécra-
tion'.[4] It is for this reason that it is central to childhood recollection.
By the time the narrator has grown up and become a connoisseur of
ecclesiastical architecture, things are no longer the same. The church
is no longer the focal point of the community, and in any case the
individual has come to the realisation that even revisiting places
from our past will not restore them, since their existence is not an
objective geographical reality, but a personal construction:

> Les lieux que nous avons connus n'appartiennent pas qu'au monde
> de l'espace où nous les situons pour plus de facilité. Ils n'étaient
> qu'une mince tranche au milieu d'impressions contigues qui for-
> maient notre vie d'alors: le souvenir d'une certaine image n'est que
> le regret d'un certain instant; et les maisons, les routes, les avenues,
> sont fugitives, hélas! comme les années.[5]

Pierre Nora appears to have seen this perceived shift from the
collective to the individual as a challenge, a stimulus to recreate
public history on a national scale. The rich collection of essays
under his editorship, *Les Lieux de mémoire*, which has been one
point of departure for the present book, as it has for many other
attempts to grapple with memory and history, is also a thoroughly
French undertaking, as he makes quite clear, arguing that apparently unconnected items are linked in an invisible network of associations, re-creating a collective memory, in this case shared by
French people. 'Les lieux sont notre moment d'histoire nationale'.[6]

4. Ibid., p. 64. 'it was the belfry of Saint-Hilaire which provided the shape, the
crowning point and the consecration for every occupation, every time of day, every
vantage point in the town'.
5. Ibid., p. 427: 'The places we have known do not just belong to the spatial world,
in which we place them for the sake of convenience. They were only a slim section
in the midst of the sequence of impressions that made up our lives in those days: the
memory of a certain image is no more than nostalgia for a certain moment; houses,
roads and avenues are all fleeting, alas! like the years'. (On this occasion, the narrator is describing the parade of carriages in the Bois de Boulogne, lost forever.)
6. P. Nora, *Lieux de mémoire*, I, p. 42. Cf. the back-cover statement in the new
paperback edition: 'The rapid disappearance of our national memory today calls
for an inventory of the places in which it has been selectively embodied and which,
through human will-power or the work of centuries, remain as its most striking
symbols. [This will be] a history of France between memory and history... the
selective and learned exploration of our collective heritage'. See also Nora's claim
that a further 'formidable décrochement' (a great dislocation), took place in the
1980s to inspire the project, *Le Monde des Livres*, 5 February 1993, and ibid., a discussion of the 'Frenchness' of the collection in Stefan Collini's review; cf. for a view
of the contents of *Les Lieux de mémoire*, P. France and S. Reynolds, 'A post-modern
cathedral' in *Modern and Contemporary France*, NS4 (2), 1996, pp. 227–30.

Nora's project had an explicit agenda then, to compensate for loss of a vanished France. It may be tempting, considering French history over the last century or so, to consider France as a special case, to see the vogue for memory, the mushroom growth of the heritage industry or 'la sauvegarde du patrimoine' as a particularly French form of displacement activity. Where once there was an apparently coherent sense of nationhood and national culture, it is now sometimes suggested that this is under threat and at risk of splintering. Globalisation has brought cultural threats to France from both outside and inside: from Japanese technology and American television, from the English language and from foreign popular music; and from several immigrant cultures within France, which appear to have encouraged an allergic home grown reaction in the shape of the *Front National*. France can no longer claim to be quite the world leader it once was in cultural production, whether automobile design, the cinema, or even gastronomy: the competition has become more intense. If one looks at some of the topics covered in this book – such as the Breton fishing industry, and the old and new *produits de terroir* – it certainly looks as if the vanishing of the 'real thing' has prompted an effort to reproduce it in some form: the replica fishing vessel, the new 'local' cheese based on modern technology. The reconstruction of the past in the form of heritage sends a clear signal that it is not easily recoverable by other means. That in turn has prompted fears in some quarters that the French past is somehow irrevocably lost and even that any attempt to 're-package it' is an admission of defeat.

One can nuance this view in a number of ways. Firstly France is far from alone in this endeavour, although the strength and variety of the French commemorative effort is certainly remarkable. As many British observers have pointed out, Britain too has a spectacular 'heritage industry' which has reflected a similar process of loss both of economic reality and historical certainty, and it too has attracted criticism.[7] As an old industrial country, Britain has its share of mining museums where there were once, quite recently working coalpits. The phenomenon is not only confined to 'old' countries. The Museum of Canadian Civilisation in

---

7. Cf. R. Hewison, *The Heritage Industry: Britain in a Climate of Decline*, London, Methuen, 1987. This and other critiques of 'heritage' by 'the metropolitan intelligentsia' are discussed by Raphael Samuel in an essay which reads as if it is slightly tongue-in-cheek: 'Heritage-baiting', in *Theatres of Memory*, London, Verso, 1994, pp. 259–273. The title of Samuel's book nods homage to Nora, while being rather different.

Ottawa contains an extraordinary juxtaposition: a collection of ancient totem poles from the West Coast – uprooted, displaced but undeniably genuine – alongside a sophisticated reconstruction of Canada's past, concentrating on the period of European (mainly French) settlement. The display contains a ship's interior, a whaling station, a main street and so on, lovingly constructed to give a sense of the past, with full explanations, but hardly any of the objects on show are 'real'. Almost all of them are acknowledged to be replicas. It is very popular with visitors, though specialists are divided. This seems an extreme case of the literal fictionalisation of the past, just where we would expect to find its reality: in a museum. This suggests that the creation of the global village has prompted a belated search for the ancestral village everywhere.

This leads to a second question in the French context. What should be the relation between the real and the fictive or reconstructed? Is the current combination of objects and narrative in museums, in France and elsewhere, a good or a bad thing? Is there even any difference between a replica and an original? Does it matter that the caves at Lascaux have been painstakingly reconstructed alongside the original, in order to preserve the paintings from disintegrating under the breath of the visitors? Yes and no, perhaps. The authentic artefact is certainly a thing of value to the curator, while the historian professionally sets great store by the authentic document in the archives. Both are surely 'the real thing', the evidence that cannot be faked. I would argue, though, that the archive document and the object in the museum have very similar status – and we need in both cases to be simultaneously very respectful and very wary – as we would more readily perhaps with oral history and the témoignage. There is a fetishism of the archive among historians, as once there was a fetishism of the artefact among museum curators. Yet both need to be contextualised if their authenticity is not to be exaggerated.

Let me give a French example. The city of Grenoble has a new Musée de la Résistance (see Chapter 5). Educational in design, videos, photographs and texts structure the visitor's progress. Its publicity describes it as having 'a resolutely contemporary museographic approach'. Yet the only item in it which really imprinted itself upon my memory when I visited this museum, was an authentic set of wooden doors from the police cells, in which Resistance suspects were locked up, and on which graffiti from the war years still survive. Rescued by chance from demolition, they carry an electrical charge which is very moving. The critical historian has a problem with these doors: they have been taken out of their original 'place' and re-erected in the artificial setting of the museum; furthermore, the narrative surrounding them – to anyone aware of the crisis of historiography about France's experience of the Second World War – perpetuates a certain heroic view of the Resistance which is open to challenge. Like the archive, when the counter-evidence has been destroyed, the real thing too can give a partial view. The problem is to decode what we are being shown, in other words to ask questions.

But who are the 'we' in that sentence? The third point I would make is one about the consumers of heritage culture, who need not be assumed to be innocent of preconceptions. It is true that today the majority of visitors to museums are schoolchildren on organised visits.[8] They are certainly too young to have many memories of their own, but it would be unwise to assume that they therefore have no access to collective memory. We are all provided with the elements of such a memory if only by our school days: the emphasis may change as different concerns govern the syllabus. In my own childhood in Wales, heroes and heroines of Welsh history played a leading role in our history lessons; my children, growing up in the 1970s, were subjected to several doses of cavemen, Romans, Tudors and Stuarts; for today's high school pupils all over Britain, the twentieth century and its wars have come to dominate the history syllabus. As for their cultural consumption, television has given students and schoolchildren a shared culture as homogenous as some cultures of the past. Significantly perhaps, many of the contributors to the first and most coherent volume of *Les Lieux de mémoire* belonged to the last generation to have experienced personally the Third and Fourth Republican version of the *école Jules Ferry*, another supposedly homogeneous culture. Their sense of loss had a particular thrust, shaped by their own schooling and collective memory, and that volume both celebrated and demystified the golden legend of the Republic 'one and indivisible', before the enterprise snowballed into a much larger and inevitably more diffuse undertaking.

So the 'we' who visit monuments and museums, who watch heritage festivals – like the Bastille Day pageant in Paris in 1989 – do so with our own cultural baggage, acquired at school or at home, and have questions to ask. Depending on our date of birth and education, we may be more or less skilled at deciphering the

8. J. Winter reports that 45,000 of the 70,000 visitors to the *Mémorial de la Grande Guerre* at Péronne were children (see J. Winter, Chapter 4).

objects and contexts offered to us: there are after all more old people in the western population than there ever have been in the
past. Even little schoolchildren today tour museums with ques-
tionnaires in hand, to prompt their spirit of enquiry. Our students
may not all turn into professional historians, but they can all
become critical citizens who visit museums. As the late Raphael
Samuel put it in his cheerful essay on 'heritage-baiting':

> There is no reason to think that people are more passive when look-
> ing at old photographs or film footage, handling a museum exhibit,
> following a local history trail or even buying a historical souvenir,
> than when reading a book. People do not simply 'consume' images
> in the way in which, say, they buy a bar of chocolate. As in any
> reading, they assimilate them as best they can to pre-existing
> images and narratives.[9]

So is history too important to be left to the historians – or to put it
another way, are we all historians once we step into a museum?
Should we welcome as a challenge all the theme parks, new museums and television documentaries which undoubtedly manipulate
the past in some ways, creating new myths? 'The new museology'
in France and elsewhere is in part a reaction to the perceived anti-
quarianism of the museums of the past. Yet as the chapters in this
book show, the museums of the new generation can take many
forms, being more or less explicit about narrating the past, encouraging more or less critical reflection on the part of the visitor, providing more or fewer 'magical' objects in which memory reposes. If
one can hazard a value judgement here, a pedagogical approach
may be most valuable at local and specialised level; there are perhaps more obvious risks in the idea of museums as repositories of
national identity (see Chapter 1). So let me end by evoking an
example from the past, an international project, located in France
just a hundred years ago, and which might usefully be remembered
as a possible inspiration for the museums of the future.

In 1900, Paris was the location for the 'Universal' Exhibition.
The whole of the West End of the city was devoted to displays and
pavilions, with a number of countries from all over the world
being represented. The energetic Scottish scientist and popu-
lariser, Professor Patrick Geddes, had persuaded intellectuals and
scientists from France, Britain, Germany and Russia to set up an
International Summer School, giving lectures on the exhibits in
their own languages to hundreds of visitors. When the exhibition

9. R. Samuel, *Theatres of Memory*, p. 271.

was on the point of closing, in the autumn, Geddes conceived the scheme of rescuing for semi-permanent display the series of national pavilions running along the left bank of the Seine, and known as La Rue des Nations. Instead of being preserved as national monuments, each pavilion was to become the site for all that was best in a certain field: thus the British pavilion would celebrate Pasteur and his contribution to science, the Finnish pavilion geographical exhibits, the Greek pavilion archaeology, the American pavilion comparative education, the Austrian pavilion music – and so on, thus deconstructing the national identity of the buildings, while recognising some national claims. Despite attracting support from many eminent people, the scheme in the end foundered for practical and financial reasons, and has been described both as 'a magnificent failure' and as a prototype for UNESCO. It corresponded however to Geddes' own very original thinking about museums: that they should be international, cross-frontier and collaborative, providing an encyclopaedic 'index' to the whole world. Real objects, diagrams and models could be combined to present a truly global view – in contrast to the very 'national heritage' approach of most of the museums which had been founded all over Europe and the U.S.A. in the late nineteenth century.[10] Geddes's French friend, the geographer and anarchist Elisée Reclus, had particularly wanted the 1900 Exhibition to display a massive terrestrial globe, embodying state-of-the-art earth science – another scheme defeated at the time by practical and financial problems, but more realisable a hundred years on.[11] Elsewhere in this volume, an example is given of successful international cooperation on French soil[12] and this may be one way of

10. The fullest published account of this incident is in P. Boardman and P. Geddes, *Maker of the Future*, Chapel Hill, University of Carolina Press, 1944, p. 304–5. For a full study of Geddes' life see H. Meller and P. Geddes, *Social Evolutionist and City Planner*, London, Routledge, 1990. Geddes wrote an unpublished memoir 'Museums, actual and possible', which has been used as part of the title of this chapter, as it is Chapter 4 in Meller's biography. The text is in the Geddes archive, University of Strathclyde, with papers relating to the Paris initiative.

11. E. Reclus, *Projet de construction d'un Globe Terrestre à l'échelle du cent-millième*, Editions de la société nouvelle, 1895, copy in University of Strathclyde Archives. Reclus's nephew, Paul, costed the project at 20 million francs, not counting ground rent. An international environmental exhibition in Rotterdam in 1998, used a great globe as an audio-visual device, and plans for the Millennium Dome in Britain envisage large-scale pedagogical models.

12. See J. Winter , 'Public History and the *Historial* project, 1986–1998', Chapter 4 of the present volume.

adopting a clear-eyed approach to a national heritage, keeping what is most valuable, while encouraging the spectator to think of the wider context: in other words both celebrating and seeking to demystify the past.

PART II
MEMORIES OF WAR

3

WAR MUSEUMS IN FRANCE

Marie-Hélène Joly

The museum is just one element of commemorative public policies and the way war is remembered. In fact, there are many other vehicles for memorialising war besides museums, ranging from social care for war veterans and the management of military cemeteries, to the politics of commemoration (the choice of Remembrance Days, the organisation of commemorative ceremonies) and the erection of physical memorials (wall plaques and tablets; war memorials and large commemorative monuments) as well as the naming of streets. Given all this activity, museums form only a very small part of the way in which memories of war are perpetuated. Nonetheless they are of particular interest, for they are open to the general public. This takes them beyond the relatively small sphere of the war veteran to the wider arena where memory and cultural activity meet.

The *Inspection générale* (Inspectorate General) of the *Direction des Musées de France* (French Museums Directorate, hereafter DMF), is the official arm of the Ministry of Culture with responsibility for the regulation of the whole museum sector in France. Inspection determines whether new museums are given state recognition, which brings with it public funding. Working for the *Inspection générale* therefore provides an excellent overview of museum development and state policy. We have recently witnessed an historic watershed in the lives of French war museums: the fiftieth anniversary of the Liberation of France in 1994 was probably the last occasion for the principal actors and those who lived through the period to be actively involved in the commemorations. This fact acted as a catalyst, prompting a sudden rash of projects and funding requests from *anciens résistants* (Resistance veterans), many of which were supported by local authorities who were also anxious to mark this important anniversary. After 1994, the number of such new projects and applications entering the DMF in-tray trailed off, with none recorded in 1997. However, projects pertaining to the First World War are now increasing in number. Although it is still too soon to generalise, it appears that the feverish construction of Second World War museums has given way to a new interest in the First World War.

Before looking more closely at war museums, it is useful to establish their place within the French museum sector. They are relatively numerous: of the three thousand institutions in the country, between one hundred and eighty and two hundred remember the three Franco-German wars. Of these, the majority (one hundred and forty) deal with the Second World War, some twenty to thirty deal with the First World War and roughly a dozen remember the war of 1870. These figures are based on a broader definition of what constitutes a museum than that generally adopted by the DMF, which focuses on the particular national importance of the museum collection and the quality of its management. This wider definition reflects the criteria which are important for the originators of the projects and their potential audience, for whom the legal status of the collection or official funding classifications are not a primary concern.[1] If one adds to these figures all those generalist museums which devote a gallery or space to the three wars, one can see that Franco-German conflicts dominate history museums in France: previous hostilities hardly get a look-in. This can lead one to put forward the hypothesis that these wars represent a strong element underlying French national identity, which is characterised by commonly-held values and which can also be defined as opposition to a common 'enemy'. This chapter will deal in the main with those museums dedicated to the Second World War, which is by far the largest and most controversial group. However comparisons will also be drawn with museums of the First World War.

1. These figures are based on an analysis of only those institutions dealing exclusively with the two World Wars, in order to show their relative importance in the collective memory and cultural practices. Museums having just a small display devoted to the subject (local history or military museums) have not been included. If they were, several hundred museums in France could be seen to deal with Franco-German conflict.

The role of the museum in the memory of war

There is one fundamental difference between the way in which the First and the Second World Wars are remembered: the First World War is marked throughout France with public war memorials listing the name of the dead, standing in every *commune* (parish). The massive building campaign carried out in the 1920s bears witness to the unanimous national memory of this war, with no apparent divisions in national unity. This may explain the relatively small number of existing museums dedicated to this war.

On the other hand, the memory of the Second World War is divided and conflictual: no consensus exists in relation to the fall of France and the Armistice, the position adopted by the Vichy regime or collaboration. Similarly there are many conflictual interpretations of the causes of victory (the roles of the Allies and the French Resistance, the role of external as opposed to internal resistance, the roles of the Gaullist and Communist resistance). Even if, at the time of the liberation of France, a political consensus was achieved to safeguard the heritage of the Resistance, no unanimous national memory of this heritage or unequivocal commemoration was possible. Those groups which found it difficult to make their specific voice heard had to find their own modes of expression, as has been clearly shown in the work of Jean-Yves Boursier on the proliferation of small war museums.[2]

It is probable that the large number of museums to the Second World War is also a response to the lack of 'concrete' monumental commemoration. Ceremonies and speeches come and go, the wall plaques and tablets are tucked away in corners, the names of those who fell in the Second World War are simply added to the end of the list on First World War memorials (and only in some cases for the Resistance dead). This lack of durable or individual recognition of the deeds of the many *combattants de l'ombre* ('soldiers of the shadows'), with only the actions of a favoured few receiving all the public and political acclamation, has led to the desire to create museums.

This over-representation of Second World War museums in relation to those of the First World War must also be understood in the developing context of cultural and heritage activity. At the

---

2. J.-Y. Boursier, 'Les enjeux politiques des musées de la Résistance: multiplicité des lieux', in Grange D. and Poulot D. (eds), *L'Esprit des Lieux, le patrimoine et la cité*, actes du colloque d'Annecy de Septembre 1995, Grenoble, Presses Universitaires de Grenoble, 1997.

time when the veterans of the First World War were active and able to exert their influence, museum creation was not an obvious answer to questions of remembrance. This course of action only really came to the fore in the 1970s. It was during this period that the phenomenon of heritage conservation and museum-building caught the attention of the public, and the war veterans – the principal group to generate remembrance projects – joined the increasing numbers of those involved in this movement, which also sought to safeguard the memory of traditional rural ways of life, as well as that of industrial communities faced with massive economic change. The dates of the opening of museums of the Second World War and of the Resistance confirm this hypothesis: only a few isolated examples exist for the immediate post-war period (Joigny and Le Mont-Mouchet in 1946). Roughly a quarter of the museums date from the years 1954 to 1979 (including some important collections: the museum of the *Ordre de la Libération* in Paris, the Besançon museum and the Jean Moulin Centre in Bordeaux). But three-quarters were opened or significantly up-dated after 1981, above all after 1984. These dates reflect the ages of the Resistance veterans: the post-1984 proliferation can be interpreted as a consequence of an increasing sense of urgency – to bear witness and transmit the memory of their experiences before it is too late – and also their reaching retirement age and having more time to devote to such projects.

One further element is the very crowded list of commemorative dates in France, which gives a strong structure to the nation's pattern of remembrance and which it would be interesting to compare with the practice of other countries. The inaugurations of many of the museums of the Second World War are linked to the major commemorative dates (years ending in 4 and 9). In this respect, 1984 and 1994, the fortieth and fiftieth anniversaries of the liberation of France and the two final major commemorations for most veterans still alive, were peak years.

Above all, the huge wave of creation of museums dedicated to the Second World War clearly follows the widespread and increasing interest in heritage and museum activity in France.[3]

---

3. The fact that museums dealing with the First World War are generally fairly late creations, dating from after 1965 (therefore being the creations of the following generation rather than the actors themselves) supports this hypothesis of 'general museification' being the main explanation.

'First' and 'second' generation war museums

War museums in France can be divided into two distinct generational groups linked to the date and impetus for their creation.
First generation museums were almost solely created at the initiative of the *anciens résistants* (Resistance veterans) associations
themselves. Even if the public authorities did offer them modest
financial help, most still operate on a shoestring, with a small budget and limited number of visitors. Their museum narrative is
memorial rather than historic, based on personal, lived experiences, without recourse to the professional help of historians,
museum curators or exhibition designers.

Second generation museums began to appear in the 1980s.
They are far more ambitious and costly projects, with clear didac-
tic or publicity-orientated ambitions, and which call upon outside
professional expertise, as shown by the striking example of the
Mémorial at Caen.

Two reasons for this generational change can be identified. The
first is the demand for a higher standard of presentation, which
results from the increased professionalisation of the museum sector on the one hand, and the rising expectations of a public faced
with an ever-widening range of leisure activities on the other. The
second and without doubt more important reason is the result of
decentralisation and the rise in power of local authorities with
their increased budgets and their proactive approach to cultural
and leisure-tourism policies. Resistance museum projects can be
highly attractive to local authorities, given the political or publicity opportunities they afford, and such projects may benefit from
increased public funding. Apart from these generational changes
affecting the size and shape of war museums, one can note a further shift: that of the *intention* of the museum. Memory takes a
back seat as museums are exploited to put across a party line or to
reinforce the policy choices of the local authority. At the same
time, in some cases economic preoccupations such as local economic development or the demands of tourism drive the museum
project. This may be evidence that the role and significance of the
museum is undergoing major change.

It is interesting to observe what happens when a first generation museum is renovated and transformed into a second generation museum. In these cases, the changes are usually generated by
a group of *Résistance* veterans who nevertheless still wish to
express their own remembrances in absolute freedom. This group

will however have to fit in with the demands of a variety of outside interests, which it may see as simply giving financial support (the local authority) or technical advice (professional historians, curators or museum designers). A power-sharing struggle ensues, often accompanied by a divergent understanding of the transmission of memory: how should the museum shift its focus from the direct recollections of actors and eye witnesses towards a mediated historical analysis? How should the museum seek to speak to generations who have not lived through the war? This question had been sidelined in most first generation museums, where – despite their declared intentions – the *Résistance* veterans spoke only for and to themselves or did not feel obliged to offer an analysis of their subject. How should the museum shift from being a place of memory to a place of history, with wider perspectives offering critical, comparative and background analysis? Finally, how should the museum avoid distorting or submerging the core message of the *Résistance* veterans? These are crucial questions to raise, especially when faced with the renovation of a museum where the process will destroy the original décor created by the veterans. They are generally very attached to their creation and had no intention of modifying it, having approached the public authorities only in order to seek financial help for the creation of new exhibition rooms. However the result *will* be a completely new 'product', which they probably had never foreseen, but which can be deemed a success if the veterans manage to claim this new space as their own.

Who makes a museum? Looking at the role and the degree of involvement of each of these collaborators gives a good indication of the social purpose attached to any project. The most strongly involved partners are the associations of veterans and those who lived through the period (former *Résistants* in the main) who are the driving force behind the project. Next there are the local authorities, who are the main allies and financial backers of the *Résistants*, but whose intentions can be radically divergent. Finally there is the state, whose role is modest, due to the lack of any clear policy towards war museums.

Lest we forget: veterans and conflicting memories of war

The memory of the Second World War and of the Resistance is divided into many distinct parts, which is reflected in museums, as analysed by Jean-Yves Boursier in 1992.[4] No one museum project offers a synthesis of all these divisions, as each group or faction wants to put across its own message in its own words, excluding any other view of the Resistance. However, the main division is that between the Gaullist and Communist Resistance factions, a division which has remained irreconcilable until very recently. The decision to include an exhibition text about the Communist resistance group FTP (*Francs Tireurs et Partisans*) in a Resistance museum set up by Gaullist veterans in central France was only possible after several years of negotiations. Communist resistance groups set up their own network of museums centred on the museum opened in 1985 on the outskirts of Paris at Champigny-sur-Marne. Using local associations of communist resistance veterans, this network has been extended during the 1990s to include five very small Resistance museums in different regions.

Political differences are far from being the only divisive point: each group of Resistance veterans is seeking to express and protect the memories of their own personal experiences, with their museum expressing the view of a very limited number of people bonded by a common experience. Rarely are these views presented as part of a unified regional or national perspective. To this end, the museum functions as a repository of partisan views or micro-memories.

For more recent second generation museum proposals, these diverse groups have often been called to work together, as the public authorities offering financial backing are anxious to create a single unifying project. The associations take this collaboration to mean that each of them will work out their individual discourse and will be allocated their own exhibition space or room. So it is a very long and arduous process to try to arrive at a genuinely collaborative project, which goes beyond the simple juxtaposition of parallel voices. However, as the association members become more aware of the urgency of putting across the ideals of the Resistance, they will now more readily consent to sacrifice part of their specific political or local claims than they might have been ten or fifteen years ago.

When one examines the factors which motivate Resistance veterans to create a museum, their statements of purpose[5] highlight a

4. J.-Y.Boursier, op.cit.

5. These statements of purpose are taken from the statutes of the associations, the introductory remarks to applications for financial support, or museographical projects, also with interviews. This is only a summary conclusion, but the statements merit a more systematic study.

clear set of objectives. It is interesting to note that these objectives rarely change, whatever the political stance of the association, and are often rather repetitive and hidebound.

Their main purpose is a 'duty to remember' (*devoir de mémoire*), a widely adopted epithet borrowed from Primo Levi. The Second World War is presented in a mythic fashion ('this glorious and heroic past') but is never put in a concrete historical perspective. Rarely does one find reference to the fight against the forces of occupation, patriotism and the defence of national territory, all of which are however often an integral part of commemorative discourse. This duty to remember is accompanied by the desire to transmit this memory to the generations which did not live through the war, particularly the young, but this desire generally does not come across in the museum presentation, where little effort is made to interpret or explain the period to younger visitors.

This duty to remember usually means recalling the sacrifices made by Resistance victims in a variety of visual forms: lists of the dead (akin to those on war memorials) or pictures of the dead (in some museums this means horrifying images of torture victims, photographed after a massacre). The museum is used to pay homage, to express the debt of the nation to these politically committed and courageous men and women. It might also be used to put across the Resistance ethos (*les valeurs de la Résistance*) but, in the majority of cases, this is not clearly defined. When some attempt at definition is made, it is usually put across in general terms such as 'humanist' and 'spiritual values'; the talk is of courage, liberty, hope, self-sacrifice.

Finally, since the 1980s, the duty to remain watchful, has become an integral part of their purpose: the object being to avoid a repeat of the tragedies of the Second World War and to give a lesson in politics and civic virtue. In most cases, these aims are fairly vague so it is difficult to distinguish whether the motivation is to promote international peace or to combat fascist and nazi ideology. This humanitarian and pacifist stance is gradually beginning to appear in project proposals, at the instigation of local authority partners, who view this as an opportunity to make a political statement. Sometimes even the name given to the museum might reflect this: the Mémorial museum in Caen is called the 'Memorial for peace'. The same phenomenon can be seen with First World War museums: Verdun now has a 'World Centre for peace'.

However, when one reads between the lines of all the written statements of the Resistance veterans which accompany their project submissions, it becomes clear that the prime motivation is not the explicit 'lest we forget', rather an implicit 'lest we be forgotten'. The nation is called upon to finally pay its debt of gratitude. 'France owes it to us' were the words used by one veteran bringing a museum project before the *Inspection générale*. This sentiment is accompanied by a wish to create a social space not afforded by commemorations or monuments or memorial tablets: creating and running a museum is seen as a collective operation, the creation of a space in which veterans can meet and do things together, rather like a club. The museum also has the advantage of widening the veterans' social circle, their fellow citizens constituting a flesh and blood audience, to whom they can transmit in a very immediate and direct way their acts of the resistance. So the museum makes up for the lack of opportunities to tell one's own story. This would seem to bear out Serge Barcellini's conclusion that there is a huge difference between 'cold spaces' (*lieux froids*) – war memorials – and 'warm spaces' (*lieux chauds*) – museums.[6]

The role of the local authorities: faithful representation or instrumentalisation?

Although they are rarely the originators of any war museum project, local authorities are very active associates, entering freely into partnerships with the associations who usually do not have the means to get this kind of facility up and running. It is usual to deal with 'municipal-association' partnerships, wherein the local authority guarantees the majority funding (by providing a building, capital investment or running costs) and the association looks after the day-to-day life of the museum (care-taking duties, putting together the museum collection, organisation of museum events and activities). The reasons which lead local authorities to lend aid and endorsement have greatly evolved over the last decade, and they are often not easily identified.

With first generation museums, any political motivation was generally easy to spot and any similarity between the intentions of the associations and local politicians was clearly understood: many local politicians were themselves former *Résistants* or the immediate inheritors of the Resistance ideals, such as Jacques Chaban-Delmas in Bordeaux. Political solidarities clearly played

6. Interview with Serge Barcellini, *Inspecteur général* at the Ministry for War Veterans, January 1996.

their part in museum projects: very often the museum originated as a homage to a founding act of local or national political life. Sometimes one can find traces of political vote catching, as the Resistance veterans formed an important pressure group at the heart of many local networks.

The significance of local politics is still relevant when it comes to second generation museums, but now other issues are also at stake. In the 1990s, some significant local politicians who had not lived through the period of the war become actively involved in ambitious projects for museums dedicated to the Second World War (for example Michel Noir in Lyons and Alain Carignon in Grenoble). Whilst still overtly adhering to the principle of the duty to remember, the duty to be vigilant is introduced, as outlined above, against the backdrop of the rise of the *Front national*. One needs to question whether this increased involvement in museum projects is an act of self-justification on the part of local councillors who are trying to create their own political identity. The *valeurs de la Résistance* therefore become part of the institutionalised identity of the locality and are used to enhance it. In this, new war museums could be seen as pure and simple products of political decentralisation.

Further motives linked to regional and local development complete this picture. The past becomes a local resource which can be promoted for economic gain. In the majority of museum projects received from small *communes*, the desire to promote local economic regeneration through tourism is very openly expressed. In the near future, the Caen Mémorial plans to double its exhibition space and create a section devoted to the Cold War from the end of the Second World War to 1989. The motivation for this is entirely commercial and looks to the success of interactive amusement attractions. This doubling in size will mean that the visitor will stay for a whole day and spend more money indirectly on site.

The role of the state: impotence or indifference?

The state has tended to play but a small role in the creation of war museums in France. Government policy towards the collective memory of war has been concentrated elsewhere, particularly in the selection of dates for national commemorations, and there is no national museum to either the First or Second World War. Most of the initiatives have been taken by associations and local authorities, as we have seen, and it was only in 1996 that the state made any high-level positive input. As early as 1955 the French parliament was debating the possibility of creating a national museum commemorating resistance and deportation. This resulted in an exhibition at the Invalides in 1962, but the project foundered as it failed to gain the support of General de Gaulle. As he felt himself to be the living incarnation of the French Resistance, he was unwilling to reassess his role or allow other figures of resistance to be in the picture.

This lack of official state recognition has latterly been challenged. Representatives of the *Forces Françaises Libres* (Free French Army) petitioned President Chirac in 1996 who gave his backing to a project for a 'museum of Free France and its leader', which would pay homage to de Gaulle. Financed by the Ministry of Defence, this museum is due to open on 18th June 2000 as part of the Army museum at the Invalides. Whilst this might not be a large-scale creation (two thousand square meters of exhibition space within an existing museum), its symbolic value is immense: recognition *in extremis* for the resistance movement and confirmation of its importance through the backing of the President of the Republic. During the Mitterrand era, presidential interest was concentrated on the financing of the *Mémorial associatif des Enfants d'Izieu* (collective memorial museum to the children of Izieu) in the Ain *département* which was opened in the early 1990s in the memory of Jewish children deported from France.

Echoing this relative lack of interest, the two governmental ministries which could actively promote and finance war museums – the Ministry for War Veterans and the Ministry of Culture – have been slow to show their support. The Ministry for War Veterans (*Ministère des Anciens combattants*) was responsible for the development of a genuine policy towards war remembrance with the creation of a *délégation à la mémoire* (remembrance delegation) in the 1980s. However museums never featured as a central element of this policy, which focused on the organisation of commemorative events and education initiatives. In the past the Ministry had become directly involved in the planning of some large-scale projects for national memorials (le Mont-Valérien in 1960 and le Mont-Faron in 1964) but has never overseen a major war museum project. Moreover, it has only ever offered limited financial support to a very small number of association or local authority museums. The one exception has been its substantial financial backing of the Vassieux-en-Vercors Mémorial, opened in 1994 to commemorate the fiftieth anniversary of the Liberation.

But despite this lack of positive action in the museum field, it was the Ministry for War Veterans, rather than the Ministry of Culture, which, in 1985, was behind an initiative which could have led to the development of a genuine policy for war museums, with the creation of a cross-ministerial commission for the two World Wars (*Commission interministérielle des deux guerres*). Chaired by the Minister himself, this commission brought together representatives from the Defence, Education and Culture Ministries as well as the Home Office. Its objective is to advise on the nature of support to be offered to public authorities and associations wishing to open a museum and to offer advice and recommendations in response to requests for assistance received by the state. Fully aware of the growing number of museum projects, the Commission set out to centralise all requests for help by bringing together each administration involved in war museum creation in order to offer a concerted response on behalf of central government. This formed the basis of a coherent museum policy initiative – we shall see below why this policy was to fail in its objectives. The criteria which had to be met by any project in order to receive a favourable response were the following: they should possess an inalienable collection of artefacts which should be accessible to the public (a criteria already established by the Ministry of Culture); they should fit in with other commemorative projects in the same region and should be economically viable, meaning that they should have the backing of a local public authority.

The Commission sought to limit the proliferation of war museum projects. On the one hand, by decreeing that the State should finance only one project per region (twenty-two in total), it tried to encourage different project leaders to work together. This measure had little success. On the other hand, it tried to make project leaders improve upon their original plans. With endless requests for supplementary information, project files could be in the process of examination for a considerable time with no guarantee of success. In the ten years between 1985 and 1995, the Commission examined ninety project applications, of which only 30 per cent were successful. Since the commemorations in 1994 applications have trailed off, and now the Commission meets very infrequently. It is entirely possible that the Commission might be wound up altogether.

After over twelve years of existence, it looks as if the Commission has failed in its objectives: a large number of the museums which opened during this period resulted from projects which never came before the Commission and therefore dispensed with the validation or financial backing of central government. Also, some applicants who had seen their project turned down did actually receive state backing, following forceful political intervention to overturn a negative technical recommendation. The most spectacular example is that of the Caen Mémorial, which amounted to a public rejection of the activity of the Commission. Finally, some projects which had been upheld by the Commission never received state funding as they failed to meet further requirements.

One other reason for so many refusals was the Commission's wariness of the new and very spectacular, theatrical museographical concepts included in the proposals received, despite the fact that these have now become the norm. However, the main reason for the failure of the Commission was its very limited legitimacy. Its role remained purely advisory – it had no budget of its own. Any positive recommendation on its part meant that the proposal would have to be sent to the Ministry of Culture who retained sole financial aid for museums. Given this, the Commission was bound to function according to the criteria set by the Ministry of Culture, which established that the central part of any project must be a well-managed collection of historical objects. However, a collection of material artefacts is often but a small element of any war museum project, where the main focus will have been the desire to bear witness to personal experience regardless of the medium. This shows two different understandings of the term 'museum': for the project instigators, a museum is 'a place where we can talk about the war and the Resistance', whereas for the state officials a museum concentrates on the conservation of material heritage. It must be said that the state has not fully grasped the full scope of the politics of remembrance. No attention has been paid to how best to offer financial support to enterprises working to safeguard the personal and immaterial memory of war.

So it fell to the *Direction des musées de France* (DMF), the main source of financial backing for the museum sector within the Ministry of Culture, to support the majority of war museum projects. But the DMF failed to produce a clear set of guidelines for dealing with this specific group which, in legal terms, has always been treated just like any other museum establishment.

Prior to 1982, a museum could receive the official status of *musée contrôlé* (designated museum) and thereby benefit from government funding, simply by writing to the Ministry of Culture, without any specific quality control being carried out. Despite this relative simplicity, very few war museums made requests for designation – only seven between 1947 and 1979. Only two war museums, both housing very significant collections, asked for and received funding in the usual way open to all. Most other projects never solicited state aid, which is hardly surprising, as the veterans associations were unlikely to be familiar with the activities of the Ministry.

After 1982, the regulations governing the *musées contrôlés* were tightened up to include a qualitative and quantitative assessment of the collections. Each application was to come before a DMF commission called the *Conseil artistique des musées de France* (the Artistic Council of the French Museums Directorate). The name is significant: most of the members of the commission were and are art historians. War museums, as well as ethnographic, technical and industrial museum projects, all had to battle it out to show that they were of wide appeal and could boast good management strategies and a dynamic mission statement. A further condition was attached for war museums: to receive consideration, the project must have received the backing of the *Commission interministérielle des deux guerres*, mentioned above. This constituted an extra hurdle and discouraged many from applying. The *Conseil artistique* received six applications from war museums between 1985 and 1993, all of which were successful and therefore able to benefit from the technical assistance and major financial support of the Ministry of Culture in the same way as any other type of designated museum.

This might paint a fairly positive picture, but the fact remains that the composition of the *Conseil artistique* makes it very difficult for war museums or any other non-artistic museum to present their application. Similarly, those war museums which have received significant capital funding (a few Second World War museums plus the Historial in Péronne) form only a very minor part of the total capital aid given over this period of huge-scale museum development. It also highlights the discrepancy between the public demand for museums to promote social memories and the response of the Ministry of Culture. With the DMF retaining its strong orientation towards material culture, it is regrettable that no administrative structure exists which is able to examine projects linked to questions of memory in all its forms, beyond this strict understanding of cultural heritage. This situation affects many other institutions, not only war museums.

The visitor: a partner in the museum enterprise?

Museums are created to serve the general public, so in theory they should be one of the main partners in the enterprise. In practice, very little is known about who visits museums. Visitor surveys are usually only interested in numbers and are never carried out in any systematic way. An unpublished study by Emmanuelle François in 1995 for the DMF (see bibliography) gave the visitor figures for sixty-five war museums. The figures need to be viewed with caution for they were provided by the museums themselves. These sixty-five museums total between them one and a half million visits per year, but the picture is one of contrasts: the Caen Mémorial and the museum in nearby Arromanches account for 630,000 visits between them; two other museums exceed 100,000 visits; several have over 30,000 visitors per year but many will struggle to attract over a thousand visits, with some only receiving around five hundred visits.

Visitor figures reveal an interesting phenomenon. Most visits are made to museums associated with a historic battlefield site (Arromanches and Sainte-Mère-Eglise in Normandy; the Mont-Mouchet in the Auvergne; the Vercors in the Isère). So the main pull for the visitor is the site itself, with the museum benefiting from the many tourists who come as an act of pilgrimage. At Verdun, local councils have created museums in the hope that they might gain some economic fallout from the large numbers of tourists coming to visit the battlefields. The Caen Mémorial, with the largest number of visitors per annum (an average in excess of 300,000) is an exception. Located well behind the landing beaches, it owes its success to the massive and very professional campaign to market the museum as an innovative 'product', using marketing methods never before seen in a history museum. In this, as well as in its creative and spectacular exhibition museography, the Mémorial marks a watershed in the historical museum sector and is the kind of facility most politicians dream of having as one of their cultural institutions.

Only a few establishments which are keen to establish details of their client base, such as the Mémorial, offer any detailed qualitative analysis of their visitors. Most war museums, as others in the sector, appear to have two captive audiences: senior citizens on coach tours and school visits motivated by the study of wars in the national curriculum. The programmes of educational activities offered vary greatly in quality. Some are excellent, but most museums do little more than distribute very superficial museum question sheets. As with all museums, the visit will only have been successful if the teachers have prepared well and make use of the visit later in class.

Overall, the pedagogical aims of museums are hardly ever clearly defined, and very few evaluations of the impact of museum visits on school children have been carried out, despite the fact that they form an easily identifiable audience to follow-up. What does a trip to a museum bring to the school programme? What information is gleaned, what lessons are learnt, and how has the consciousness been raised? What do school children remember of their visit after a few months? The question of the social utility of the history museum, and its role in political and moral education, is only now being addressed by a handful of curators.

Visitor figures show that the French like visiting war museums. Why? What do they gain by their visit? For the moment these questions remain to be answered, quite simply because not enough institutions are asking them.

The portrayal of war in museums

Over the last ten years, the way in which war is presented in museums has been transformed. New methods of display which are the result of increased collaboration with professionals – historians and curators – can be found in those few museums which have been renovated or are recent creations: many older museums remain unchanged, with a purely bellicose or war-driven vision of their subject. The presentations have evolved in two ways. On the one hand, the involvement of historians has led to a widening of the perspectives and issues raised in the display. On the other, new 'fashionable' ideological concepts are finding their way into the presentation (peace, human rights, the birth of Europe).

This shift is very easy to observe in the small number of First World War museums. Before the building of the Historial in Péronne, opened in 1992, all museums presented a purely French-focused and primarily military view of the hostilities. With its international *conseil scientifique* (expert steering committee), Péronne revolutionised thinking by creating a tripartite presentation, with the three main warring parties given the same space. The Historial also moves beyond pure military history with displays concerning the home front. It mentions every nation involved, and develops themes which are rarely treated elsewhere: childhood and war, questions of belief. The Historial reflects the specific circumstances of its international *conseil*, but it is also a product of the notion of European construction, and as such would not have seen the light of day some thirty or forty years ago. Similarly, the Verdun projects – the *Centre mondial pour la paix* opened in 1995 and the project in Meuse, still in preparation – both used an expert panel and take the wider view to include more universal, less uniquely French perspectives. With the passing of the generation of those who lived through the First World War, it is possible to take a more balanced and less revanchist attitude to display and to include a historical perspective. The First World War can now be revisited and reinterpreted.

This is however far from being the case with the Second World War, where many of those who participated in events are still alive. Display is further complicated by the fact that the complex controversies over the inheritance of the war are far from over. It is interesting to note that the narrative of museums and contemporary debate are at variance over the role of the Vichy regime. For the last fifteen years or so, various trials and revisions of the roles of many political figures right up to the highest levels of the state have meant that the issue of Vichy dominates the news and weighs heavily on the collective consciousness. Yet museums have continued to present an image of a France in which every citizen resisted. In the oldest museums, the Vichy regime and the subject of collaboration are barely alluded to, and when they are it is largely to settle local, personal scores. Examples of museums dealing with the French internment camps remain rare. A specifically Jewish memory of the war is finding its way into museums, having been totally obscured for many years, or alluded to only in gallery displays dealing with deportation. This memory now has its own legitimacy and led to the creation of the Izieu children's memorial and with other projects now being developed.

For the Second World War, micro-memories predominate. The growing involvement of local authorities and academics is leading to attempts to define more federal, synthetic projects, but most museums remain local expressions of war and resistance. In this they join many other history museums, where local narratives predominate. So museums continue to deal with the Resistance in the Forez, the Morvan or the Vercors, to the detriment of the larger picture.

Today we are witnessing an increasing desire to transmit remembrances, but there is a shift away from direct recollections to a form of mediated analysis of memory. In museums, this mode of transmission generally relies on the intervention of the *conseil scientifique*. The museum in Besançon, opened in 1971, was the first to use historians to shape the museum narrative, working alongside associations in a free and exemplary manner. In the 1990s, the use of a *conseil scientifique* became standard practice for large-scale projects: the centre for the History of the Resistance and Deportation in Lyon (1992) or the Mémorial Leclerc-Jean Moulin museum in Paris (1994) for example. The Mémorial at Caen falls into a category of its own, as its creation is owed to a CNRS (French national research institute) research centre and the *Institut d'Histoire du Temps Présent*, without the involvement of any veterans or associations. This experiment ended with an acrimonious split between the *conseil* and the museum management. Contrary to what one might believe, the use of a *conseil scientifique* is not the norm: most museums dispense with any input from professional historians. At best, a secondary school teacher might be called upon to offer advice

Most museums of the Second World War are confronted with the added difficulty of having to take on board the views of the veterans who will be taking an active role in the development project. Direct and personal oral testimonies must take their place alongside scientific historical research and teaching. The selection of 'important' facts and events will be difficult, as will their interpretation. Whilst seeking to introduce a historical and critical perspective, the testimonies of the Resistance veterans must remain intact, as it forms the most precious historical artefact of these kind of museums. The example of the Resistance and Deportation museum in Grenoble (see Chapter 5) shows how collaboration between veterans and historians can result in the successful transmission of remembrance.

The most decisive role of the professional historian working with a history museum is the widening of perspectives and issues covered. Often national and international events begin to take their place, even if the local region remains at the heart of the narrative. The Caen Mémorial and the Péronne Historial moved beyond a simple treatment of the Normandy landings or the Somme battles thanks to the actions of their *conseils scientifiques*. Besides these well-known examples, some more intimate projects should also be cited, such as the small resistance museum at Estivareilles in the Forez, currently undergoing renovation. This is the only museum of war in which the curator and the historical advisors have dared to move outside the chronological time-scale of the Second World War in order to look at the impact of the major or national events of the twentieth century on the life of this small isolated rural area. This example is ripe for emulation: indeed, in some cases, thematic diversification might ensure the survival of the museum. Can one really imagine that one hundred and forty small museums, already fighting for financial support, will outlive the generation which lived through the war?

If it is easy to see what history can bring to the museum, it is much more difficult to assess what the museum brings to the historical discipline. The museum cannot be said to be the best medium for history – books or television programmes probably do the job in a more efficient and faithful way. The finer points of historical inquiry are sometimes difficult to put across in a museum, and the lessons learnt from material culture do not in themselves tell of the complexities of the situation. Most museums of the Second World War display parachute containers. At the most, given a good display, they will show *how* a parachute drop was made, but will never be able to explain the important question of *why*.

One should not ask more of the museum than it can offer, but it is possible to make the museum a place of intelligent popularisation of history, where new research findings can be swiftly and faithfully presented, and where the visitor can be invited to reflect, not only to remember emotionally. Emotion is however an important conductor, which should be used advisedly. The emotions aroused on listening to testimonies or at seeing 'real' objects can be the contribution of the museum to a world which is becoming increasingly imitative and virtual. This emotion can push the visitor to ask questions, to take on board some new information, and to seek to deepen their knowledge, somewhere else, in some other manner, of what they have glimpsed in the museum.

4

PUBLIC HISTORY AND THE 'HISTORIAL' PROJECT, 1986–1998

Jay Winter

My subject is public history, history outside the academy, linking historians to the broad population interested – sometimes passionately interested – in historical inquiry. Public history is defined by this extension of the domain within which the scholar operates. The audience for historical literature defines the discipline as much as the professional credentials of the practitioner. Public history is thus an attempt to flee from the increasing specialisation and decreasing readership of professional academic work, both in journals and in monograph form. It is also a recognition that historical scholarship is intrinsically tied to concepts of educating the public, and not only university students. Public history is an act of civic responsibility.

There are other features of public history worthy of note. Work in this field is almost always collective, in that it deals with issues too large for one lone scholar to master, express or explain. There's the rub. Public history matters, but its collective character stops many people from going into it. Why? Because the fundamental ethos of the historical profession is individualistic. Collective venture is daring, risky, and rarely yields the recognition that young scholars in particular need at a time of vanishing university posts and cut-backs in university funding.

And yet the field of collective historical writing is not only thriving, but also almost certain to expand rapidly over the next decades: either through television and video audiences, in interactive systems easily plugged into a desktop or portable computer, and in the growing world of museums and historical exhibitions.

The contradiction is clear: at a time of stagnant or shrinking academic audiences, public audiences have never been larger. While the profession of history is under siege in the universities, it has a clear avenue to expand. The audience is there; the public service is there. The argument for expenditure, always essential to academic ventures, is one based on utility and (in the broadest sense) on the development of public support for historical scholarship through historians' support of the public. Both private investment and public support is necessary for public history to emerge as a thriving enterprise.

The obstacles facing such an approach are formidable. The means to arrive at the destination challenges cherished assumptions of our profession: namely, that what we do is individual; and that the 'authorial voice' is the core of our enterprise. But even if individualism is worshiped among many academic historians as the *sine qua non* of wisdom, there is still room to share our profession with another kind of colleague, the public historian, who speaks primarily, though not exclusively, to society at large, and does so as part of a group of scholars and other professionals working together.

One way to appreciate the attractions and the difficulties of aspects of work in public history is to survey a project on which I have had an insider's perspective: the creation of a multinational museum of the First World War at Péronne on the river Somme. I would also like to suggest some ways in which this kind of project, while likely to play a more and more important part in historical study, has difficulties imbedded in it: difficulties better faced when exposed to the light of day.

First the bad news. In a nutshell, the problem is that public history is publicly funded history. This is true with respect to state, foundation or corporate funding. No one else will pay the sums needed for public history projects – television series, museums and exhibitions. The private sector has a critical role to play here, but the state sector is now and is likely to remain the essential source for the cash needed to develop projects in public history. As soon as official or state organisations commit themselves to pick up the tab for collective projects, then the autonomy of the individual scholar may be curtailed. It need not happen all the time, but in every major documentary produced by the BBC in Britain, issues of public sensitivities overlap with concerns for the presentation of historical events. One way or another, our holy of holies – the right to speak out about the past without financial or institutional shackles – has been invaded. These brief remarks aim at opening a debate about the benefits and costs of public history with special reference to the expanding domain of museums dealing with twentieth-century history.

Collective history and public history

First, is public history worth the aggravation, the dangers, the effort? My answer is a resounding yes. The first point about collective projects in public history is that they are unavoidable when confronting gigantic issues of wide public concern. With certain notable exceptions, no individual can produce by him or herself a history of most of the major subjects in contemporary affairs. The documentation is too vast, the issues too complex, the linguistic skills needed too daunting. Either we work together, or we do not work at all on a host of issues. Some such subjects spring to mind easily: Fundamentalist Islam, international migration, urbanisation, the information revolution. No one scholar can even keep up with the mountains of documentation produced day by day, let alone add to it in a rigorous manner in academic publications or in other ways.

There is another, less parochial, reason for doing this kind of work. Collective history is the only way to break down the hold of national history in our discipline. There is nothing wrong with national history: it simply throttles comparison. The celebration of the 'peculiarities of the English' (or Welsh or Scots or French or Germans) assumes the other, but the pursuit of such comparisons in Britain – and in France – is virtually non-existent. Public history can cross boundaries, and does so in Europe at precisely the moment when the creation of transnational histories parallels the emergence of transnational institutions and (in time) transnational identities too. The jointly funded Franco-German television station, Arte, is one such venture; the Erasmus exchange programme for university students in the European Community is another.

The concept of collective work is, therefore, *not* one we can do without. Yet as university jobs are decided on the basis of the individualist ethos, it is unlikely that young people will put their careers on the line by embarking on risky projects in which their personal contribution cannot easily be specified. This must mean that universities – in France, in Britain, in the United States – will continue to be bastions of individualism in scholarship. The people who can 'risk' collective projects, such as those which reach a television audience, are those already established in the profession, that is, middle-aged and tenured. The logic of appointments (and inertia) is driven by conservative forces in Europe as well as in North America. Public history is not, because it is intrinsically collective. Creating a museum, or an exhibition, or a television series can never be a one-man show. Collective work is how it has to be done, and if the lead is to come from anyone, it will have to be from those of us sheltered from the job market with an already established reputation as 'conventional' historians, or as curators or workers in the field of heritage.

The case for this kind of public history is clear. Historical understanding is part of the equipment of citizenship. Those millions of people outside the academy who care about history are part of our profession whether we academics admit it or not. Their craving for some kind of history in museums or on the television screen creates jobs which apprentice historians may find compelling and even rewarding. Evidence that this market exists is more abundant in France and the United States than in Britain, but here too the interest in historical issues goes well beyond the well-manicured grounds of the National Trust.

Resistance among professional historians

Public history is, therefore, both a reality and a necessity. But there the problems start. Some are internal to the trade. No one should underestimate the resistance inside the academy against such collective historical work. Partly this is simply old-fashioned elitism. Partly it reflects a style of life, in which subtlety and irony are valued to the point that at times nothing clear-cut can be said; or rather, it underlies the notion, more commonly voiced than you may suppose, that anyone who speaks clearly is presumed to think simply. Public history, from this point of view, is simple-minded history. Any academic who engages in it is, therefore, risking his or her professional reputation.

Then there is the old goddess of jealousy. Most academics I know are either politicians or actors manqué; they like performance, but only when *they* are on stage. Those who speak to them through a museum or from a television screen are bound to touch nerves among a profession both craving public attention and at times suspicious – even contemptuous – of it.

Finally, there is the question of 'objectivity'. Any one approach to a major problem in history is bound to select evidence and material on the basis of a particular *problématique*, a set of questions a generation of historians chooses to address. What about the questions historians of the 1960s, 1970s or 1980s addressed? Do they get a look in? In some cases, the answer is no, and that is one point where the fur flies.

When the field of study is the history of war, the quarrels intersect with more general fault lines separating military history from cultural history, as if either could live in majestic isolation each on its separate peak. No one who enters this field is likely to leave it unbruised, another reason why young scholars may be prone to stay out of it.

The 'Historial de la Grande Guerre'

To do so would be a mistake, because the opportunities are there for the taking. Let me try to illustrate this point by reference to the genesis of one particular project in public history – the 'Historial de la Grande Guerre'. The idea of building a museum of the First World War on the battlefields of the Somme originated in the bureaucracy of the *Conseil Général du Département de la Somme*. An hour and a half north of Paris, the *Département* is one of the less attractive sites for tourism in France. The cathedral of Amiens and the coastal region of the Somme bring visitors to the region by the thousands, but what of the east of the Département? Its claim to fame is the fact that it is a vast necropolis, the traces of which are visible throughout the countryside. French, German and Commonwealth War Graves are everywhere. They testify to four years of trench warfare between 1914 and 1918 and two massive offensives: that of 1 July to 10 November 1916 initiated by the British army between Amiens (their headquarters) and Péronne (German headquarters), and the last major offensive of the war, initiated by the German army on 22 March 1918 and ending up with the armistice of 11 November.

For both British and German survivors of the war, the Somme is iconic. For the French, it is Verdun that symbolises the horror of industrialised warfare, as well as the capacity of the French army – fed into the cauldron in a giant conveyor belt or 'noria' – to successfully defend their soil. Yet one hundred and fifty kilometres further north and west, between Amiens and Péronne, the British and the German army fought out a battle no one had ever seen before. Ernst Jünger has written that there, on those flat fields, the twentieth century was born.[1]

The scale of Verdun was so great, and its symbolic existence so powerful that it seemed to obscure the fact that the French had also suffered and died on the Somme. This chapter of the war has recently been treated wonderfully in Sébastien Japrisot's novel *Un long dimanche de fiançailles* which surprised many French readers by its emphasis on the futility of the war waged not at Verdun, but on the Somme.[2] This classic example of what cognitive psychologists call 'interference' – the overlaying of one set of memories by another[3] – has made the Somme a virtual non-event in French history, despite the quarter of a million casualties suffered by the French army there in 1916 alone. Here was a hidden memory, a hidden story, and a hidden site to attract not only British and German, but also French visitors to a place of significance in their history.

One critical point historians must recognise is that history was (and remains) family history for most visitors. That is to say, their link with these huge and devastating events is through family stories, at that time primarily relayed not by the survivors, but by the children of the survivors. The transmission of messages about the past – especially about the Great War – occurred between grandchildren and grandparents, leaping over (as it were) the intervening generation of adults between them. The fact that family narratives in the 1970s and 1980s frequently took the form of the imparting of historical knowledge from a first to a third generation is hardly surprising. The silence of the middle generation – active during the Second World War – covers a multitude of sins for millions of German families and French families as well. Talking about the past of 1939–45 is to enter a dangerous domain; but when grandparents reach a certain age, it is their place and pleasure to reach out (as it were) over the heads of their own children to their children's children and to do so by storytelling, stories of an earlier age, the age during and after the Great War. This is what Georges Brassens has captured so ironically in his lyrics 'Qu'est-ce que c'est la guerre que je préfère, c'est la guerre de 14–18'.

The 'Historial de la Grande Guerre' arose from this specific and fleeting generational moment, when history became family his-

1. E. Jünger, *In Stahlgewittern*, Berlin, 1929, p. 22.

2. S. Japrisot, *Un long dimanche de fiançailles*, Paris, 1994.

3. On the phenomenon of 'interference', see J. Winter and E. Sivan (eds), *War and remembrance in the twentieth century*, Cambridge, 1998, chapter 1.

tory, and therefore could include scripts not yet inscribed by the French in their national narrative of the war. Here was a way to justify a major French investment in a story very few Frenchmen had acknowledged as of fundamental importance to them and to their sense of the past.

The man who saw this opportunity was Max Lejeune, president of the Conseil Général, and a former Defence Minister at the time of Suez. He was a characteristic Fourth Republic politician, skilled in the byways of Parisian infighting, but whose power rested on a personal fiefdom and following in his own Department of the Somme. Tourism mattered to him, but so did the memory of his father, an *ancien combattant* of the Battle of the Somme, who had returned from the war a troubled man. The childhood Lejeune recalled was not a happy one; the war had broken his father, and seventy years later in the 1980s, Max Lejeune wanted to find a way to put those memories to rest.

For Lejeune, the idea of a museum originated in family history, his family history. His insight was in seeing that such a museum was a means of turning national narratives into family narratives. 'Il ne passeront pas' is etched in words and in stone all over the Western front. It was the nation as a whole which blocked the German advance in 1914 and for the four bloody years which followed. But the nation did not bleed and die on the Western front; individual men did, and each one had a family, who took in the tragedy as part of its own particular story, its own family narrative. What Lejeune saw was that respecting this familial element in national history could help bring French children at the end of the twentieth century into contact with the world of his childhood, in the 1920s and 1930s, shadowed as it was by the Great War.

With the support of a *notable* of the eminence and power of Lejeune, it was possible to envision the financial investment necessary for the creation of a museum in the late 1980s or early 1990s. However, its scale and character were still uncertain. To frame its design, two groups of people were assembled. The first were designers, chosen by a remarkable filmmaker and entrepreneur, Gérard Rougeron, a native of the Somme, and a man whose family went through the Great War, there, at the front; the second were historians, there initially for quality control alone. Rougeron, a writer and artist with a vivid imagination and an explosive temper, invented the term 'Historial', as a marriage of Memorial and centre of historical study.

This choice of nomenclature constituted a crucial step forward, with practical consequences. First, it enabled the Somme project to stand apart from one just completed at Caen in Normandy on the Second World War landings. That museum was called the 'Mémorial'. We wanted something different; something much more explicitly linked to the world of *international* academic scholarship; hence the name 'Historial' blended our concern with rigorous scholarship and pictorial expression. Thus the word chosen by Rougeron was a symbol of another kind. When he asked three historians – Jean-Jacques Becker, Wolfgang Mommsen and me – to serve as advisors to the project, he announced its international character, very unusual for a French-financed operation. He also opened the door to another development, of particular importance for the project as a whole.

Lejeune and the civil servants of the Department were fortunately sensitive to the argument that the danger of creating a museum is the speed of its atrophy. The antidote to sclerosis of the kind that attends fixed projects gathering dust and little else, I argued, was to locate within the museum a research centre. This would be a focus for the then burgeoning historical literature on the First World War in general, and on its cultural consequences in particular. It would also operate as a means of updating the museum, of giving it some room to breathe, as it were, so that as historical interpretations changed, so did the design and geometry of the museum. Lejeune nodded, the *fonctionnaires* noted, and the research centre was born, with a line item in the proposed annual budget of the museum. The sums were not great, but the principle was.

This achievement transformed the project for two reasons. First, it enabled historians to be in on the design of the museum from the start, because the research centre existed before a single stone was placed on the site. Secondly, though we did not know this at the time, our presence was of critical importance, for as the project unfolded, the designer (or museographer), Gérard Rougeron, came into increasing conflict with the bureaucrats. The issue was not his approach, which was imaginative; the conflicts were temperamental and financial, and led to his departure from the project after it was more than half completed.

It is important, therefore, to recognise his early contribution to the project. His notion was to purchase hundreds of artefacts – British, French and German alike. More importantly he saw the value of trawling through the film archives of the French army, and other European archives and thereby making visual images the centrepiece of the museum. Through the placement at eye level of fifty video screens scattered throughout the museum, contemporary films of astonishing quality would be shown permanently. He also created a film of his own about the British veterans of the Somme, the poignancy of which was deepened by the death during filming of one old soldier, Harry Fellowes, who had fought at Pozières on the fateful 1 July 1916. His signature for the museum was to be a life-sized plastic *poilu*, or French infantryman, standing in a transparent space like a telephone booth, and through a simple water-circulating system, Rougeron placed this iconic soldier permanently in the rain.

All that remains of Rougeron's major contribution to the museum are his films. Before the final stage of construction, he got into a massive conflict with the bureaucrats, not surprisingly over money. By 1990, the cost of the project had spiralled to one hundred million francs or double the original budget. Using a rough rule of thumb in this business, he calculated that ten per cent of this sum should be his. The *élus* thought otherwise, and Rougeron walked out. It was a miscalculated poker hand: he guessed that no other professionals would touch a project mostly completed, since he, Rougeron, had copyright on the design. Thus the team taking on the project would have to start from scratch.

That is where the historians came into the act. We were able not only to choose a successor, but to work with that successor to design an entirely new project with no resemblance whatsoever to Rougeron's ideas, and to complete the job in two years. The work was done by Adeline Rispal, a Paris architect, responsible for an austere and beautiful design of the *Institut du monde Arabe* at the end of the Boulevard St Germain in Paris. It suited us perfectly, since what we wanted to develop was not Rougeron's vivid romanticism, but a more abstract and simple design avoiding pseudo-realism, the real danger of museum design. No one can convey the 'trench experience', and to pretend that we can is to violate the intrinsic strangeness, the otherness, of the past we wanted to represent.

What we offered was a double design. We used the horizontal axis for the floor space, and the vertical for the *vitrines* on the walls. In four large spaces, we placed *fosses* or dug-outs about five feet by fifteen feet long at various points in the floor at a depth of about ten inches. In these spaces we scattered the artefacts of ordinary life in the trenches – toothpowder, combs, tobacco, pencils, needles, playing cards, bullets, knives and so on. The *fosse* for German soldiers uncannily resembled the British *fosse* and the French one too. Parallelism announced our central point: that here was a common history, one making national differences pale on the everyday level of *Kriegserlebnis*, the war lived by the ordinary soldier, of whom there were six million on the Somme alone.

Other museum curators felt the design of the *fosses* was impractical: children would fall in; thieves would be tempted. However, nothing of the kind has happened. The effect is something like an archaeological dig, or a cemetery uncovered, and this sense of contact with the sacred has been noticed time and again in the visitors' books.

On the walls, we used a vertical organising principle. Civilian objects were arranged in thematic groups, but with German, French and British examples one on top of the other. Yet again, the European character of the museum was announced, and we were able to show how wartime life and what we call *la culture de guerre* converged in the major combatant countries.

We were committed to a certain degree of thematic overlap between the walls and the floor space. The reason was our belief that front and home front were in fact much closer together than many accounts of the war suggest. Films showed the wounded coming home, and the presence of civilians, farmers in particular, among the soldiers camping on their land. Civilians stayed in Péronne throughout the war, and watched the German army come and go four times in four years. In March 1917, they retreated from Péronne forty miles east to the Hindenburg line. They levelled most of the buildings in Péronne to preclude their use by the Allies and as a calling card, the Germans put up a big placard over the ruined town hall. It said 'Nicht ärgern, nur wundern' (do not be angry, just be amazed). It is that sense of astonishment at what war had become that we aimed to project in the museum's treatment of civilians and soldiers alike.

The design of the museum building emphasised this fundamental contrast between the horizontal and the vertical. The architect, Henri Ciriani created the design of the museum to resemble both an armed encampment, coming out of the ground, and a tomb. I found (and still find) the design highly original, in suggesting a kind of ecological disaster, in which the war permanently injured and indelibly marked the landscape. That motif of a tomb helped us move from tourism to pilgrimage in the ambiance of the museum. The architect here worked on his own; we adapted to his notions, which had important implications for the representation of war we wanted to develop. He helped us mix the sacred and the profane, both abundantly present in wartime, in a beautiful and quiet space.

In 1990 I had been engaged for some years in writing a history of mourning after the First World War, and was struck by the space Ciriani had provided for us. Anyone travelling around France will note that most war memorials express hope through verticality. By choosing the horizontal as the central axis of the museum, we were blunting hope – or rather raising questions about the hope of some kind of redemption, aesthetic or otherwise, emerging from war. The opposite vision I took from Hans Holbein's 'Christ in the Tomb' of 1524, now in the Kunstmuseum in Basle, where the dead Christ is completely horizontal; no one looks on; there is simply death and absolutely no hope of the Resurrection. For Holbein this may have made the miracle of the Resurrection even more powerful, but for us, the message was different. It was the use of the horizontal to avoid giving a positive gloss to the war, one in which its glorification is possible. The Imperial War Museum in London is one such powerful statement about war from an older, more patriotic point of view. We wanted to move in another direction, and used the horizontal to do so.[4]

Issues of design matter intrinsically, but they also illustrate how historians can and must contribute to the design discussion of historical museums; this was only one level on which the link between professional architects and museographers on the one hand and historians on the other operated. Even before Rougeron's resignation in 1990, the bureaucrats wanted to test the waters and see whether I was right in saying that a research centre could and should be set up at Péronne, which is a small market town. Here French academic politics came into the equation. French university life is spectacularly underfunded; this is even more marked if one contrasts the meagre resources and rundown physical plant of provincial universities – or even the Sorbonne – with the separate and better-equipped facilities of the *grandes écoles* or the CNRS, the national research foundation. Most French historians teaching in universities have little experience with research centres because there is virtually no funding for them, outside the CNRS. In addition, French historians of the First World War are a fractious lot; to choose one group to run this research centre, and through it, to guide the museum's work, would be to offend the rest. In conse-

4. For the full statement of this argument, see J. Winter, *Sites of memory, sites of mourning,* Cambridge, 1995, chapter 4.

quence, they asked an outsider – me – to gather together in the Somme forty of the leading historians of the First World War from around the world. The French bet that I could not do it, and waited to smile benignly at the failure. To their surprise, forty colleagues from Australia to Israel came, and on 20 September 1989, inaugurated the research centre. Then and only then did *nos chers collègues français* become full and active collaborators in the project.

In 1990, two years before the opening of the museum, it had a corporate life, a visible existence because of the research centre. Part of that presence showed another linkage between museum work and historical scholarship. We decided to use our annual budget in such a way as to earmark about FF100,000 for scholarships for graduate students who needed a short period of time to complete research or writing on the Great War, and to do so anywhere in the world. Then in the Thatcher years, the future for graduate students was bleak in Britain; such funding was a blessing. For French students, it was completely unprecedented.

This braiding of research centre and museum is the central element in the 'Historial' project. When the museum opened on 16 July 1992, we could all breathe a sigh of relief that it had come off. There were some costs, perhaps inevitably so. The opening ceremony was organised by the Department without consulting the historians. As a result, they celebrated the event by inviting and fêting Ernst Jünger himself, the author of *Storm of Steel*; a man who had fought there, at Péronne, seventy-six years before. The problem was timing: 16 July 1992 was fifty years to the day after the notorious *'grande rafle'*, the round-up of Jewish children in Paris, en route to Drancy and Auschwitz, an event conducted by men who had their offices adjacent to those of Jünger, then responsible for army propaganda in Paris. His hands were far from clean, and I for one did not want to shake them. But there he was, embodying the ugliness of one war at a museum exploring the history of another. Public funding meant public compromise.

Conclusion

The years that have passed since the opening of the museum have been successful ones. The Historial has managed to attract the approximately 60,000 visitors per year needed to cover recurrent expenditure. The museum has won the 'European museum of the year' award. We are in the process of revising the design of the last room in the museum, on the post-1918 years, in light of recent scholarship. The research centre and its activities have made a mark in both French and international awareness of the Somme as one of those *lieux de mémoire* of which the French are so fond.

We have done so without the names of the historians associated with the project being visible at any point or place in the building. Here we return to the question of collective history. No one of us – and here I can only speak indirectly for Jean-Jacques Becker, Stéphane Audoin-Rouzeau, Gerd Krumeich and Annette Becker, the original *comité directeur* – created the design; it was hammered out in interminable meetings of maximum disorder in the French style, but hammered out it was. Fortunately, Stéphane Audoin-Rouzeau and Annette Becker, both young and dynamic scholars, found posts in the region, at Amiens and at Lille, where they now hold chairs. They could therefore handle the day-to-day tasks of running a research centre. They were also unmistakably French, and hence less likely to draw fire than foreigners when we dispersed an entirely French-funded budget.

If our names cannot be seen on the museum, the museum can certainly be seen in our historical scholarship.[5] Each of us in different ways has drawn on the project. We were all engaged in the construction of comparative cultural history, something more than the history of representations, and less than the exploration of a timeless *mentalité*. The museum enabled us to direct our attention more acutely to the codes, gestures and objects created by contemporaries to make sense of the world in which they lived – the

5. For our collective work, see *La très grande guerre*, Paris, Le Monde, 1994 by J.M. Winter, J.-J. Becker, A. Becker, S. Audoin-Rouzeau, G. Krumeich; *Guerres et culture, 1914–1918* (edited by J.-J. Becker, A. Becker, J. M. Winter, S. Audoin-Rouzeau and G. Krumeich), Paris, A. Colin, 1994. For our several contributions, see A. Becker, *La guerre et la foi: de la mort à la mémoire, 1914–1930*, Paris, A. Colin, 1994; J.-J. Becker, *La France en guerre: 1914–1918: la grande mutation*,Bruxelles, Editions Complexe, 1988; J.-J. Becker and S. Audoin-Rouzeau, *La France, la nation, la guerre, 1850–1920*, Paris, SEDES, 1995; S. Audoin-Rouzeau, *L'enfant de l'ennemi, 1914–1918: viol, avortement, infanticide pendant la Grande Guerre*, Paris, Aubier, 1995; S. Audoin-Rouzeau, *La guerre des enfants, 1914–1918: essai d'histoire culturelle*, Paris, A. Colin, 1993; S. Audoin-Rouzeau, *14–18, les combattants des tranchées : à travers leurs journaux*, Paris, A. Colin, 1986; G. Hirschfeld, G. Krumeich and I. Renz (eds), *Keiner fühalt sich hier mehr als Mensch : Erlebnis und Wirkung des Ersten Weltkriegs*, Essen, Klartext, 1993; J. M.Winter and J.-L. Robert, *Capital cities at war: Paris, London, Berlin, 1914–1919*, Cambridge, Cambridge University Press, 1997; J. Winter and E. Sivan (eds), *War and remembrance in the twentieth century*, Cambridge, Cambridge University Press, 1999; J. M. Winter and B. Baggett, *1914–18 : the Great War and the shaping of the 20th century*,London, BBC Books, 1996.

world at war. Without the rough and tumble of the construction, my guess is that none of us would have written history as we have come to do.

I cannot speak for my colleagues on this point; their voluminous scholarship speaks for itself. However, there is a sense that by working on objects, on the presentation of artefacts in space, on the explication of what some have called 'material culture', we have been able to avoid falling into an idealist trap present in much contemporary writing in the field of cultural history. The danger is to see representations as not only a significant reality, but the *only* reality.[6]

One instance may illustrate this problem, and our attempt to find a solution. At the entrance to room three, covering the period 1917–18 are three *fosses*. They include, on the left, a range of weapons, in the middle, an array of defensive equipment, much of it frail, indeed medieval in its chain-like character, and on the right, a trunk full of the possessions of the French author and surgeon Georges Duhamel, including the flute he used to play to regain his composure between operations. Here is a simple trilogy: attack, defence, outcome. Combat, and in particular combat in trench warfare, is in no sense a text, a semantic construction. It is about metal and the way it tears soldiers apart. In case the visitor might think that we were making a strictly materialist point, adjacent to these displays are video screens which present some of the same objects, and the men subjected to them, in training and in use. Film, itself a cultural code flourishing during the war, contextualises the objects, locates them in space, time and a kind of language whose power derives in part from its silence.

Doing this kind of material history has informed the way we, the historians at the centre of the 'Historial' project, do cultural history. There is also a second way in which dealing with objects has affected our own sense of cultural history. It is in forcing us to consider the limits of representation itself. Between rooms two and three, which cover respectively 1914–16 and 1916–18, is a white space, with the simple legend, 'The Battle of the Somme'. That is the only direct representation of it. Nothingness conveys the problem of representing a reality about which we have no direct evidence. There is no film of the battle; there are images of mines exploding, and there is the notoriously staged scenes of

6. R. Chartier, 'Le monde comme représentation', in *Annales. E. S. C.*, Nov.–Dec. 1989, pp. 1505–20.

'Going over the top' in a contemporary film made during the battle for domestic consumption.[7] Yet of the battle itself, we have very little *direct* evidence.

Presenting an empty space invites the visitor to imagine battle; using objects to create a sense of combat is a dangerous game, easily moving into the realm of kitsch. What good would it have been for us to show a rat, mud or staged destruction, when none of these things remotely approaches the sheer terror of the moment of attack and counter-attack? The Imperial War Museum has tried this, and has fallen into the trap of pseudo-realism. Such an approach is attractive, and visitors flock to the Imperial War Museum by the tens of thousands. Nevertheless, we wanted to show another way. All the displays are austere, clean, beautiful, perhaps too beautiful, according to some commentators. Yet by adopting a minimalist attitude, in which we suggest, rather than instruct, we offer a language of visual representation not only aware of the material realities behind it, but explicitly aware of its own limitations.

On the day the museum was to open, it was far from complete. All the objects had been put in the showcases and the *fosses*, and the highly polished wooden floor and cement pillars completed. Cleaning the lot on the day before the opening had produced the opposite of what we had intended: it had deposited a thin white film of dust on everything. Entering the museum was like going into a catacomb. You could not see a thing. Then, after we got out the industrial vacuum cleaners and worked at a terrified speed, it all suddenly appeared, as if a fog had lifted. What I saw for that moment was magical – a beautiful place to mark an ugly war, a visualisation of history that suggested much more than it showed. It was a creation that had a few of my own notions in it, but they had been transformed by a collective effort that had effectively effaced them. The whole was much, much greater than the sum of its parts.

It had – and has – the capacity to touch ordinary people. I like to wander around overhearing snatches of conversations from family groups visiting the museum. They bring many things to the museum, but time and again it is the family narratives that are heard: snatches of memories of a great-uncle or grandfather's lives in the early part of this century. To the extent that we have transformed formal history into family history, and thereby have

7. See the comments of Nick Hiley in episode 4 of the BBC/PBS series 'The Great War and the shaping of the twentieth century', 1996.

enabled families to place themselves in these stories, we have found a way to break out of the isolation of professional historians, speaking to smaller and smaller groups of readers about narrower and narrower themes. Public history has its dangers – trivialisation or oversimplification being among them – but they exist in every corner of our profession, and not just in historical work outside the academy.

Perhaps it is time to insist upon the risks of *not* doing this kind of work. One of the clear dangers of historical writing is its tendency to mistake cynicism for wisdom, to place historians in the position of knowing more about the world than did the people about whom we write. Of course we know more than they did; we know the outcomes. However, working in the framework of a museum establishes a kind of complicity between professional historians and laymen and women. We share the same narratives, many of which are family narratives, though we may express them in different ways. Outreach may not only be creative and exciting, though it is both; it may also be an act of moral responsibility for a profession which at times turns its back on the millions of people outside the academy who are our allies, our audience, and our subject.

5

LEST WE FORGET:

Memories, History and the Musée de la Résistance et de la Déportation de l'Isère

Sarah Blowen

On 1August 1994, under a blistering sun, hundreds of *Grenoblois* lined the streets of their city to watch a drive-past of historic military vehicles. A military band played and a local choir sang the *Chant des partisans*. The crowd, moved to tears, reported the Dauphiné Libéré,[1] watched on as local children, dressed in white, collected around a huge urn. Some carried flaming torches, while others carried phials containing earth from the fifty-eight cantons of the departement of the Isère, which were solemnly emptied into the urn. There were speeches, dignitaries were present, the accent was on the ceremonial.

The occasion was the fiftieth anniversary of the Liberation of the city of Grenoble at the end of the Second World War and the opening of the new *Musée de la Résistance et de la Déportation*. This inauguration was significant for the inhabitants of Grenoble but it was not only the local press which carried the story. For the new museum was the fruit of an unprecedented collaborative effort between former members of the Resistance and deportees and local cultural agencies. It also attracted much professional attention for its state-of-the-art displays. That a provincial city in south-eastern France rather than a national capital should be responsible

1. E. Louis, 'Un lieu de mémoire au coeur de la ville', *Dauphiné Libéré*, 2 August 1994.

for such a venture might at first seem incongruous. However Grenoble has a distinct place in both the development of a new museology – the philosophy of the museum institution – and in the memory of the Second World War, and these specificities find their nexus in this project. It is unique in many ways, but at the same time representative of many contemporary debates on the role of cultural institutions in forging collective identities.

This chapter charts the various stages of the development of the museum up to its inauguration, whilst exploring a series of wider questions thrown up by the museum creation process. How does a museum strike a balance between the narrative of history and that of memory? How does it allow for a plurality of voices and representations? What form should the exhibition space take, so that the past is not reduced to a purely decorative function? Does the museum's relationship with the public authorities make it hostage to political imperatives? Can local past experiences be translated to draw wider conclusions, both geographically and temporally? Who, ultimately, is a museum for?

Marie-Hélène Joly offers a helpful and comprehensive typology of museums of the Second World War in Chapter 3. She distinguishes between 'first' and 'second' generation museums, the former being those instigated by veterans themselves, the latter being those created as part of the commemorative zeal of the 1980s and 1990s. The Musée de la Résistance et de la Déportation in Grenoble fits this typology exactly, but with an interesting twist: it began life as a first generation museum, only to reinvent itself as a second generation museum thirty years later. We shall now trace the steps of this transformation.

The first generation museum: 'an emotional hotch-potch'

There is a long-established perception of wartime activity in the Isère: the fiercely independant *maquis* in the Vercors mountains around the city; the 'phoney' Italian occupation followed by the repressive German occupation with its mass deportations of local citizens; the subsequent distinction given by de Gaulle – Grenoble as one of only five French localities to be awarded the *insigne de Compagnon de la Libération* (Order of the Companions of the Liberation) for the city's suffering and courage. Due to its strategic and symbolic importance, this period of Grenoble's past has been turned into something of a national myth. Grenoble was a large university centre which had sheltered many intellectuals and activists during the war. After the Liberation former soldiers, members of the Resistance and returned deportees made their way back to the city, and this critical mass was to play a significant part in the drafting of the *programme d'action du Conseil national de la Résistance*, a series of political measures and policies which were to shape France in the post-war period.

It was these Grenoble veterans who were also to be the driving force behind the creation of a museum dedicated to resistance and deportation. They had found that their wartime experiences had taught them more about liberty, responsibility and personal initiative than any formal schooling ever could. As a consequence, they spearheaded the movement for education for the masses and in 1945 founded *Peuple et Culture*, an association dedicated to the right to education and instruction for all, whatever their age or social origin.[2] Many of the veterans had entered the teaching profession and were anxious to organise a collection of documents, objects and testimonies which could be used to transmit the ideals and the legacy of the Resistance to younger generations who had not known the war. The significance of this pedagogical focus should not be underestimated: such ventures were few and far between at this time when 'collective forgetting' was common in much of France, as the country nailed her colours to the mast of modernisation and sought to put the war behind her.

Plans for a museum were first mooted in the late 1950s. A committee was formed which brought together representatives of no fewer than twenty-seven veterans' organisations, ranging from the Communist to the Gaullist Resistance, and which covered the whole geographical spread of the Isère. In 1963, when an initial display of their collected material in the Departmental archives attracted much positive interest, the search for a permanent site for their collection began. The committee took the name of *Comité du musée de la Résistance dauphinoise*, and although the *Comité* was to run the museum as a private venture, links with the municipal authorities were inevitable as many of the city's elected officials were also members of the same network of veterans' groups

2. The development of the *éducation populaire* movement (education for the masses) will be of great interest to the reader of this book, due to the major role it has played in restructuring the cultural and social sectors of post-war France. See 'Education Populaire, le retour de l'utopie', *Politis magazine*, 29, February - March 2000, hors-série.

which flourished locally. The mayor Albert Michallon, himself an *ancien résistant*, offered premises in the building where the writer Stendhal had been born, in the rue Jean-Jacques Rousseau at the heart of the old quarter. On 23 April 1966, Deportees Day, the Musée de la Résistance et de la Déportation opened to the public. The small appartment was crammed full with displays and objects giving an exhaustive presentation of the actions of the Resistance and the horrors of deportation. No wartime battle was forgotten as local and international perspectives jostled for space. A contemporary tourist brochure described it as *'un fourre-tout émouvant'* (a hotch-potch which tugs at the emotions).

The transformation process: museum politics

The museum attracted a respectable five thousand visitors per year, many drawn from local schools on organised visits, in line with the pedagogical intentions of the veterans. By the 1980s however it was clear that the size of the museum and the static displays were no longer adequate to their purpose. Other cultural attractions held more appeal for an increasingly demanding audience. Younger visitors gained little from the peeling black and white photographs and did not stop to read the long explanatory notes. The *Comité* therefore put forward an ambitious and coherent plan for renovation. It was argued that the importance of the ever-expanding collection should be recognised through the attribution of local, regional *and* national financial support. The plan listed the need for new premises, a new museographical display based on the latest museum design, the cataloguing of the collections and the appointment of a qualified curator.[3] Presented to the mayor of Grenoble, Alain Carignon, in his capacity as president of the *Conseil général of the Isère*, this plan was given the official go-ahead in October 1986. In 1987 the *Conseil général de l'Isère* approved the creation of a new *musée départemental de la Résistance et de la Déportation*, a public structure which would replace the private museum, with the veterans remaining in control of its day-to-day running. This was to be under the curatorial guidance of the Musée Dauphinois, the regional history museum in Grenoble. The Musée Dauphinois and the ethnographic approach it favoured

3. J. Paquet, 'Le musée de la Résistance et de la Déportation de l'Isère', *Evocations*, 1993–94, p.60.

had long been central to the cultural policy of the city and using its expertise to guide this project was viewed favourably on all sides. The *Comité* had begun an active campaign to attract sponsorship, but with little success. Its members recognised with much foresight that a partnership with a respected existing museum would improve their chances of securing funding in the increasingly competitive market for cultural capital investment.[4]

In early 1990, Jean-Claude Duclos, assistant curator of the Musée Dauphinois, began to work with the *Comité*. An ethnologist by conviction, he had previously curated several very successful community-led exhibitions which had entailed working closely with various sectors of the local population such as the Greek and Italian communities and agricultural small-holders struggling at the margins of urban life. The first task that he identified was the drawing up of a computerised inventory of the existing collections in order to assess their historic value. The *Comité* understood that enthusiasm and commitment were not enough: to secure funding for a major overhaul, the museum would need to convince the *Direction des Musées de France* (National Museums Directorate, hereafter DMF) that it had a material heritage of some note. This, along with a strong museographical design for the display of these collections, was a central criterion for obtaining the DMF's classification of *musée contrôlé* (designated museum status). Such certification would add weight to the museum's applications when it competed for public funds. As highlighted by Marie-Hélène Joly, the DMF emphasis on material collections is at odds with the objectives of many museums of the experience of war, where immaterial ethnographic remains – oral testimonies, memories, shared values – predominate. However, the Grenoble veterans had unwittingly helped their cause in pursuing a relentless search for documents and objects of all kinds during the entire post-war period. The wide range of Resistance and Deportee groups involved enhanced not only the quantity but also the quality of the collection, which included complete runs of some of the clandestine publications produced in occupied Grenoble. These fragile papers were of highly symbolic value reinforcing a certain idea of resistance, but they also singled out the collection as an invaluable research resource.

---

4. Interview with Pierre Bolle, member of the *Conseil Scientifique du musée de la Résistance et de la Déportation*, May 1995.

The application process was slow and protracted. The DMF was however following the developments in Grenoble with great interest. Severely criticised by cultural commentators for its reluctance to move away from its narrow definition of the museum institution, it had long been seen to favour *Beaux Arts* art galleries and elite cultural forms. By the early 1990s the DMF had to acknowledge that heritage was more broadly construed by the visiting public who were flocking to the new industrial, historical and rural-life museums. It was also the slowest administration of the Ministry of Culture to embrace decentralisation and, as most of these popular, dynamic museums were geographically remote from Paris, was no longer representative of the whole museum sector. Recognising that it needed to widen its remit to keep in step with the evolution of the sector, the DMF looked for potential allies and advisors. The Parisian *Musée des Arts et Traditions Populaires*, long-regarded as the main ethnographic museum in France, spent most of the 1980s and 1990s in a state of organisational disarray. Therefore the DMF looked to the Musée Dauphinois as a benchmark of best practice, endorsing its achievement in moving forward the boundaries of museum practice in this domain(see below). In June 1993 the future musée de la Résistance et de la Déportation was granted the status of *musée contrôlé* following a DMF inspection of both the collections and the initial plans for the museum layout which had been drawn up by Duclos. As a result of this favourable inspection, Ministry of Culture funding became available via its devolved *Direction régionale des affaires culturelles* (Regional Directorate for Cultural Affairs) for the Rhône-Alpes region. This was decisive in prompting the *Ministère délégué aux anciens combattants* (Secretary of State for War Veteran Affairs) and the Conseil régional to offer their backing also. The main source of finance for capital costs was, however, the Conseil général, which contributed FF 14.5 million, compared with the FF 2.5 million allocated by the Ministry of Culture and FF 500 thousand by the War Veterans administration. In 1991, a large municipal building in the rue Hébert, which had been earmarked as a possible home for the new museum, was purchased from the city by the Conseil général. Close to the city centre and a minute's walk from a tramway stop, the location was ideal. The guarantee of funding meant that renovation could begin: the new museum could now become a concrete reality.

The relative ease with which the project attracted the backing of the public authorities merits attention. Cultural institutions are increasingly finding themselves at the heart of political decision-making, as shown by Susan Milner and others in this volume: was there a hidden agenda in the promotion of the museum project? Did the political will of specific personalities play a role? It would appear that the Gaullist RPR *(Rassemblement pour la République)* mayor of Grenoble, Alain Carignon, saw in the renovation of the museum a consensual project for the city. However, it must be noted that, like so many of the generation too young to have fought in the war, he held a passionate fascination for the Resistance and this personal interest undoubtedly helped to speed the project on its way.[5] However, the city authorities were already financially committed to the building of the *musée d' intérêt national* (MIN) launched as a regional *Grand Projet* under President Mitterrand, which was to house the city's exemplary art collection. By 1986 Carignon was not only mayor, but also Minister for Communication and brand new President of the Conseil général. Locally, it was rumoured that the MIN benefited from his hotline to Paris for attracting massive central funding whereas other equally worthy projects languished. Similarly, the attribution of departmental funds to buy the new premises for the Resistance museum and to provide the majority of the capital costs was seen by some as Carignon wanting to secure his power base in his new function. The veterans were fully aware of these arguments when they pressed for the status of departmental museum. They felt that playing on Carignon's *cumul des mandats* (concurrent occupation of several public offices at different levels of government) would help their cause. They believed that the heavy financial burden of the MIN on Grenoble rate-payers would scupper their chances of backing at municipal level, and so appealed to their mayor in his other capacity.[6] The gamble paid off and the museum was to become truly representative of the whole of the Isère.

Would Carignon, an ardent Gaullist, seek to guide the narrative of the museum in the General's favour? All the indications are that he did not interfere in curatorial decisions, deferring to the

5. Interview with Jean Paquet, president of the museum association, May 1995.

6. See aforementioned interviews with Paquet and Bolle. The veterans recognise that this move on their part was fortuitous: in 1995 Alain Carignon was arrested for misuse of municipal funds and served time in prison. It should be noted that the Musée Dauphinois was also transferred from municipal to departmental control during this period. In this instance, the transfer was formal recognition of the fact that the museum was already carrying out much technical and advisory work to support other institutions in the area. It kept its name but now also has a function as the *Conservation départementale de l'Isère.*

judgement of the veterans and Duclos. Anecdotal evidence does however exist to suggest that Carignon tried to have the opening brought forward to coincide with the one hundredth anniversary of the General's birth. This did not happen, and the date remained one which could have a symbolic resonance for every veteran, regardless of their political motivation. Nevertheless, the budget for the inauguration was to be FF 1 million,[7] and the event would offer numerous publicity opportunities for the dignitaries of the Isère and Grenoble who were present.

The second generation museum: defining a purpose

Jean-Claude Duclos did not only have to oversee the structural transformation of the museum. He also had to tread a sensitive path in order to reconcile the objectives of the veterans (who retained legal ownership of the collection on behalf of the various veteran and deportee associations) with the imperatives of contemporary museum creation. If the project was to succeed, the veterans would have to modify their understanding of their role as both key players in the events on display and as guardians of that heritage. In the four years between the initial involvement of the Musée Dauphinois and the inauguration of the new Musée de la Résistance et de la Déportation, this was to be a major challenge facing the curator.

To find common ground and unity of purpose, it was necessary to define a rationale for the museum, and to agree its function as a new cultural institution for Grenoble and the Isère. In this, the influence of the Musée Dauphinois was to be decisive. The Musée Dauphinois is pre-eminent in a group of institutions which had in many ways anticipated that the socio-economic reshaping of France would need accompanying spaces in which communities could both reflect upon these changes and rebuild some sense of identity. They called themselves 'musées de société', a term which is difficult to translate for folk-life museums, ethnographic and industrial collections, rural or urban site museums all fall under this title. Recognising this complexity, Emilia Vaillant interprets it not as a definition of type, but rather as a banner bringing together a variety of institutions united by a common aim: 'to study the evolution of humanity from a social and historical point of view,

7. Interview with Gil Emprin, museum education officer, June 1995.

and to provide means and markers for the understanding of cultural and social diversity'.[8] Since the 1970s, the Musée Dauphinois had pioneered this approach based on radical museum ethics which came to be known as *le style grenoblois*. This stipulated that the museum must collaborate with the local community it serves, as well as the general visitor, to articulate collective or personal memories. In so doing, these memories are restored to those who have no voice of their own, with the museum acting as a kind of psychoanalytical tool to explore contemporary society in the light of past and present experiences. This is 'committed' museum practice, often referred to in the profession as New Museology: the exhibition space is utilised as an act of restitution and empowerment. The veterans understood this philosophy perfectly as it paralleled their own motivation in setting the original museum: using their wartime experiences and the legacy of the Resistance to show the role and responsibilities of the individual in society today. Therefore it was decided that the new Musée de la Résistance et de la Déportation was to become a *musée de société* rather than a history museum. Terminology is a difficult matter, as all museums and heritage sites tend to qualify their stance in relation to other competitor institutions and so any label tends to be relative rather than absolute. Jean-Claude Duclos argues however that every museum with the Resistance as its focus should be categorised as a *musée de société* due to the nature of the past which is its currency:

> The kind of experience of the past which is usually found in the *musée de société* is one which is nearly always inextricably linked to the process of memory. This memory carries a mixture of warnings from the past and projections into the future and it can call up moral and possibly even utopian sentiments. This is why any musée de la Résistance is a *musée de société* first and a *musée d'histoire* second. It is actively committed to a single objective: that of fighting totalitarianism, anti-Semitism, racism and social exclusion.[9]

This supposes that a history museum is something else, as borne out by a further quote:

---

8. E. Vaillant, 'Les musées de société en France: chronologie et définition', in *Musées et Sociétés*. Eds E. Barroso and E. Vaillant, Association Musée sans frontières, Mulhouse, 1993, p.37.

9. J.-C. Duclos, 'Les résistants, les historiens et le muséographe: histoire d'une transaction et de ses enseignements', unpublished conference paper, 1996. (All translations into English are by the present author).

The museum must be able to adapt to the evolution of historical knowledge and must be able to draw upon developments in current affairs. The evolution of the relationship between collective memories and history will mean that the museum narrative will constantly be reassessed. This is why the Musée de la Résistance et de la Déportation is a *musée de société* – it must move with the times.[10]

The distinction is therefore drawn between a treatment of past events which isolates their specificity in time and space and one which allows comparisons to be drawn across generations. Paul Ricoeur qualifies the distinction thus: 'It is memory that has a future, whereas history provides an interpretation of past events which forgets that they have a future'.[11] Other scholars do not necessarily support this view and argue that historical events are created from a unique set of circumstances and it would be dangerous to suggest that they can be used to teach us how to react to events in the present.[12] The dialectic between history and memory is central to much contemporary thinking in the historical profession, and the veterans, in their consideration of the rationale of the new museum, were joining in the debate. They became aware that history and memory both use the past to tell a story, so the museum would inevitably become a place of discourse. Yet the narrative will not be the same: as François Bédarida tells us, history aims at truth and encourages critical distance, whereas memory aims at *fidélité* – faithfulness – which encourages identification with the event from within.[13] This distinction was at the heart of the veterans' thinking and they realised that their initial display had been too resolutely historical for their initial purpose. With its encyclopaedic presentation of wartime events, it had attempted to answer questions on behalf of the visitor. Museums may tell a truth, but they can never tell the *whole* truth: to acknowledge the subjectivity of the truth on offer should allow the visitor to engage with it, reflect upon it, and make up their own mind. This was highly liberating for the veterans, who now understood that their purpose would be better served by focusing on the narrative of memory, which would encourage visitors to ask questions on their

10. Interview with Jean-Claude Duclos, May 1995.

11. P. Ricoeur, *La critique et la conviction. Entretiens avec François Azouvi et Marc de Launay*, Paris, Calman-Lévy, 1995, p.189.

12. See, for example, P. Bordes, 'Les musées et l'histoire'. In *Musées et recherche, Actes du Colloque*, Dijon, OCIM, 1995, pp109–119.

13. F. Bédarida, 'La mémoire contre l'histoire', *Esprit*, July 1993, pp7–8.

own behalf therefore actively involving them in the museum experience. The veterans' remembrances would provide a human link between the past and the present and could send out a message of hope. This was to be their contribution to the life of the Department: 'Tant que nous nous souvenons, tout est possible' (So long as we remember, everything is possible).[14]

As the memorial approach focuses on the transmission of experiences lived from within, the scope of the new museum would have to be pared down to those events and processes in which the veterans themselves had participated. The choice was made to jettison an exhibition of the Second World War from a global perspective, which at first worried those veterans who felt that the museum would nevertheless need to be located in time and space by some historical markers. A compromise was reached by the plan to include a preliminary area of the museum space which would rapidly place the specific events in Grenoble and the Isère in the wider context of the unfolding war in Europe. In the end, external factors also played their part in this narrowing of focus. In the run-up to the fiftieth anniversary of the end of the Second World War, the DMF began to receive large numbers of applications for support for new projects from cities, towns and even villages throughout the country, anxious to record their own contribution to the war effort and the Liberation of France. It would be impossible for every planned museum to receive funding; a country can only have so many collections of unexploded bombs and ration books maintained at the public expense. As the Heritage Lottery application system has recently made clear in Great Britain, success would depend upon the demonstration of some original or specific appeal. Duclos therefore insisted that the Grenoble application should play heavily upon its local specificity and the originality of having so many of those who had participated in the events to be displayed associated with its development. Countless other museum projects which had retained their universal presentation of wartime events never saw the light of day, and they conceded that without the presence of a professional museum curator who understood the selection process at their side, the Association would never have been able to make the most of the many assets they possessed.

---

14. The words of Elie Wiesel, recited by Alain Carignon in his speech at the inauguration of the museum.

Finding a voice: narrative choices

The decision to adopt a memorial approach was undoubtedly liberating, but how could all the memories represented by the twenty-
seven different associations represented find their voice?
Jean-Claude Duclos had been aware of this potential pitfall from the
first and so had insisted on the setting up of a steering committee
(*conseil scientifique*) drawn from a broad representation of most of
the groups, which would guide the writing of the museum narrative on a collegiate basis. The curator could not advance without the
backing of the veterans, and vice versa. Steering committees are an
integral part of the *style grenoblois* and are now much used elsewhere.[15] Dominique Vieville gives a useful typology of these committees, highlighting that in the main they draw upon specific
academic expertise which the generalist curator cannot hope to
command. They exist either for the limited duration of the planning
of a temporary exhibition, or for framing the overall mission of the
museum.[16] He stresses that the steering committee should enrich
the work of the museum, but at the same time be careful to limit its
involvement to that of the provider of specialist advice. The steering
committee of the new Musée de la Résistance et de la Déportation
varies from this model in that its members were also the museum
managers and, as we have seen, their memories were to become one
of its major historical resources. Some specialist historians did join
the committee, but it was clear that in order to uncover the various
strands of memory which should find their way into the display, the
veterans would have to be at the heart of any technical discussions.
Similarly, the committee would have to meet over a long period of
time to allow these narratives to work their way to the surface. The
group of roughly twenty people met regularly for two years to
thrash out the narrative choices which would dominate the exhibition space and the concrete episodes which would be chosen to
illustrate them. In order to focus the discussions, Duclos made the
committee first put together a temporary exhibition in the Musée
Dauphinois in April 1993. Called *Les Années Noires – la répression à
Grenoble pendant l'occupation* (Dark Times: repressive measures in
Grenoble during the occupation), the exhibition concentrated on

15. For another example of the *style grenoblois* procedure, see S. Blowen, 'Images
of Exile and the Greeks of Grenoble: a museum experience'. In *New Readings*, Vol.4.
Eds C. Gorrara and F. Meyer, Cardiff, University of Wales, 1998, pp55–66.

16. D. Vieville, 'Les conseils scientifiques dans les musées'. In *Musées et recherche,
Actes du Colloque*, Dijon, OCIM, 1995, pp215–218.

the efforts of the various groups of the Résistance to continue their under-cover activities in defiance of the French *milice* and the Gestapo. This 'dry run' was a popular success, but it revealed to Jean-Claude Duclos that a great strength of feeling and resentment was dividing the various factions represented on the committee.

The Communist Resistance complained that their wartime activities had been sidelined in the exhibition. Others insisted that General de Gaulle should stand at the heart of any such exhibition and if he did not, it would look as if the Liberation of the Isère had come about more by accident than by design. The Jewish community were angry that they were still cast in the role of victims: when would their own resistance be recognised? Veterans from the north of the Isère challenged the narrow focus of the exhibition: many of the significant acts of resistance and sabotage had occurred a long way from Grenoble. Fifty years on, the divisions were as strong as they had ever been. Indeed, Duclos was amazed that the various factions had been able to work together thus far, given the reactions of many of the *ancien combattants*. It was evident that while they agreed about the global purposes of the war, the focus on the local was causing this unity to unravel.

The solution lay in the presentation. Duclos decided that the emphasis must be upon *mémoires juxtaposées* (parallel memories). The heart of the museum space would be given to the central notion of *entrée en résistance* – the reasons that motivated individuals and groups to take a stand against occupation. This would bring together the different points of view, whilst at the same time allowing them all to have a specific voice. It would be wrong to view this decision simply as a judicious compromise. The more points of view the museum could project, the more it could claim to be representative of the local community. Even if they did not agree on the reasons why they decided to resist, all recognised that there had been a specific moment and a specific set of circumstances which had caused them to take a stand. The veterans warmed to the idea, as did the professional historians who were working alongside them on the steering committee. Any remaining doubts about whether the museum should have qualified itself as a *musée d'histoire* disappeared. It was clear that a purely objective historical approach would not have allowed for such juxtapositions and that differently refracted points of view would have been hard to accommodate. The provision of temporary exhibition space alongside the permanent galleries further eased the tensions. Temporary exhibitions are increasingly the mainstay of museums and today all newly created museums and heritage centres are designed to cater for them. By ringing the changes, visitors can be encouraged to return time and again. In the case of the Musée de la Résistance et de la Déportation, it was an added incentive to the associations involved, with each planning their own temporary exhibition.

The past on display: object choices

Once the steering committee had begun to sketch out their narratives, an appropriate museography had to be put in place. The interior of the rue Hébert premises had been ripped out and four levels built giving a total surface area of 1,165 square metres. Three of these floors would be used for the permanent exhibition, with the fourth given over to offices, the documentation centre and museum store rooms. The museum architect Bernard Dutel, the scenographer Jean-Noël Duru and Jean-Claude Duclos were anxious that the display should be far removed from that of the rue Jean-Jacques Rousseau with its surfeit of objects and information. Their museographical plans were totally in keeping with the concepts of New Museology. Broadly speaking, objects, the usual museum currency, are deemed important only in so much as they highlight specific human experience. If an object cannot be anchored to the central narrative thread of the museum, it has no place in the display. Glass cases still exist in many museum institutions which are the direct descendants of the encyclopaedic collections of nineteenth-century national and municipal institutions. These subscribed to the belief that knowledge is power and the exhibition space could be used as a bulwark of social control. In focusing not on power but empowerment, New Museology and the *musées de société* place the visitor to the museum at the centre of the institution's priorities. A visually dramatic *mise en scène* is used to bring the events to life and make them accessible to the visiting public. Sounds, lighting and 'props' – non-original artefacts – are all utilised to encourage the visitor to respond emotionally to the display. With this approach, any museum can of course run the risk of being nothing more than the institutional equivalent of a vacuous costume drama. Yet when a strong and coherent narrative underlies the display, the effect can be to create '*les conditions esthétiques de la pensée*' [17] – an aesthetic environment which encourages critical thought.

17. J.-M. Frodon, *Le Monde*, 27 February 1997.

The steering committee was to produce the libretto and the museography was to be its score: any text should find its echo in the scenography, and vice versa. Five overarching principles were established to guide the development of both within the museum space available.[18] Firstly, the content must be accessible to a wide-ranging audience, with particular reference to children, in a visit to last an hour and a half. This would have implications for the written elements which would have to be simplified and reduced to a minimum. Similarly, the themes presented would have to be easily identifiable. This would mean dividing the space of the exhibition into coherent sections through varying the scenography used from one to the next. Secondly, the exhibition should respect the chronology of events, whilst clearly drawing out thematic strands from each: it was recognised that many visitors may have only a tenuous grasp of the chronology of the Second World War. Thirdly, the decision to narrow the focus to the geographical limits of the Isère in the main was formally adopted. The veterans understood that this should not be construed as a limiting gesture; rather, using concrete events and their parallel memories of them would allow for a more complete extrapolation on the part of the visitor. Fourthly, it was agreed to make good use of the already extensive collections of the old museum.

Although fewer objects or documents would find their way into the exhibition space, the direct link between those objects on display and the narratives of the veterans themselves would inevitably invest the objects with greater power and meaning. Finally, the content (themes and debates) and form (scenography) of the museum must be as easily malleable as possible. This supports the thesis proposed by Jean-Claude Duclos and adopted by the steering committee, which recognises that the museum must 'evolve through time'. That this should be actively encouraged by the veterans, rather than imposed upon them by curatorial demands, highlights one of the unique aspects of the Grenoble project. Marie-Hélène Joly suggests that many veterans are motivated to become involved in museum projects in order to mark their own place in history. This usually leads to a very static, hermetic display, with the museum becoming some kind of reminiscence therapy. The Grenoble veterans, sensitive to the responsibilities which accompanied their will to transmit messages to future generations,

18. J. Paquet, 'Le musée de la Résistance et de la Déportation de l'Isère', *Evocations*, 1993–1994, p.66.

were clear from the outset that this museum would only partially be theirs. The message and presentation would have to evolve so that future generations could continue to relate to the exhibition and its debate and the museum move on in the hands of curators. Guided by these five principles, the steering committee refined their narrative choices in order to arrive at sections which would present the chronological and thematic development they required. After presenting the initial background to the run-up to war and occupation, the visitor would be taken through spaces devoted to the *entrée en Résistance*, the role of the underground Resistance, the *maquis*. Then the period of German occupation would be presented in a space devoted to repression and deportation, before a section devoted to the Liberation and the restoration of Republican values in France. So the itinerary would be a movement from the specific to the general, with the general extrapolation firmly rooted in the role of the Isère Resistance groups in the creation of post-war values. A final space would however take this extrapolation even further, and was to prove highly controversial: the relevance of the values of the Resistance for the world today.

The exhibition space: from local to global

The historical background begins on the ground floor and uses wall displays of photographs, posters, newspapers and small objects as it spirals upwards, quite literally taking the visitor through the ascent into war in Grenoble and the Isère. Displays of pre-war life are followed by images of the fall of France and the setting up of the Vichy government. A stopping place on the spiral gives access to an audio-visual presentation of the main periods of the Second World War which situates the local events in a wider context. At the centre of this section devoted to pre-occupation Grenoble and Isère, is a film clip of the visit to Grenoble of Maréchal Pétain in March 1941. It is chilling in its enthusiastic gaiety and the place Verdun looks pretty much as it does today, foreshortening the historical difference between then and now for the viewer. A short text tells the visitor that the local *députés* were amongst the few who voted against giving full powers to Pétain, but no attempt is made to excuse the local flag-waving. This marks a first significant point in the new museum. No other exhibition had dealt with the Vichy period in such a direct way. Museums were still part of the collective amnesia which meant that little mention was made of popular support for the Vichy Regime. The steering committee had been categorical: this is part of our past, and so it has to have its place in the museum. The stilted moving images made a powerful point about collective responsibility.

On the first floor, the visitor is presented with the different *entrées en Résistance* and it is here that the parallel memories find their place. Tightly designed and low-lit spaces, some with original artefacts, but most reconstitutions of specific locations, evoke different meeting places and atmospheres. The office of Major Seguin de Reyniès at the Bonne barracks is recreated, the desk cut away to reveal a cache of arms and explosives and highlighting the specific contribution of the army Resistance. The façade of the Café de la Rotonde, a landmark which had just disappeared to make way for Grenoble's Europole business district, is also ressurected: its shutters drawn, the subtle clink of glasses suggests clandestine activity within. It is here that the *Francs Tireurs* organised their sorties into the Vercors. Here is the genteel dining room of Marie Reynoard, teacher at the lycée Stendhal. It was in this room that she set up the discussion group that would become the *Combat* Resistance group. Chairs surround a small stove. The chairs are empty and speak of loss: Reynoard was to be arrested and deported by the Germans in 1943 and died in deportation. All strands of Resistance find their place in this dramatic portrayal of sites and sounds. There is hardly any text here, and the main narrative is carried by these visual and aural markers. These different *entrées en Résistance* are spatially juxtaposed, but at this stage no links are made between these spaces, challenging the preconception of the Resistance being a monolithic entity.The exhibition continues by drawing these threads together, showing how the various groups came to work together and establishing the geographical spread through the Isère by the various networks. Radio transmitters, parachutes and camouflage equipment are displayed alongside photographs showing the various hideaways of the *maquis* groups in the mountains. The complex genealogy of the *maquis* necessitates a more conventional presentation here, with maps and diagrams.

On the second floor, the visitor is confronted by the German occupation of the Isère from September 1943, following the abortive Italian administration of the area. The visitor sees three wooden doors, lit so that the various graffitti on them can be read clearly. These were the doors of cells at Gestapo headquarters in Grenoble. Names of seventy imprisoned Resistants and locals can be seen carved on them, along with messages, poems and drawings. Forty of these names have been identified, and the stories of five people are recounted alongside the doors. This reveals much of what went on behind these doors – torture, suicide – and they provide an emotionally charged link for the Grenoblois of today to their wartime predecessors. The doors are original artefacts isolated from their original location, but this does not lessen their impact. A short text tells the visitor that the Gestapo headquarters were at 28, cours Berriat. This information provides a powerful juxtaposition. It is to this site that many locals now flock each week as the building houses a major city centre supermarket. Universal significance can be drawn from these doors, but they speak loudest to those who are so closely linked to them in time and space.

The device of isolating original artefacts to highlight their significance is used elsewhere. More than three thousand men, women and children were deported from the Isère, of whom only just over a thousand were to return: on 11 November 1943, a patriotic demonstration in Grenoble was to result in the arrest and deportation of four hundred inhabitants. The experience of deportation is evoked by a length of railway track, leading off to an unknown destination. Small box-shape holes in the walls invite the visitor to a close inspection of their contents: each contains a 'treasure' or an object fashioned in one of the concentration camps, which belonged to a local deportee. In the old museum, deportation had been depicted with graphic images of mass graves and unbearable physical hardship. Here, the approach is different. As the visitor stands face to face with the isolated object, the experience of deportation is vividly humanised, with one individual simply contemplating the life of another. The boxed-in isolation of the object reinforces the isolation of the deportee. The everyday nature of these objects – a drinking bowl, a child's toy – creates an empathy which again transcends time and space.

The Liberation of the Department follows, with the display centred around the *Comité départemental de Libération nationale* (the Department Committee for National Liberation) and its role in re-establishing the Republic. The final section of the exhibition presents *mémoire et actualité de la Résistance*, and brings the visitor right up to date with a contemporary call to arms. This is a space of both allegory and reality. In the darkness, the visitor perceives four peripheral pillars upon which continuous messages flash in red: *attention, discernement, réflexion, vigilance*. A central pillar inscribed with the Republican values of *Liberté, Egalité* and *Fraternité* tramples a large

Swastika underfoot and is crowned by an image of Marianne, the symbol of the Republic. In the corners of the room television screens relay images of examples of contemporary totalitarianism and intolerence.[19] On the wall at the exit to this space contemporary newspaper cuttings are displayed which relate other abuses of human rights as they occur worldwide. A final text gives the watchword: '*Rester vigilant, prêt à dire non et à se battre, telle est l'attitude de la Résistance*' (Remain watchful, ready to say no to wrong and to fight for what is right, is the message of the Resistance).

This section has strongly divided both museum curators and the historical profession. Some see it as a remarkable and compelling way in which to teach moral and civic values. Others view it as a gross oversimplification and misrepresentation of the past. Commentators from outside France generally welcome this widening of perspective but regret that the presence of Marianne limits the extrapolation to the specific French context. The form the room should take was the subject of intense debate by the steering committee and sketches in the museum archive show the many different scenographic possibilities examined. The veterans freely admit that they do not all like the form of this section and that it does represent something of a compromise. Yet they all agreed that it had to have a place in the museum to put across their message that their battle was not an isolated one. Future generations must act as they did, in line with the educational intentions underlying the veterans' project since its beginnings in the rue Jean-Jacques Rousseau. To attack the museum for this closing theme would be to miss the point that the choice was made to be a *musée de société* first, and a *musée d'histoire* second, in order to allow for such extrapolations. It could be said that if the rest of the museum has achieved its function, the final room should not be necessary. Yet this would be to ignore the fact that the world in which we live is not one where lessons are easily learned from the past. The veterans would agree with Yannick Guin when he writes that the end of the twentieth century is characterised by an inability to think '*dans la durée*'[20]. Guin argues that our information society presents us with a mass of data, but not the critical capacities

19. In January 2000, video images showed Klu Klux Klan gatherings in America; Neo-Nazi rallies in Eastern Europe; the desecration of Jewish graves in a French cemetery.

20. Y. Guin, 'Musées d'histoire et crise de conscience historique', in *Des Musées d'histoire pour l'avenir*, eds M.-H. Joly and T. Compère-Morel, Paris, 1998, pp343–349.

to analyse it. Paradoxically, faced with this surfeit of information, all certainties are washed away and the past, viewed as a more certain and value-led 'place', is given renewed currency. It is increasingly called upon to provide markers against the accelerated pace of change which characterises contemporary life. As part of this process, the museum will be looked to as a mediator between past and present and as offering certain values. The Musée de la Résistance et de la Déportation fully understood this in placing mediation at the heart of its mission and in insisting on the transmission of personal experiences to enlighten visitors and encourage questioning of the responsibilities of citizenship. Blunt and debatable as it may be, the final section of the exhibition goes some way to providing the analytical tools necessary for the visitor in today's disenchanted world to appreciate that they are part of a rooted historical continuum.

Conclusion

In this chapter, the museum creation process has intentionally been viewed from within. All too often, exhibitions are 'deconstructed' without reference to the museological stance, political background or hands and minds which have shaped them. These elements must be sought out if one is to understand the full significance of the institution in its wider setting and to establish what message it hopes to bring, and to whom.

So who is the museum for? This basic question is, surprisingly, a new one for much of the museum world. Visitor figures are easy to establish, but the quality of the experience for the visitor less so. The recognition that this must be taken into account accompanies a societal shift: museum professionals in all types of institutions are increasingly anxious that the museum should become more than a mere consumer product, and provide a *service culturel* to the visiting public. As such, the Musée de la Résistance et de la Déportation is for the museum community. With its strong educative function, it seeks to provide more than a mere moment of drama and has been instrumental in the evolution of the sector. At another level, the museum is for the wider population of the Isère and Grenoble, making precisely those links through time and space mentioned above to understand the significance of some of the events which still cast their shadow over local life. In this, it has a vital function as part of a current of cultural policy which values institutions with social functions. By extension, the museum is obviously aimed at the young visitor. A vast programme of activities is coordinated by the museum's education officer, Gil Emprin, and an average of eight thousand school children visit it each year. The Musée de la Résistance et de la Déportation was one of the first to commission research into the impact of written texts in the exhibition [21] and has rewritten some texts in order to make them more accessible to youngsters, highlighting its insistence that the museum must evolve to remain pertinent to its visiting public. The comments of the school groups which pass through the museum are often full of emotion and never fail to make a link between the past, present and future: 'Fascism isn't dead. It could always come back'. 'They fought and died for us. If we forget their example, they die a second death'.[22] This developing historical consciousness is encouraged by the fact that the veterans themselves often act as guides for these visits. Questions are asked and answers given which go beyond those offered by history textbooks. The museum is, of course, for the veterans who created it. In bringing to life their memories, the museum is an act of acknowledgement and restitution. It is significant that on the day of the museum's inauguration, the association passed the museum collection into the trust of the departmental authorities, relinquishing ownership, one may say, of the past.

The Musée de la Résistance et de la Déportation is a mirror for some and a window for others, but for all, it raises questions as to the construction of identity and the role of the past in that process. In the words of Jean Paquet, president of the museum committee:

> We must not forget that the only human reality we can know is that of our past, a past which is never fixed, but which is continually being reworked, according to the problems we face, the means at our disposal and the needs of the present. To some extent, we can be seen to choose our past and in so doing, we choose our future. [23]

21. M.-S. Poli, 'Le texte dans un musée d'histoire et de société', *Publics et musées*, no.10, 1996, pp9–25.

22. Comments made by local sixteen year olds on a school visit, as told to the author, May 1995.

23. Jean Paquet, *Discours de réception à l'Académie Delphinale*, 26 November 1994.

PART III
MARITIME HERITAGE

6

CONSTRUCTION OF A BRETON MARITIME HERITAGE:

Processes and Signification

Françoise Péron

It is fairly common in France to speculate as to why it has taken such a long time to recognise the importance of preserving and promoting the heritage linked to France's maritime past. This slow awakening applies to harbours and quaysides, rope-works, military dockyards as well as merchant craft, naval vessels and fishing fleets. The French, compared to the British or the Dutch, have in the past shown only a sporadic interest in the 4,500 kilometres of coastline which circumscribe their metropolitan territory. For the French, their country has been first and foremost a land mass: its coastal regions were for a long time considered as peripheral areas, 'land's ends'. This vision also prevailed traditionally among the nation's geographers.

Over the last fifteen years on the other hand, a widespread interest in everything related to the maritime past has been clearly in evidence. It includes not only the sea itself but also the coast and man-made heritage, and affects all strata in society. The growing popularity of television programmes such as *Thalassa*, sailing and sailboarding magazines, books of photographs, posters representing waves, storms, ships, lighthouses photographed in different lights and from different angles bears witness to this love affair. This development has in fact led to a paradoxical situation. On the one hand, the economic importance of the fishing industry and the merchant navy has been dwindling; more generally all the traditional components of a classical maritime economy have been plunging deeper and deeper into crisis to the point that their future is now seriously under threat. On the other hand, sailing has been rediscovered for leisure purposes in the form of boat trips, regattas, gatherings of traditional sailing craft and festivals of the sea. This has led to an enthusiastic renewal and reappraisal of a sometimes totally recreated maritime heritage, around which festivals of the sea are regularly organised. A few examples are Douarnenez 1986, Douarnenez 1988, then Brest -Douarnenez 1992 and Brest-Douarnenez 1996. These last two festivals attracted more than 2,500 sailing vessels over four days in Brest harbour for the pleasure of more than a million visitors. A maritime event on such a scale had never before been witnessed in France.

The scale of these events, the proliferation of festivals on a smaller scale, scattered, in Brittany at least, over the whole coastline, bear witness to a change in mentalities and perceptions as regards maritime affairs. This new awareness, for which the French have coined the word *maritimité*, lures crowds to the seaside for reasons unrelated to work or to the traditional pleasures of the beach and has a strong leisure and holiday character as it mainly takes place during the summer holiday season. However, it is also part of a wider quest for authenticity and identity on the part of individuals as well as coastal villages and small towns which engage in it.

This observation leads to four questions:

- What particular social and cultural conditions are at the root of this heritage process?
- What is the nature and significance of this 'new maritime heritage'?
- How did the various prime movers involved in the process develop different yet sometimes converging strategies?
- What, from a social and geographical perspective, are the consequences and limits of this movement? Is this a fashion which will soon run its course or is it a more deep-rooted phenomenon reflecting the development of a neo-urban society whose nature and role will have to be appraised in the context of the current restructuring of the use of space, characteristic of our time?

In order to find an answer to these questions, the experience of the Brittany coastline will be used as a case study. Geographically Brittany is the cradle of this resurgence of interest in French maritime heritage and the region where it is most strongly felt. It offers the whole range of maritime heritage activities, from the building of replicas of fishing boats by local associations, to the opening of a large sea life museum in Brest (*Océanopolis* is now the main tourist attraction in the town) or the project to create a national marine park of the Iroise Sea, close to Brest.

To throw light on this complex phenomenon, an analysis covering three discrete phases is necessary. We shall look first of all at the characteristics of French maritime heritage in the period before the 1980s, that is to say before the main heritage movement got underway. We shall then move on to the passion for maritime heritage which has characterised the last fifteen years and found its expression in a real cult of the boat as an object, including the building of replicas whose sparkling newness has not jeopardised their status as heritage products. Finally an analysis will be made of the meaning and consequences of this vast movement which goes far beyond the simple building of a fleet of traditional working boats: the dynamics created around traditional sailing craft has contributed to the transformation of the coastline in keeping with the new socio-economic needs of French society at the end of the twentieth century.

French maritime heritage: the historical perspective

First, a rapid outline of the main ways in which maritime heritage evolved in France over time. To begin with (see Chapter 7 below), the complexity and fluctuating nature of the concept of heritage needs to be underlined. The word encompasses three aspects: unifying, subjective and strategic. Heritage unites people who identify with a corpus of artefacts and inherited values which are considered worthy enough to be transmitted to the following generation. It is subjective in as much as what is included as heritage varies from one period, one culture or one social group to the next. Inventories of what constitute heritage need constant updating because of the vast choice between a nearly unlimited potential number of artefacts and inherited values. Ships, buildings, wharves, tools, seamanship, rituals, sea shanties, artefacts produced by sailors, letters, memoirs, etc, are all inherited from the past; not all can be preserved by the living. As with the construction of other heritage activities, maritime heritage is the result of a sorting process carried out at a given time among remnants inherited from the past. What is at a given moment seen as heritage is the subjective result of the relationship between each social group and its past, in keeping with its present needs. What constitutes the heritage of a given social group is the collection of artefacts and traditions constituted by the group for its own use. Finally all heritage construction is strategic as it is ultimately a way of perpetuating a group by asserting its difference vis-à-vis other social groups.

Heritage therefore is in constant flux: each period focuses on the content of its own heritage. It has a social nature and projects into the future: it can exist only through the society which holds it together, maintains it, takes responsibility for it, uses it and attempts to transmit it. Each new heritage activity which emerges is an indicator of social change and it is therefore from the angle of changes and processes that the whole subject needs to be tackled.

Until the 1970s five discrete components were identifiable in French maritime heritage. The first was an architectural and military component dating back to the seventeenth and eighteenth centuries. Wharves, city walls, rope-works, warships belonging to the French Navy were from the start of more than a little interest to the enlightened public of the time. This public was proud of the nation's achievements, which were seen as the results of human reason at work. However, behind the scene, the state was orchestrating this movement. The commissioning of a series of paintings of French ports by Joseph Vernet[1] and of engravings of the port of Brest by the Ozanne brothers was intended to disseminate an exalting representation of French maritime power at its peak. However, after the defeats of the Revolutionary and Napoleonic era, a waning of sea power followed and during the first half of the nineteenth century, part of this maritime heritage either disappeared or was abandoned. Compared to Great Britain, maritime policy in France has lacked historical continuity; national maritime heritage is still paying the price for this. The recent proposal to move the *Musée de la Marine* from the Palais de Chaillot in Paris to a less prestigious site is a reminder that French maritime identity still holds a minor place in national priorities.

A second component in maritime heritage was the result of civilian maritime life in the nineteenth century with its functional and material nature whose value was publicly acknowledged at different times: lighthouses have from the outset been considered as works of art, worthy representatives of the technical ability of the nation; on

1. Joseph Vernet (1714–1789) was a French painter of the Pre-Romantic period. He completed a series of fifteen paintings called 'The ports of France', a commission from Louis XV, between 1753 and 1763. He became a member of the Royal Academy.

the other hand, fishing boats linked to small-scale fishing such as tuna and lobster boats, fish-canning factories and similar functional buildings have long been ignored and despised. As late as the 1960s and 70s, the last wooden sailing boats used for fishing or coastal trading were rotting away in Brittany in estuaries and harbours. They would have all disappeared in turn if it had not been for two seminal works which brought traditional sailing boats to the forefront of the heritage movement: *Groix, l'île des thoniers* (Tuna fishing on the Isle of Groix) by Dominique Duviard, published in 1978, and *Ar Vag, voiles au travail en Bretagne Atlantique* (Sailing boats at work on the southern coast of Brittany) edited by Bernard Cadoret and published in 1984 in Douarnenez. Previously, Jean Baudouin's *Les Bateaux des côtes de France* (Boats of the French coast) was published in 1974 but was known only to a few specialists.

The third component in maritime heritage is of a social and cultural nature and can best be described as the seafarers' dimension. The division of the maritime community into seafarers and shore-based people took place at a time when the economic development of the coastline followed the expansion of the railways. The coastline was no longer cut off from the rest of the country and small-scale fishing grew with the opening of new markets. A coastguard system and network of lights and beacons was established in order to aid long-haul shipping. At the same time the urban middle-classes, including numerous painters, writers and journalists took advantage of the railways and of the first steam boats – the main lines were open between 1885 and 1890 – to visit the coast and islands of Brittany. These newcomers on the coast were concerned that their world was changing rapidly because of the impact of industrialisation. In these remote lands' ends, they were looking for a part of humanity which had remained unaffected by the decadence of the age: primitive, pure, honest and courageous human beings, unaffected by the 'evil of civilisation'. They naturally had a tendency to idealise fishermen and their families; they described the tragedies that affected them; they focused on the cult of death which, in their view, characterised the inhabitants of these islands. For example, around 1900, the painter Charles Cottet [2] made a

2. Charles Cottet (1863–1925) was a painter of the socialist realist movement and a follower of Gustave Courbet. At the time when Pierre Loti published *Pêcheurs d'Islande*, he was painting the seafarers with whom he was in daily contact around the coasts and islands of Lower Brittany (Camaret, Island of Sein and Ushant). In his pictures he brought out the noble qualities of the fishing community and the profound effect that death had on these families, constantly at the mercy of the implacable sea.

series of austere and beautiful paintings based on scenes from fishermen's lives in Camaret, Ushant and the Island of Sein. Breton writers such as François-Marie Luzel [3] and Anatole Le Braz [4] took an interest in legends, traditions and death rituals peculiar to fishing communities and linked them to ancient civilisations which had disappeared elsewhere.

A few observations can be made as regards the research carried out on maritime and coastal societies during the century 1870–1970. First of all it it significant that the lives of merchant sailors, who were very numerous during that period, did not interest French writers and anthropologists specialising in the maritime world; consequently a great part of the heritage linked to the merchant navy has disappeared. The second point is a more general one: the lives of fishermen inspired writers such as Victor Hugo and Pierre Loti [5] and held an interest for their readers, but objective observers of the maritime world were a minority among researchers and the approach adopted by the Breton writers mentioned above was short-lived. Maritime anthropology was born late: in the debate about Breton regional consciousness in the 1930s–1960s, the rural world was deemed to encompass all the essential values making up Breton identity. At Brest University, the *Centre de Recherches Bretonnes et Celtiques* (CRBC, Breton and Celtic Research Centre) organised its first international conference on a maritime theme only in 1996. The conference entitled *La ville maritime* (The Maritime City) was organised when Brest was the centre of a large gathering of traditional craft for the second time, ten years after such gatherings started in Douarnenez.

3. François-Marie Luzel (1821–1895) dedicated a large part of his life to compiling a collection of oral traditions of rural Breton folk (tales, narratives, legends, songs). Via articles in a great number of magazines and newspapers specialising in Celtic affairs, he helped to develop an appreciation of the originality of this popular type of literature. Luzel is considered to have been one of the great folklore specialists of the nineteenth century in France (*Contes populaires de la Basse-Bretagne*, 1867). He also took an interest in Breton seafarers (*Voyage à l'île d'Ouessant*, published in 1874 in the *Revue de France*).

4. Anatole le Braz (1859–1926) was another writer in the Celtic tradition who also compiled collections of Breton tales and legends (*La légende de la mort*, 1893). He had an affection for people of humble background whose oral testimonies were considered by him to have greater value than most written works of literature. He took an interest in the maritime world and also extended his work to the coastal populations.

5. Still on the theme of seafaring life, we should note two novels which enjoyed enormous success in their time: *Les travailleurs de la mer* by Victor Hugo, published in 1866, and *Pêcheurs d'Islande* by Pierre Loti, twenty years later.

The fourth component of Breton maritime heritage was linked to the notion of the seascape. Unlike the other aspects previously mentioned, this aspect developed continuously from the middle of the nineteenth century onwards. It originated in the vision of painters, writers and the first railway visitors, whose descriptions and paintings of seascapes initiated an inventory of beauty spots along the coast, out of which emerged the major sites still so heavily visited today. Colonies of writers and painters of French or foreign origin spread from one year to the next along the Brittany coastline at a time when small-scale fishing was booming, creating an international reputation for sites unknown until then, such as the Pointe du Raz, Camaret harbour and the bay of Douarnenez on the West coast of Finistère. Postcards very quickly took over from painters' easels; inspired by writers' descriptions, tourist guides also spoke highly of the beauty of the coast and listed those circuits and beauty spots not to be missed. In 1975 the *Conservatoire du littoral et des rivages lacustres* (national body in charge of coastal protection) was created. Its objective was to protect the most famous natural sites, that is to say those which were part of the emotionally charged inventory drawn up at the end of the nineteenth century by landscape spotters at the time of the Impressionists. As a consequence, the current vision we have of the Brittany coast has to be seen in the light of the interpretation given to it by artists more than a hundred years ago.

Finally, maritime heritage had an ecological, moral and leisure component, which developed in France later than in Great Britain and coincided with the democratisation of nautical sports. After the successes of Alain Gerbaud and Bernard Moitessier in single-handed sailing, Eric Tabarly caught the imagination of French youth in the 1960s, opening their eyes to the virtues of sailing as a discipline, the beauty of a hull slicing through the waves, the purity in the lines of sails when they are in perfect harmony with the wind which fills them. Here, the originality of the French and particularly the Bretons lay in the importance attached to single-handed transatlantic races. A generation of yachtsmen was trained by the designer of all the *Pen Duick* yachts, the name given to a whole generation of sailing boats designed for speed by Eric Tabarly when he adapted traditional sailing boats to incorporate the most recent technical developments. This movement played a major part in the heritage awakening of the 1980s–1990s.

The renewal of maritime heritage in Brittany: instigators and strategies

The rapid historical outline of the various heritage strata over two centuries described above brings out some of the specific features in French attitudes, which were characterised by a wavering and sporadic acknowledgement of their maritime cultural heritage. It is therefore impossible to understand what is happening today on the Brittany coastline as regards maritime heritage without referring to the major social, economic and cultural upheaval which took place in the 1960s and 1970s, and brought about significant changes in France, particularly an indisputable heritage fever.

Until the 1960s France remained an essentially rural country. The following decade saw an acceleration in economic change and a rapid transition to an urban society in which tertiary employment played an increasingly important part. The rural population diminished; towns expanded; the work place became distinct from the home; individual mobility increased at all levels. The face of French society changed rapidly and the French became suddenly aware that a long phase of their rural past was on the verge of disappearing forever. The rural sociologist Henri Mendras called this brutal end of peasant life 'the second French Revolution'. It is no coincidence that in 1975 three books dedicated to traditional country life were published in the prestigious Plon collection, *Terre Humaine*. Their success surprised everybody involved in publishing. They were *Le Cheval d'orgueil* (The Horse of pride) by Pierre-Jakez Hélias, a Breton-speaking professor of French; *Montaillou, village occitan* (Montaillou, an Occitan village) by the historian Emmanuel Le Roy Ladurie; *La France rurale* (Rural France) by another well-known historian, Georges Duby. The relationship between the French and their past was about to be completely transformed.

To quote from Pierre Nora, editor of the original collective work *Les Lieux de mémoire* – three huge volumes were published between 1984 and 1992 – (see general bibliography at the end of the volume), 'heritage is no longer the inventory of totemic masterpieces of national stature, but a collective asset belonging to particular groups of citizens who, by appropriating it, decode an essential and constituent part of their identity'. This explains how various heritage activities emerged: Corsican, Breton, rural, industrial... and maritime. The nature and social function of heritage also went through a profound change. French heritage, which used to be made up of easily inventoried material elements of an essentially national and historical character, has become more intangible. Interest in artefacts still exists, but so too does an interest in the rituals and practices of the people who used these objects; hence an interest in the reminiscences of old people – indeed as old as possible – in order to collect an authentic account of how things used to be in former times. The social base has become more diversified, with each group tending to create its own heritage. Official curators have been overwhelmed by this heritage fashion which is blossoming in a spontaneous way, fostered enthusiastically by individuals and local associations intent on 'preserving our heritage'. All sorts of museums have been created, dedicated to horses, cider, schools, bees, seaweed farming, etc. However, a feature of these developments is a new concept, the eco-museum. The *Ecomusée des arts et traditions* on the island of Ushant, which opened in two small houses on the island in 1968 was one of the first of a generation of new museums intended to create a positive image of local life. In this way, the notion of heritage expanded considerably and became the concern of the whole population.

This is the context in which Brittany reinvented its maritime heritage, essentially via traditional sailing craft. At the beginning of the 1980s, the alarm was raised. France was letting its traditional sailing boats disappear without trace, and with them a whole maritime culture was dying. Several events explain how public opinion was brought to focus on this situation. First of all, a 'Ministry for the Sea' was created and Louis Le Pensec (from Finistère) was the first to be offered the post of Minister. The Ministry of Culture headed by Jack Lang became very active and within it, the Heritage Department, created in 1978, played an important part. Under its auspices, a high profile conference was held to promote the preservation of maritime heritage. This took place on board the *Belem*, the last French three-masted barque, in the presence of the two ministers. Secondly, far from the political world, the growth in nautical leisure activities meant that sailing became accessible to great numbers of people; the nation began to take pride in the values associated with sailing. At grassroots level the pressure from local associations increased. In 1979 the *Fédération Régionale pour la culture maritime* (FRCM) was created in Douarnenez under the direction of Bernard Cadoret. In Brest Roads, in 1981, a working boat named *Notre-Dame de Rumengol,* an old *gabarre* built in 1945 in Camaret, was taken out of service. For over thirty years it had transported wine from Algiers to Port-Vendre, then strawberries from Brittany to England, and finally sand in Brest. A local associ-ation was created to buy the boat and restore it. Fifteen years later, after it was totally refitted, the boat was launched during the Festi-val of the Sea in 'Brest 96'. More than 40,000 people were present at the launching and *Notre-Dame de Rumengol* was the star of the fes-tival. In 1981 too, in the wake of that growing enthusiasm, Bernard Cadoret assembled a team of young enthusiasts to publish the magazine *Le Chasse-Marée*, which was devoted to traditional sail-ing vessels and techniques. Although it started out on a subscrip-tion basis, it immediately struck a chord for a growing readership which tended to be drawn from the wealthy middle-classes, hun-gry for enlightenment about traditional boat building. It was the ingenious policy of the editorial team to involve the readership in the process of locating and preserving the forgotten heritage. This enhanced sense of the maritime past was in tune with the growing contemporary feeling for ecology. This stakeholder strategy gave subscribers a feeling of belonging to a like-minded community. The *Chasse-Marée* initiative was then followed up by others in the region, notably when the Douarnenez Boat Museum (the first in France) was created at Port-Rhu in 1988.

This awakening had two essential consequences. It gave pre-eminence to the maritime as an aspect of Breton identity; secondly, it focused first and foremost on one object above all others, the boat. After the Second World War, Breton cultural identity found its expression in two types of festival activities, organised at two different levels. On the one hand, small-scale local fetes in country villages were special occasions celebrating customs and rituals which had been part of traditional life in rural parishes; on the other, large-scale festivals in cities such as Quimper (*Les Fêtes de Cornouaille*, organised by Pierre-Jakez Hélias) and Brest (*La Fête des Cornemuses*, which became the *Festival Interceltique* when it moved to Lorient). These festivals with their processions of people dressed in traditional costumes, songs, bands, even Breton food, were often the opportunity for extremist groups with a separatist message, such as the *Front de Libération de la Bretagne* (FLB) to get their mes-sage across to a wider public, sensitive to the need to take action if Brittany was to survive economically and culturally and not endure a slow death like other French peripheral areas. However, from the 1980s onwards, land-based cultural events progressively gave way to maritime festivals, and the success of the latter has shown no sign of declining for the last ten years. This develop-ment is in a way more attuned to the needs of a new generation and has helped to regenerate the Breton movement. For these people separatist claims are hardly a consideration at all; what matters is the development of a modern Breton culture (the present transformations of Breton music are proof of this), open to the outside world. These maritime festivals, which often attract huge crowds, in which Bretons and non-Bretons, locals and tourists, happily mix on the quaysides in a harmonious and easy-going atmosphere, are the sure sign of a re-alignment of the Breton regional movement and the adaptation to modern life of a 'minority culture'. This term in a way is no longer valid as Breton culture in its modern form has now become a model imitated by other regional populations, who are searching for stronger roots in their local environment.

In this process, the traditional sailing boat has become the pride and joy of every maritime festival and as such has played the role of catalyst for new identities and attachment to a particular location. The creation of the FRCM and the launching of *Le Chasse-Marée* have inspired an enthusiasm for preserving every aspect of maritime culture: sea shanties, songs of the workers in canning factories, ex-votos, naive paintings by merchant seamen, etc.; but it is above all the boat that is at the heart of this vibrant maritime heritage movement in Brittany in the last fifteen years. Consequently, traditional sailing vessels have been listed since 1983 as heritage items to be preserved, classified and inventoried by the Department of *Monuments Historiques* in Paris. Boats eligible for listing were immediately assessed by experts from *Le Chasse-Marée* magazine, the FRCM, the Amerami (an association speedily created by Luc-Marie Bayle of the *Musée de la Marine* in Paris for this purpose). In 1990 there were only thirty-one listed traditional boats. It is worth noting that being listed does not automatically mean that the boat in question will be restored; hence in Camaret the last lobster boat, *La Belle Etoile*, was listed in 1983 but is still sinking into the mud in the port. The demand was strong but the supply weak. A few boats were purchased abroad but these purchases were not sufficient to correspond to the surge of enthusiasm for maritime identity at the time. The only solution was therefore to build replicas of boats which existed previously: the 'new' traditional boat with a rather ambiguous heritage status made its appearance.

The first replica was built in Cancale. The initiative for this project came from an association of young people from Cancale, inspired by an enthusiast called Jean Le Bot. The basis of the scheme was public subscription, with local people purchasing shares in the project: it was a winning formula. In 1989 *Le Chasse-*

Marée and the daily newspaper *Ouest-France* launched a competition 'Boats of the French Coast' by way of preparation for the 'Brest 1992' Festival of the Sea. The aim of this was to assemble a range of boats representative of every French maritime location. Eighty building projects were registered as early as summer 1990. This movement coordinated and gave fresh impetus to those projects which were already underway. The boats built were often of modest dimensions and their designs replicated those in existence at the end of the last century, at the time when the need for a small-scale fishing and coastal trade was at its peak. The memory of local people thus played an important part in the process.

For each project, the heritage process followed a very similar pattern. Someone spotted a boat whose existence had been an important feature of maritime life of a particular place, and which had then disappeared. For example, the sloop *La Pauline,* of Le Dahouet, was built following the design of a similar boat of the same name, first built in 1901 to transport seaweed to a local iodine factory. Laid up in 1933 when the factory went out of business, all that was left of it was the faded photograph of a forgotten boat, tied up at the quay in the small port of Le Dahouet. A public subscription on a share basis was launched for the building of a replica. Depending on his or her inclination and financial means, every subscriber could contribute to the funding of a mast, a part of a sail, a pulley block, a shroud, etc. Those that were most heavily involved quickly felt a sense of ownership towards 'their' boat, which thus, from its birth, was very much a collective property. While all this was going on, serious research was carried out to find the necessary documents to build the replica as authentically as possible. Old photographs and postcards as well as customs records were collected, some more useful than others. Newspaper archives were consulted to throw some light on the boat's working life. The archives of the *Service Historique de la Marine* in Paris were also called upon, including some which had never before been consulted; in this way were the enthusiastic researchers able to find out everything about the boat, its crew members, and the nature of its trade. The memories of the older generation in the community was a precious asset, as oral history records provided a fragile and irreplaceable documentary source in this quest for knowledge, especially as regards the life onboard the boat, the skills involved in sailing it, the special technical know-how used onboard. The yard where such boats were built was generally fairly public. A committee of local experts monitored all phases of the building.

The work progressed under the admiring gaze of the local population who were regularly invited to witness the most significant steps in the construction of the boat. On each occasion a little ceremony took place around the boat and in all these places rituals soon developed: the completion of the hull, the launching, the stepping of the mast, the completion of the rigging, the unfurling of the sails, all of these stages were public events. The first time the boat sailed was the biggest event of all, with a cohort of every other local vessel accompanying the new boat out to sea. From this point onwards, the big moments in the life of the boat take on a new dimension. She leaves her home port to take part in the major festivals in Brest and Douarnenez. Here, she is surrounded by crowds on the quaysides, and is also visited by crowds onboard. The success of these first maritime heritage festivals is in large part due to this mixing of crowds. The participants and the general public mingle happily, in a new shared identity, singing, feasting, dancing alongside the boats as well as on them. The atmosphere is hospitable, colourful, festive. It is reminiscent of the traditional Breton rural festivals (*pardons*); but now, this is all taking place by the sea.

The number of people involved and the media coverage of these events, the positive refocusing of Breton identity on maritime life went beyond the reaches of Brittany. The region attracted attention nationally in a way which had never been known before. Within a few years, a whole fleet of Breton boats was built, the most spectacular examples of which were the bisquine in Cancale, the Odet lugger *Corentin*, the Saint-Malo privateers' cutter *Renard*, the Brest schooner *Recouvrance*. From then on, for a few days every year, these vessels put on a magic display, criss-crossing the Brest Roads in full sail, heading out through the narrows into the Iroise Sea towards the Bay of Douarnenez, and all this before the eyes of thousands of admiring spectators. These sailing craft seem like an incredible challenge to the recession which affects maritime economic activities, a defiant response to the Mellick Plan of 1991 set up to scrap fishing boats in order to modernise the European fishing industry without increasing its capacity.

Maritime heritage: social and spatial integration

In the general context of the surge of interest in heritage, Brittany was reborn with a maritime identity thanks to the initiative of certain individuals and the contribution of the local populations who acknowledged their attachment to a maritime culture. Then came the contribution of institutions: the local councils in seaside towns, the French navy, the county and regional councils who jumped on the bandwagon at a time when Brittany was painfully trying to restructure its economy.

However, many questions remain unanswered as to the real nature of the phenomenon and its future. Is this a final farewell to the maritime world inherited from the nineteenth century, a simple ritual, a passage from a traditional to a modern world? In this case is not the movement destined to come rapidly to an end? Is it an illusory remedy designed to make us forget for as long as possible the gravity of the crisis affecting these coastal regions which are far from the great European metropolitan centres, while deep down we all know that it represents a futile solution? If that is the case, does the movement prevent or delay the finding of true solutions to the crisis? Or on the other hand is it not the most obvious proof of a whole restructuring of our national space and a shift in present urban societies to a model based on identity, leisure and culture instead of the industrial model of the nineteenth century?

It might be fruitful to reflect further on the functions and significance of this vast maritime heritage movement in Brittany. Initially, the University world remained relatively silent on this phenomenon. Those who did voice an opinion were fairly critical. Historians expressed doubts about whether it really was a question of authentic heritage. They were the first to call for a major debate on the concept of heritage as they wanted the public to realise that the boats that they admired and worshipped were not historical boats in the strict sense. They denounced the ambiguity of this festive movement which blithely played fast and loose with historical truth, allowing the fun-seeking general public as well as the young to believe that life on board these boats in the last century was a leisurely round of singing and dancing, whereas it was in fact extremely harsh. In Chapter 7, François Chappé goes even further when he points out that through ignorance and intellectual laziness, images of traditional sailing in the last ten years are ideologically consistent with the themes of Pierre Loti's books and the songs of Théodore Botrel, encouraging the public to revel in the pathos of a sea-going existence. In his view, this amounts to a complete obscuring of the social responsibility of the nineteenth-century shipowners. Today, because of its commercial success, maritime heritage can all too easily be lured into being nothing more than a branch of the tourist industry. It will thus have little in common with historical truth or with the real sense of maritime identity which lay initially at its roots.

The accuracy of these criticisms, which were being made from 1991 onwards, is partly borne out by recent developments. The cult of the boat is difficult to sustain at the same level as in the period 1989 to 1996. First of all the maintenance of this fleet of replicas is expensive, and the aesthetic criteria which applied when they were built do not conform to present security regulations. In fact, the question of the future of these boats and of their economic viability was only raised after their construction. The use of the larger craft (including *La Recouvrance*) for cruising in the Mediterranean or the Caribbean has proved impossible, either for marketing reasons or more simply because of the difficulties inherent in sailing these heavy and ultimately fragile craft. The fact that these traditional boats were very vulnerable was perhaps not sufficiently taken into account: shipwrecks and accidents have only been reduced in modern times thanks to technical progress. For opponents of this movement, the time when sailing ships had canvas sails and hemp ropes has gone, and there are better things to do with one's time today.

At its worst, the movement led to grandiose projects such as the building of a clipper ship in Douarnenez, in the heart of the open-air museum in Port-Rhu (see Chapter 8 below). In 1994 no one paused to wonder what possible useful role this clipper could play; transporting food to the Third World was vaguely mentioned. Nobody knew either how the hull, once it was completed, would get through the narrow locks when leaving the museum docks. These questions in any case became irrelevant once the project collapsed, as the result of the financial debacle of the whole Port-Rhu enterprise. At its best, it can be said that a return to traditional lines in boat-building, associated with a renewed interest in sailing has popularised new designs of sailing boats based on traditional Breton hulls and rigs but incorporating modern techniques.

In fact, the stakes involved in maritime heritage are higher than this debate about the nature of new 'traditional' craft. In addition to the reshaping of Breton identity, it can be argued that maritime heritage in its present form plays a territorial and spatial role, enabling Brittany to adjust to the modern world in three different ways.

At the local level, it helps to bring together fragmented communities and create a new feeling of solidarity. The associations for the preservation of maritime heritage very often create a link between the local population and visitors from inland urban areas. Heritage celebrations also enable generations to mix: the fixed and older populations of coastal villages, the young and mobile populations from urban areas mix and fraternise around a common passion or interest. In a way, it does not matter what this interest is; what matters is that people of different geographical origin, with a different individual and family history, assemble in a certain place which becomes theirs, following not the traditional model of territoriality, but a modern one made of disjointed spaces characterised by mobility (work places, living space, leisure areas); this fragmentation in terms of space is bearable only if at least one fixed point can constitute a sort of anchorage and create permanence and identity. This is the case for Breton maritime culture.

At the institutional level, local councils were at first hesitant to get involved. Then they realised that the investment in a handsome sailing ship symbolising the town was a good public relations ploy, an opportunity to transform the image of their town and to acquire an appealing asset as part of a whole tourist campaign. This process took place in Quimper when the city attempted to regain its image as a river port with its Odet sailing lugger, moored during the winter at a short distance from the famous Quimper Cathedral. In the summer, river cruises reinforce the image of a town whose influence stretches far inland. As for Brest, its strategy was slightly different. The schooner *La Recouvrance* was intended to play the role of an impressive ambassador for the city to other countries. The festivals of the sea were used to give Brest the image of a dynamic and modern maritime city on a European scale, thus hiding the reality of the deep recession which affects this city with a large working class population dependent for three centuries on the French Navy and the dockyards. The focus on a reinvented maritime heritage was only one of the aspects of the strategy for the redevelopment of the town. The Sea Life Centre *Océanopolis* opened in 1992 and now receives more than 500,000 visitors per year and its extension is planned. It is a major tourist facility for the city and the council would like to see it complemented by the future Iroise marine park, so that both of them can constitute a pole of attraction fostering an ecologically sound and sustainable use of the marine habitat. Finally the major project to restore the natural site at the Pointe Saint-Mathieu completes the wide-ranging programme aiming at restructuring the use of space which is taking place presently in the most western part of Brittany.

At the regional level, as has already been stressed, the rural image of Brittany has now been replaced by a maritime image present on the front page of almost every local newspaper and in magazines luring tourists every summer to Brittany to discovers ports, boats, lighthouses and seafaring people. Throughout France, Brittany is now considered to be a 'tonic experience', the regenerative power of surf and spray having no equal.

By accumulating photographs, videocassettes and television programmes with an increasingly stereotyped and bland content, presenting an idealised image of maritime life, Brittany ends up being packaged in the most simplistic fashion. Yet, if we look at it more closely, the whole process of the making of the Breton maritime heritage is far from negative. It contributes to the modernisation and the redefinition of the use of space in depressed areas: for example, the little island of Molène has become the favourite place for launching new Breton products. If we take the example of Finistère, with the festivals of the sea, the Océanopolis Sea Life Centre in Brest, the reorganisation of the Port-Rhu museum in Douarnenez, the Isle of Ushant lighthouse museum, the imminent marine park, the *Department* already has many valuable tourist facilities. If we add to this list a number of smaller-scale events, newly-established coastal paths, sporting activities which take place throughout the year, we can see how much in the course of a few years, the Breton coastline has changed, how maritime heritage, authentic or not, has contributed to a dynamic process of complete geographical reorganisation of space.

Acknowledgement

To map out the construction of Breton heritage and understand its significance and socio-geographical implications, numerous sources have been called upon: articles in newspapers, magazines and scholarly journals, conference proceedings (in particular those of the conference 'River and maritime heritage', organised by the Ministry of Culture in 1992), personal observations and university research carried out in the Geolittomer-Brest research centre. For six years micro-social geographical studies have been carried out by undergraduate and postgraduate students as part of University studies in the West of France on the theme of seafaring societies.

7

HERITAGE AND HISTORY:

Rocking the Boat

François Chappé

> Les outils du grand-père recueillis par le conservateur des ATP (Arts et Traditions Populaires) sont-ils encore des outils du grand-père? Elément du patrimoine, l'objet change de nature et de fonction. Il sert à autre chose. A quoi alors? Sinon à illustrer le patrimoine. (J.-P. Babelon, A. Chastel)[1]

> Are grandfather's tools collected by the curator of the museum of 'Arts et Traditions Populaires' still grandfather's tools? Once it becomes part of our heritage, the artefact changes its nature and function. It has a different purpose. What is that purpose other than to illustrate heritage?

If only because of who its authors are, this apparently light-hearted quotation deserves a detailed analysis for several reasons: in fact practically every word in it poses an interesting problem; it ends with a question, the answer to which, while misleadingly tautological, is a stimulating enigma for all those concerned with heritage. The maritime scene will be the focus of our present study, but the difficulties encountered are of the same nature whether we consider rural, industrial or maritime heritage.

By definition, and this is the only definition possible, heritage is a human activity with a universal application in time and space even if it is performed with varying intensity and methods. These

---

1. J. P. Babelon and A. Chastel, 'La notion de patrimoine', *Revue de l'Art*, 49, 1980, p.30.

differences make it virtually impossible to arrive at a final definition of heritage. In accepting this we can apply to heritage the
same statement used by H. Seton-Watson about the concept of
nationhood: 'I am led to the conclusion that no scientific definition
of a nation can be established...yet the phenomenon has existed
and still exists'.[2]

We will explore the reasons for it being impossible to arrive at a
scientific definition of heritage, using J.-P. Babelon and A. Chastel's
question as our framework and pursuing it to the limit of the contradiction that they expose, a contradiction which is far from ster-
ile. We will then examine the reality of heritage work; we shall ask
ourselves in what way it can or cannot be distinguished from the
work of the historian and what are the consequences of this possible independence of heritage relative to the discipline of history.

Let us start therefore by analysing the quotation at the head of
this study. The word 'tool' refers to a technical, manual or craft
activity, but a natural extension of its usage leads us to adopt the
word 'artefact' (*objet* in French) which Babelon and Chastel also use
in their study. At the end of the Nantes *Estuaire 1992* conference,
Hervé Couteau-Bégarie, in answer to the main question 'what is
heritage?' saw a return to 'the confrontation between two concep-
tions, one centred on artefacts, the other on human beings. The former is naturally more dominant'. He proceeded to refine this
difference by distinguishing between those people for whom 'heritage is first and foremost, if not exclusively, made of artefacts' and
'the followers of the anthropological approach which basically
tends to identify heritage with collective memory'.[3] This distinction
is valid in practical and administrative terms, but fundamentally it
is difficult to justify in the light of the following statement: as Edgar
Morin[4] stressed, 'the biggest mistake is to isolate an object from its
human environment'. An artefact only attains its full significance
when it is viewed in its cultural context. It would seem that a fundamental problem is posed from the outset regarding this contex-
tualisation which is an indispensable part of heritage activities.

In an exhibition it is of course possible to display artefacts – a
pebble from the beach for example – without any commentary or

---

2. H. Seton-Watson cited in B. Michel, *Nations et nationalismes en Europe Centrale
XIX–XX S*, Paris, Aubier, 1995, p.15.

3. H. Couteau-Bégarie, *Estuaire 92; le patrimoine maritime et fluvial*, Paris-Nantes,
Ministère de la culture, Direction du Patrimoine, 1993, p. 449.

4. E. Morin cited by B. Lesueur, *Estuaire 92; le patrimoine maritime et fluvial*, Paris-
Nantes, Ministère de la culture, Direction du Patrimoine, 1993, p. 62.

label, and trigger off an infinite variety of imaginative responses. We shall return later to the dangers which this type of cultural display entails, especially when it is a matter of artefacts created for a precise purpose, the understanding of which may be obscured by the manner in which they are displayed. If the artefact is displayed with the intention that this purpose be understood, the cultural imagination of the beholder is called upon and directed towards this purpose; even then this cultural imagination has to be fed with a certain number of references concerning the artefact. A sextant from the last century might be thrown away as rubbish if the person who has stumbled across it has not the slightest idea what its use may have been. At all events the artefact exists only when it is 'examined' by the human gaze.

Conversely, the collective memory, which is the subject of the second concept of heritage mentioned above by Hervé Couteau-Bégarie, cannot be created or transmitted without a technical and physical support, in a word without artefacts. The ex-voto is perhaps the most characteristic example of the impossibility of separating spiritual life from its related material objects. The most immaterial aspect of maritime culture, thriving on legends, traditions, superstitions and sayings, was created on boats and quaysides. It was then committed to books, posters and charts, before being transmitted orally in specialised places such as sailors' bars. No approach to religious culture for example is possible unless one traces its transmission via statues, altars, churches, chapels, processional routes or stained-glass windows. Without denying the existence of differing approaches to maritime heritage, it is important to underline the fundamental *human* unity of the heritage process. If this process places the emphasis entirely on artefacts, the latter can be 'understood' only if one knows of the human cultural context in which they were made; if the process centres on cultural practices, the latter are in turn only comprehensible in relation to those artefacts which are an essential part of them and in relation to places in which they occurred. Ultimately, mankind is both the object and the subject of the heritage process.

The reference to 'grandfather' emphasises a time element, the generational gap in which the heritage process develops. How does time relate to heritage? The time of 'our grandfather' appears as a natural heritage time just like that of the great-grandfather or great-great-grandfather. A serious problem arises when it proves necessary to make a cut-off point between time which has become heritage and contemporary time, between yesterday and the living present. We are all aware of the ambiguity of the French academic convention which understandably confuses the general public in distinguishing between two periods in history: 'modern' history is that which precedes the 'contemporary' era. It is an ambiguity which is further compounded by the distinction between French 'contemporary history' and French 'history of the present time'. All heritage activity is part of a temporal context which is subdivided only by these academic conventions. This fundamental contradiction makes it impossible to define a precise cut-off point between time seen as heritage and contemporary time. The proof of this insurmountable difficulty is the use of this very word *patrimoine* in French (heritage in English) to represent the assets of a company inherited in the past and at the same time the whole of its manufacturing and commercial capacity at the present time.

Who is qualified to collect heritage artefacts? Who is responsible for sorting out the traces of past human activity in terms of those which 'deserve' conserving and those which do not? Everyone, which means no one in particular. The Babelon and Chastel quotation suggests that professional heritage specialists have priority, but the case of maritime heritage at the present time, amongst others, reveals the considerable variety of people active in heritage affairs: national, regional and local authorities, tourist boards, associations, private individuals, commercial concerns. This profusion of people involved in heritage is further complicated by the multiple roles they often fulfil: collecting, preserving, restoring, exhibiting and displaying, explaining and disseminating. Furthermore their motivation may be extremely diverse – sentimental, aesthetic, identity building, scholarly or commercial. Although techniques for conservation and restoration exist, there is no science of heritage. The impossibility of a scientific definition of heritage is further complicated by the impossibility of a definition of the tasks involved in heritage activities since those in charge of it have no single view of what heritage activity is.

When the collecting process is carried out, are grandfather's tools still tools? The question posed by this *still* has to be directly related to Babelon and Chastel's final question: does a tool become a heritage artefact when it loses its original function? Does a lightship which is no longer in operation become a heritage artefact when it is finally moored in the Boat Museum at Douarnenez? The vessel itself does not change in size or tonnage. It is the same artefact used for another purpose; this change is related to its new purpose; the artefact is inseparable from its former and new function. This clearly shows that the separation between heritage centred on artefacts and heritage centred on human beings has hardly any essential value because in any case human beings allocate a purpose to the artefact.

What is the nature of this new purpose? This is the second part of our authors' question. Behind the tautological flourish ('it has a different purpose. What is that purpose other than to illustrate our heritage') can be detected the variety of possible functions already noted: aesthetic, sentimental, identity building or historical. From the outset one can ponder on the choice of the verb *illustrer* (illustrate) instead of for example 'incarnate'. This choice suggests that heritage artefacts illustrate something which exists beyond these artefacts, that heritage is a project, an idea which therefore needs illustrating in the same way that pictures and photographs illustrate a history book or that the life story of certain human beings illustrates the destiny of a nation.

Once we have identified a certain number of difficulties inherent in any attempt to define heritage, it becomes legitimate to formulate a hypothesis which reconciles them but which rejects the definition of heritage as a thing, a substance, an end result, in favour of a perception of an activity which produces effects. This hypothesis is that heritage activity is nothing other than a historical activity. When attempting to justify this hypothesis, we shall have to analyse the risks and dangers inherent in heritage activity's claim to independence.

It may seem paradoxical to demonstrate that a heritage activity, in this case the heritage industry, does not exist. To begin with, we must acknowledge that it does exist in people's minds and in the media, as is clear from the profusion of books, articles and conferences which are devoted to it and also from the titles of books which draw attention to the public obsession with this subject. [5] We must also stress that this activity is only part of the work of the historian. Four factors seem however to justify our hypothesis.

The first is the absence of a precise word to describe the person who carries out the heritage activity. This strikes me as significant. The term 'curator' (*conservateur* in French) seems too restrictive in connection with the variety of activities which this person has to carry out. Even supposing that curating is the only activity with

---

5. E. Lever, 'La folle passion du patrimoine' in *L'Histoire*, 181, p.94. See also H. P. Jeudy (ed.), *Patrimoines en folie*, Paris, Maison des Sciences de l'Homme, 1990.

which the heritage profession is concerned, it is part of a much wider operation than just the 'keeping' of artefacts, objects and archives. The expression 'doing heritage' (*faire du patrimoine* in French) does not exist in the way that 'doing history, geography, sociology' does and this is necessarily so because 'doing heritage' is in fact 'doing history'.

To take an interest in the traces left by past human activities is from the outset to put oneself in the position of a historian. To illustrate this, we shall discuss the example of the traces left by the exploitation of the sea and coast by mankind. One can of course classify them ad infinitum: constructions of various sorts (vessels, wharves, docks, shipyards, etc.), writings (archives, memoirs, books, etc.), oral records (songs, anecdotes, proverbs, etc.), but what unites them is that they are all records of human activity, whether we deliberately intended them to be regarded as records or not. The distinction made by the positivist school between a monument and a document placed the latter above the former because it was deemed to be more objective. Their conclusion was opportunely challenged by, among others, Raymond Aron who stressed that 'the past which has disappeared into nothingness [remains] partially fixed in monuments and writings'.[6] More explicitly Jacques Le Goff is of the opinion that 'a document is a monument'.[7]

In an absolute sense, there is no hierarchy of values between traces: an ex-voto is not of lesser value than the memoirs of Duguay-Trouin; the wreck of the Jean Bart is not more valuable than La Paimpolaise.[8] During the Estuaire 92 conference, a claim was made which I consider to be imprudent to say the least: that the records of ship owners are an indispensable historical element, but they can never replace the testimony of sailors themselves.[9] The opposite could just as easily be claimed but this is not where the problem lies. A possible hierarchy of values to which we will return later cannot be avoided when it is a matter of using the traces in the context of questions formulated about them.

6. R. Aron, *Dimension de la conscience historique*, Paris, Plon, 1964, p.100.

7. J. Le Goff, 'Documents/ Monuments', *Encyclopaedia Finandi*, Turin, Volume V, p. 38–48.

8. 'La Paimpolaise' is a song written in 1895 by Théodore Botrel who claimed to have composed it after reading Pierre Loti's *Pêcheurs d'Islande*. The song was an immense success.

9. D. M. Boëll, *Estuaire 92; le patrimoine maritime et fluvial*, Paris-Nantes, Ministère de la culture, Direction du Patrimoine, 1993, p.232.

The second element, which in some respect equates the heritage observer of historical traces with a historian, is time. With considerable panache as well as profundity, Paul Ricoeur stresses the relationship between the two fundamental elements of the historian's discipline which are historical traces and time: 'Let us observe the felicitous verbal relationship between "having passed" in the sense of "having been past a certain place" and "being *passé*" in the sense of "being outdated"' (in French both meanings are conveyed by "être passé").[10] One cannot do justice to the argument here. Let us simply observe that, in his words, 'the state of "having been" is problematic to the precise extent that it is not observable, whether it is the "having been" of an event or the "having been" of a testimony'.[11] As regards the immense difficulty which makes the historian reconfigure time, using 'specific connectors', such as the calendar, in order to make time 'thinkable' and easy to handle, no difference of status exists between the historian and the heritage curator. Like the anthropologist, sociologist and geographer, both of them are irremediably confronted with time and can do nothing but accept that the past which continues into the present is no longer the same as when it was the present.

The third element, which might allow us to differentiate the world of heritage from the historian's terrain, is the written word. The heritage curator's mission is to conserve, display and divulge the evidence that the exploitation of the sea and the coast by human beings has left behind. The historian's medium is the written account.

The place of the narrative in the historian's discipline is a complex and substantial debate, as the narrative is contemporary and already historical. 'History is the story of true events'.[12] Paul Veyne analyses in considerable depth this fruitful statement but there is no opportunity to go into it further on this occasion. It is appropriate however to note that Paul Veyne's observation is enhanced by Michel de Certeau's exhortation to avoid 'the illusion which makes us think that discourse can do justice to reality';[13] enhanced also by Jacques Roncière's insistence that the work of the historian is the result of a narrative contract,[14] and by the unavoidable fact observed by Antoine Prost that 'it is not possible

10. P. Ricoeur, *Temps et récit*, Paris, Le Seuil, 1997, p.218.
11. P. Ricoeur, *Temps et récit*, Paris, Le Seuil, 1997, p.284.
12. P. Veyne, *Comment on écrit l'histoire*, Paris, Le Seuil, 1971, p.22.
13. M de Certeau, *L'écriture de l'histoire*, Paris, Gallimard, 1975, p.5.
14. J. Roncière, *Les mots de l'histoire*, Paris, Le Seuil, 1992, p.24.

to talk of the reappearance of the narrative in history because it has never been absent'.[15]

The narrative element inherent in history would thus appear to constitute an obvious factor differentiating it from heritage activity. It is hardly as simple as that in the sense that an exhibition, a museum, a gathering relating to maritime affairs narrates activities which have taken place. An exhibition *'Mémoire d'Islande'*, dedicated to the experiences of Breton fishing activities in the Icelandic seas, displays artefacts, books and other types of traces which are no more the reality of what was once the great cod-fishing history of Iceland than the words of Jean Kerlévéo's written account.[16] Finally, the last argument which points to a similarity between the historian's and the curator's discipline is the common nature of the 'questionnaire', that is to say the main 'problématique' which pulls historians in different directions. The historian's discipline is meant to be scientific, yet he knows that scholarly activities and the 'interesting' are not necessarily the same thing. Paul Veyne points out: 'what is interesting is not what is fine or beautiful or real or useful or indispensable or even important; to be more precise, if it is one of those, it is not what makes it interesting. In a word, the "interesting" is "disinterested"'.[17] H. I. Marrou also stressed that hypotheses formulated by historians are inevitably circumscribed by a degree of empiricism: 'It is quite clear that historical knowledge is not arrived at ex-nihilo. The historian already has a rough idea of the questions which he is likely to ask'.[18] Contemporary historiography has shown how the focus of historical interest can shift, as can the reasons given for this shifting emphasis, according to the different ways in which historical time and space are perceived. Hervé Couteau-Bégarie's work[19] shows the development over time of maritime history and the extension of the subjects deemed to belong to this field. In this area, the heritage curator no more possesses a scale of values for exhibitions than the historian does for the importance of historical topics.

Although historians may be perplexed by the difficulty of giving scientific value to literary narrative, they nevertheless con-

15. A. Prost, *Revue Sciences Humaines*, 1996, p.24.

16. Mgr J. Kerlévéo, *Paimpol au temps d'Islande*, Paris, Réedition Slatkine, 1980, p.135.

17. P. Veyne, *Le quotidien et l'intéressant*, Paris, Les Belles Lettres, 1995, p.63.

18. H. I. Marrou, *De la connaissance historique*, Paris, Editions du Seuil, 1954, p.59.

19. H. Couteau-Bégarie, *L'histoire maritime en France*, Paris, Economica, 1995.

tinue to seek a scientific premise for their discipline. They seek truth through the medium of intelligible discourse which lends itself to debate, in the same way for example that one particular exhibition[20] attempted (and in the event succeeded) to explain the appeal of the Breton coastline for French society between 1840 and 1940. The scientific core can be found in the coherence between the question raised and the documentation used: 'what better means of rediscovering the life of seafarers than the traditional sailing boat?'[21] – this is how the question is phrased by Roger Cougot, the respected former maritime correspondent of the daily newspaper *Ouest-France*. This is a thought-provoking question for at least two reasons. It provides a wonderful link between the discipline of the historian and the curator, and illustrates the necessity of coherence already mentioned. It so happens, as I see it, that there are many other ways of rediscovering the life of seafaring folks,[22] but the question is a real problem area for the historian. The inappropriateness of the answer implicit in the question stems from the fact that certain types of maritime artefacts and evidence are overvalued, and this is because of the deliberate efforts of those in the heritage industry to make it an autonomous activity from history. This determination is founded essentially on a definition of heritage which cannot be ignored because there is an etymological basis for it according to reputable authors.

Heritage is a fixed collective asset, temporary owners of which have the responsibility regarding its maintenance and safekeeping vis-à-vis their predecessors and successors. Another concept arises immediately from this definition: identity. Heritage is a collection of assets which authenticate the permanence of a community, a port, a region or an association, for example. Seen in this way, heritage activity is not directed towards the quest of knowledge; its goal is essentially aesthetic, emotive or identity building. Jean-Michel Leniaud[23] has brilliantly illustrated this definition which implies that heritage activity is part of the pattern of appropriating material or symbolic assets by individuals or collective bodies. Various individuals or bodies are involved in this task.

20. Y. Pallier, N. Richard (eds), *Cent ans de tourisme en Bretagne*, Rennes, Apogée, 1996.

21. R. Cougot, 'Vieux gréements, répliques' in *Cols Bleus* magazine, Suppl. No 2220, 1993, p.12.

22. As brillantly illustrated by R. Estienne and P. Hendwood in 'Archives, mode d'emploi', *Le Chasse-Marée*, no 73, 1992.

23. J. M. Leniaud, *L'Utopie française, Essai sur le patrimoine*, Paris, Mengès, 1992.

They may be officially appointed at different levels – local (curator of a museum devoted to maritime life, fishing, boats, etc.), regional (coastal protection officer), national (Director of the *Musée de la Marine* in Paris), international (UNESCO) – according to the specific requirements of these authorities. On behalf of their wider community, these specialists sift among the remains left behind by seafarers and coastal inhabitants to create a collective asset which is meant to distinguish and reflect the identity of the community which has charged them with this task of reinforcing its identity.

In a free society, these leading players can set themselves up as 'heritage specialists', 'cultural technicians', according to their interests and enthusiasms; in this case it is market forces, for example public attendance figures on the occasion of the launching of a traditional sailing ship, which justify whether a heritage enterprise (both in the sense of an initiative or a business venture) will succeed. In the end, anyone and everyone can take possession of a landscape or a boat just by looking at it ('the façade of a house belongs to the person who looks at it' in the words of Lao Tse).[24]

This last quotation brings us back to a fundamental human freedom, yet one nevertheless perceives the possibility of dangers inherent in heritage activities operating independently of the historical discipline. Indeed, if one strays away from the path of knowledge, if one avoids what D. M. Boëll in his unflattering phrase called 'the well-trodden paths of university research',[25] anything goes in the free-for-all uncharted territories in which the 'heritage craze'[26] operates (in French, *patrimoines en folie*). Since identity cannot be scientifically defined, the quest for identity is carried out in an impressionistic way and is vulnerable to the most empirical impulses. Of course, anyone who talks about dangers has the duty to say exactly why he or she deplores these impulses. Admittedly, no political, cultural or academic authority can map out the field of scientific requirements for everyone, but it is legitimate to stress the dangers incurred by those who are not willing to admit that they exist. Historians in the French University system have no say in the matter of private publishing but they have

24. Cited by Michel Parent: 'Un entretien avec Michel Parent', *Le Monde*, 30 June 1993.

25. D. M. Boëll, 'La Fédération régionale pour la culture maritime', *Estuaire 1992, le patrimoine maritime et fluvial*, Paris-Nantes, Ministère de la culture, Direction du Patrimoine, 1993, p.234.

26. Title of the excellent edition by H. P. Jeudy (ed.), *Patrimoines en folie*, Paris, Maison des Sciences de l'Homme, 1990.

the duty to denounce a certain type of 'revisionist' or 'negationist' (i.e., in French, 'holocaust-denying') writing. As regards the traces of maritime and coastal life, we all have the right to read, interpret, admire or exhibit them as we wish, but no one has the right to confer upon them a meaning which is in any way, or even totally, divergent from the one intended by those who created them.

The 'irrational cult'[27] of heritage in general and of maritime heritage in particular can create three dangers: fetishist, teleological and nostalgic. The fetishist danger has several sources and several consequences. The cult of the boat is an excellent example. Many of those passionate about maritime heritage claim that it is the love of boats which motivates their commitment to heritage; this is a worthy motivation even though it is built upon the media hype and commercial exploitation generated when historic vessels assemble for spectacular events such as 'Brest 2000'. The consequences of this fetishist cult are serious and varied.

The first is an excessive scaling down of boats and other maritime elements: preference for the 'traditional' fishing boat over the 'non-traditional' fishing boat; preference for boats over artefacts, for artefacts over archives. The book *Bateaux des côtes de France* (Coastal boats of France) [28] is an excellent instance of this. It is far from an uninteresting work but should have been entitled 'Traditional fishing boats'. A subtle semantic shift has allowed the historic sailing vessel to incarnate all boats; then in turn boats have come to incarnate all maritime heritage.

A second consequence is the scale of values which is applied to the traces according to their emotive or aesthetic impact. F. Reynaud makes a pertinent and thought-provoking observation about merchant ships in regretting their lack of physical attractiveness: 'They are less spectacular than passenger liners, less poetic than sailing ships, less heroic than destroyers and submarines. Therefore they are less attractive to the public and it is much more difficult to put a case for their preservation'.[29] This scale of values in maritime traces brings with it a similar sense of hierarchy as regards the 'importance' of the maritime spheres of interest relating to them. Roger Cougot's beloved traditional fishing boat may be useful for a study of shipbuilding but its docu-

---

27. F. Choay, *L'allégorie du patrimoine*, Paris, Le Seuil, 1992, p.198.
28. 'Bateaux des côtes de France', *Le Marin*, Brest, 1992.
29. F. Reynaud, 'Les Bateaux de commerce', *Estuaire 92, le patrimoine maritime et fluvial*, Paris-Nantes, Ministère de la culture, Direction du Patrimoine, 1993, p. 100.

mentary value is limited as regards a cultural, social and religious history of the fishing community. In France today, the history of the merchant navy is sadly neglected and the current maritime heritage emphasis on the so-called traditional fishing industry does nothing at all to remind us that the French merchant navy was once a vital part of the relationship between the French and the sea and coastal regions.

A third consequence of this 'cult of the object' is the risk that the rigour of historical discipline will be neglected at the time of the ceremonies and rites accompanying the building and launching of replica boats. Although this widespread practice is endorsed by social approval, it is nevertheless seriously defective. The tourist and commercial goals behind these enterprises are foreign to the professional aims of the original shipowners and builders. No similarity exists between the public nature of current replica slipways (even sometimes used as advertising opportunities), and the privacy of an authentic shipyard. The working practices of these replicas are also determined by a great range of incompatible needs and objectives.

The final consequence of this type of heritage activity is a kind of 'glossing over' of certain social realities. The replica of an Icelandic schooner tells us nothing about the fear, alcoholism and misery that were all part of life on board when the schooner was a working vessel. In conclusion and by way of a final example, one could apply to a replica vessel the same verdict that F. Choay passes on the practice of floodlighting cathedrals: 'by exhibiting this monument immediately and indecently, as it was never meant to be seen, the process destroys the setting which rooted it in time'.[30]

The teleological danger is no less serious. Three elements show this, and the lessons that can be learnt are worth considering. Historical traces, whether constructed, cultural, archival, were never originally created for the purpose of becoming heritage. They only become so when a heritage consciousness comes into being and the development of the latter is in itself a historical moment. 'Heritage is an idea immersed in history' as André Chastel has observed. [31] Between 1880 and 1885, the Paimpol shipowners, engaged in the Icelandic cod-fishing industry, built their first floating harbour without any qualms. Why should they have felt any?

---

30. F. Choay, *L'allégorie du patrimoine*, Paris, Le Seuil, 1992, p.167.
31. A. Chastel, 'La notion de patrimoine' in P. Nora (ed.), *Les Lieux de mémoire, II. La Nation 2*, Paris, Gallimard, 1986, p.404.

Because they 'corrected the physical geography of the site'? Jean Kerlévéo, an excellent local historian of Paimpol, wrote about this episode and absolved them of committing any sin against our heritage: 'The physiognomy of Paimpol was changed as a result but does it matter? The importance of the trade with Iceland was such that many things disappeared – the picturesque tidal water mills, the centuries-old pond, the causeway built by monks in the Middle-Ages with its historical connection to Vauban'.[32] No more than this local historian did these shipowners experience any sense of guilty feelings with regard to their heritage for the simple reason that heritage consciousness did not exist at that time.

Maritime artefacts, legends and traditions are not in themselves conceived for the purpose of becoming heritage. It is not the component parts of heritage which are bearers of a message. This message is brought home when human intermediaries interpret it; these may in many cases be professionals, preferably historians, or in other cases, those loyal to a certain image of seafaring (the sort for example who could never conceive of drunkenness being a possible cause of shipwreck in Icelandic fishing during the period mentioned – we shall return to this aspect when discussing the danger caused by nostalgia).

Without exactly being equatable with the teleological danger, the notion of a 'maritime vocation' is nevertheless capable of feeding it. R. Marx points out that 'no one would really talk about the maritime vocation of Great Britain after realising how late this notion developed in that country'.[33] The term 'maritime vocation' should be used only with the greatest care. It seems to be justified only when it describes a whole set of objective conditions, geographical, technical or cultural, which enable or accelerate the process of a widespread maritime activity involving all the adjacent seas, coasts and hinterlands. At any rate, this vocation cannot be applauded as a feat which was destined to happen; rather one should realise that it is born at a point in time which can be scientifically located. Indeed, as Michel Roux has brilliantly shown, it is possible to create a maritime vocation through sheer political will power, with vocation in this instance being taken to mean a culturally composed representation. Starting in 1898, the Second Reich in Germany succeeded in building up in the public imagi-

32. J. Kerlévéo, *Paimpol au temps de l'Islande*, Paris, Réédition. Slatkine, 1980, p.135.
33. R. Marx, *Histoire de l'Angleterre*. Paris, Fayard, 1993, p.7.

nation a maritime consciousness with the purpose of making public opinion ready to accept a considerable financial burden. This
vocation was not a quasi-religious or mystical feat, but rather was
the result of a public relations exercise with striking results. 'An
analysis of the German example shows that a nation which does
not from the outset benefit from a favourable geographic position
and whose maritime traditions are virtually lost in the past (the
time of the Hanseatic League) is nevertheless capable in less than
thirty years of landing itself up to second place amongst the naval
powers of the time'.[34]

The third aspect inherent in the teleological danger is that of
identity; everyone would like to believe that it can be defined and
yet no one suggests a definition, and this is hardly surprising. The
problem is twofold: identity in general is an extremely difficult
concept to grasp, and in this respect Fernand Braudel's warning is
salutary. He refuses to consider the identity of France as an
essence, preferring rather to talk about 'a central problem area'.[35]

Maritime identity is every bit as difficult to grasp. 'Pure' maritime activities as such can hardly be said to exist in so far as maritime, naval, merchant and fishing activities are intimately bound
up with land-based organisations. The Icelandic cod fishermen
were for the most part recruited in the rural hinterland of Paimpol.
The Saint-Malo sailing vessels (*malouinières*) which are the subject
of André Lespagnol's huge and excellent study[36] are a characteristic example of heritage which deserves the most rigorous analysis. These 'malouinères' are spectacular material proof of the
commercial success of the shipowning class of Saint-Malo who
built up their own private heritage in a special way, before it even-
tually became part of public heritage from a historical perspective.
What is remarkable is that the commercial success of these
shipowners was accompanied by a desire to acquire social status
among the land-based nobility, thanks to a maritime heritage of
the most functional sort. It would seem very difficult to distinguish in this enterprise a 'pure' maritime identity and Alain
Cabantous has in fact demonstrated this thoroughly.[37] Finally, the

34. M. Roux, *L'imaginaire marin des Français, mythe et géographie de la mer*, Paris,
L'Harmattan, 1997, p. 79.

35. F. Braudel, *L'identité de la France*, Paris, Fayard, 1986, p.19.

36. A. Lespagnol, *Messieurs de St Malo*, Rennes, Presses Universitaires de Rennes,
1997.

37. A. Cabantous, *Les citoyens du large, les identités maritimes en France, 17–19ème
siècle*, Paris, Aubier, 1995.

lure of nostalgia is the third danger to which heritage activities are susceptible when carried out independently of the historian's discipline. Because it is spectacular and attractive in tourist terms, maritime heritage activities are pregnant with dangers in two ways: dreaming up a golden age of seafaring which never existed, 'the good old days of sailing ships', etc.; secondly, turning a blind eye to the reality and problems of the present day. Sea shanty festivals, rallies of old sailing vessels, maritime museums – all of these may be extremely interesting and heart-warming but they should not be allowed to blind us to the fact that the French merchant navy at the present time is going through a very serious crisis. Pierre Nora's admirable observation can be applied to French maritime affairs: 'France should be more than just a museum of itself' (see bibliography). The nation's seafarers must surely not be confined to glass cabinets in maritime museums.

In conclusion, it may be claimed that when heritage specialists attempt to operate independently of the historian, certain technical features are valid: the restoration and conservation of artefacts, the collection of legends and songs. Certain peculiar features persist: the particular form of an exhibition, the emotive or aesthetic dimension of certain practices. Yet when a man or a woman undertakes to examine the remains of a former human activity, whatever its nature, he or she comes up against three major problems which demolish any dividing line between the disciplines of the historian and the heritage specialist: the problem of time, which Saint Augustine claimed to be able to define provided he was not questioned about the nature of it; the problem of consciousness, which may or may not be at the root of human enterprise; the problem of the 'questionnaire', i.e., the central problem which historians or heritage curators create and which pulls them in two directions, leaving them torn apart by the double dilemma of the specific and the universal, the permanent and the transitory.

8

HIDDEN REEFS:

A Case Study of the Port-Rhu Floating Museum Fiasco in Douarnenez

Jeanine Picard

It may seem paradoxical to select a failed venture in a small Breton coastal town as an illustration of the enthusiasm felt by the French for maritime heritage at the present time. Yet the present case study seeks to illustrate some of the dangers, shortcomings and excesses related to maritime heritage, already highlighted by Françoise Péron (see Chapter 6) and by François Chappé (Chapter 7). This chapter examines the conflicts and contradictions which arose between interested parties in the political, economic, cultural and social fields when a new heritage structure was hurriedly set up in the 1990s in Douarnenez. We shall focus on the way in which economic restructuring led to a reinterpretation of maritime culture towards a position favouring the interests of the local tourist industry, threatening in the process to reduce a seafaring community to the status of a museum exhibit.

A few words first of all to situate Douarnenez, a small town of 17,000 inhabitants ranking fifth in terms of population in Finistère, in its physical and economic environment. Its three ports, the fishing port, the marina, added in 1945, and Port-Rhu, an old commercial port abandoned in the 1950s, look out on a magnificent bay. From a tourist point of view, being located close to some of the most scenic sites in Brittany, Douarnenez enjoys an enviable position; however, it is less well placed in terms of the distance separating it from Paris or even from the major road system in Finistère. Since 1850, the economic history of Douarnenez has been dominated by the fish-canning industry, especially sardine canning.[1] Industrialisation was not achieved without social upheaval and in 1921 the local inhabitants elected the first Communist mayor in France, Sébastien Velly. Nowadays only three canning factories remain in activity, employing around seven hundred workers. The fishing port is also in decline with three hundred or so registered fishermen in 1993, compared with 3,100 in 1950; 2,200 direct or indirect jobs are still created by the port but compared with the more dynamic fishing ports of Southern Brittany, Douarnenez is slowly losing ground.

Breton ports from Douarnenez to Lorient are the heart of the French fishing industry, supplying 50 per cent of the tonnage and 32 per cent of the national value of the industry. In the first half of the 1990s the economic climate was particularly detrimental to the French fishing industry which went through months of agitation in 1993 and 1994. The unrest was led mainly by Breton fishermen and violent demonstrations culminated on Saturday, 5 February in the accidental destruction of the *Parlement de Bretagne* in Rennes. This fine historic building was engulfed by flames caused by a flare thrown by demonstrating fishermen. The latter were driven to desperate measures by the prospect of seeing their whole way of life and their communities irrevocably destroyed following a sharp fall in fish prices and drastic European policies to preserve fishing stocks. The decline of the industry therefore made it imperative to bring about an economic repositioning based on tourism, sport, leisure and other tertiary activities in order to ensure the survival of coastal communities. It is in that context that there occurred in Douarnenez an exceptional renewal of interest in a type of maritime heritage largely ignored until then in France, linked to ordinary seafaring activities, such as small-scale fishing and coastal shipping. The fact that a small town like Douarnenez was at the heart of this movement can only be explained by the synergy produced in the town by a group of dynamic individuals, the disquiet felt by the local population and politicians alike faced with an increasingly hostile economic climate and a widespread reappraisal in society at large of the significance and role of heritage activities.

1. For a full picture of the state of fishing in Brittany and particularly in Douarnenez, see the very detailed study by J.-R.Couliou, *La pêche bretonne – les ports de Bretagne-Sud face à leur avenir*, Rennes, Presses Universitaires de Rennes, 1997.

At the end of the 1970s, following the emergence of new research fields in anthropology and ethnology, maritime culture managed to carve out a niche for itself. Publications relating to the different types of traditional boats[2] used in the past for fishing and trading along the French coast caught the imagination of the public at large, constituting a milestone for the rediscovery of a certain type of maritime culture which was in danger of disappearing without trace. In 1981 the authors of these publications launched a high quality magazine specialising in maritime history and ethnology called *Le Chasse-Marée;*[3] its editorial office was situated in Douarnenez. Its aim was to make boats better known as objects, but also to find a rightful place for ordinary seafaring people in the wider context of maritime heritage. Until then the French had to look to foreign publications for articles about their own traditional craft and indeed French specialists had long envied the British their record of paying tribute to both their maritime and naval heroes and their ordinary seafaring folk. The success of the magazine coincided with a renewal of interest in all aspects of maritime heritage. More than a quarter of a century after its launching, it is fair to say that *Le Chasse-Marée* played a major role in raising the profile of maritime culture in French national consciousness.

In 1979 the *Fédération régionale pour la culture maritime* (FRCM), an umbrella organisation linking around a hundred different associations specialising in maritime heritage, set up its headquarters in Douarnenez and embarked upon an ambitious programme. Its purpose was to collect, save and restore the remaining traditional craft, last used for fishing and coastal shipping in the 1950s and rotting away in the mud amid the complete indifference of the general public. At the end of 1984, when a fleet of some seventy boats had been collected, an association called *Treizour* (meaning 'Ferryman' in Breton, i.e., the crossing from one bank to the other, from the past to the future), one of the members of the FRCM,

2. See F. Beaudouin, *Bateaux des côtes de France*, Grenoble, Glénat, 1990; J. Le Bot, *Bateaux des côtes de Bretagne Nord*, Grenoble, Editions des 4 seigneurs, 1979; B. Cadoret, D. Duviard, J. Guillet, H. Kerisit, *Ar Vag. Voiles au travail en Bretagne Atlantique*, Grenoble, Editions des 4 seigneurs, 2 vol., 1978, 1979 and D. Duviard, *Groix, l'île des thoniers*, Grenoble, Editions des 4 seigneurs, 1978.

3. *Le Chasse-Marée* started in 1981 in France with an initial print-run of 7,000 copies; it has since reached peaks of 50,000 copies, an exceptional figure for a relatively expensive magazine which frequently includes articles of a technical nature. The magazine is now also published in English and its first issue came out in the summer of 1998 under the name *Maritime Life and Traditions*.

contacted the Douarnenez town council. The decision was subsequently made to convert an old canning factory, closed in 1983, into a Boat Museum. The museum was soon afterwards officially accredited by the Direction des musées de France (DMF), which gave recognition and financial support to a movement which had until then been dependent on the hard work of a small group of enthusiastic volunteers.

This first phase seemed promising. The general public appeared to respond enthusiastically to new developments in maritime heritage, as was indicated by the success of initial traditional maritime festivals in Pors Beac'h (Brest Roads), at the beginning of the 1980s.[4] Further gatherings, organised by *Le Chasse-Marée*, took place in Douarnenez in 1986, in the presence of three hundred traditional craft. In 1988, the number had grown to eight hundred and fifty, and (despite grumbles about the high cost of entry) the festival attracted 300,000 visitors. This exceeded all expectations and the local council in Douarnenez became convinced that it was possible to restructure the declining activities of the town around maritime heritage. The conversion of Port-Rhu, a commercial port disused since the 1950s, into a floating and living museum was approved, requiring the construction of a dam and lock gates, a small sea wall, a footbridge and a dock in front of the Boat Museum.

In-line with the process described by Françoise Péron (see Chapter 6), by investing in a floating museum, the town council saw the potential advantages that a modern maritime image could bring to the town: the museum would be used as a showpiece helping to put Douarnenez on the map at regional, national and even international level. It was thought that the new structure would bring distinction to the town, enhance tourism by integrating it into a wider tourist circuit, and above all create new jobs, thanks to diversified activities. The capital investment was presented to local people as a sound economic choice during a difficult period of restructuring. Tourism by then had become the second largest economic activity in Finistère, just after agriculture, and the floating museum, appealing to a more varied public with its more open site than traditional museums, seemed to reflect the

4. The first rally in fact took place on 14 July 1975 when, for the first time in France, twenty traditional craft were presented to the public. There are several illustrated publications of the various gatherings which took place in the 1980s; for example, see F. Puget, *Bateaux en fêtes, 20 ans d'aventure et de rêve*, Brest, Le Télégramme Editions, 1996.

bracing image of wind and waves promoted by Breton advertising agencies specialising in the marketing of tourism. After all, so the argument went, each year, 500 to 700,000 tourists had to pass through Douarnenez to visit the Pointe du Raz – the equivalent site in Britain in terms of tourist attraction would be Land's End. – situated forty kilometres away, and it seemed to make sense to assume that 300,000 of them could be encouraged to stop and visit the floating museum on the way.

In 1992 half a million people faithfully attended the gathering of traditional craft in Brest and Douarnenez. The site of the floating museum was first inaugurated amid rejoicing on 16 July during the Festival of the Sea; at national level, this coincided with the period when the so-called 'major regional projects'[5] – including the *Historial de la Grande Guerre* in Péronne (see Chapter 4) – came to an end in other parts of France. The official opening of the floating museum then took place on 22 May 1993; FF75 million had been spent on the venture.[6]

The museum comprised two hundred and fifty boats, forty of them afloat. Among them *Scarweather*, a lightship built in Dartmouth in 1947 and acquired at the cost of FF400,000; *Saint-Denys*, a Scottish steam tug built in 1929; *Anna-Rosa*, a replica of the coastal vessels which delivered to Douarnenez the roe used as bait for sardine fishing; *Northdown*, a Thames sailing barge built in 1924. Significantly, the most interesting floating vessels were obtained from Great Britain, such was the difficulty of finding similar craft in France.[7] On the left bank of Port-Rhu, more in the spirit of a folk museum, a village was developed with marine craftsmen, carpenters, riggers, rope-makers, sailmakers, marine blacksmiths, traditional sculptors, etc., demonstrating their craft

5. As well as Port-Rhu, three regional museums were opened in spring/summer 1992 : *L'Historial de la Grande Guerre* (Péronne), *Le Musée de la Préhistoire* (Tautavel) and *Le Musée d'Art Moderne* (Céret). The four were situated in medium-sized towns, a long distance away from Paris. Their regional location was part of a national policy of cultural decentralisation. See *La lettre des musées de France*, Paris, Direction des musées de France, n° 24, August 1992.

6. Out of the FF75 million, the State contributed FF21 million, the Region FF4.75 million, the Département FF7.9 million, the town of Douarnenez FF10 million, the EU FF5 million. The rest was financed by loans (FF20million) guaranteed by the town council.

7. The purchase of foreign craft was in itself the centre of a controversy. According to René Louboutin, Vice-President of the local CDS Party, 24 November 1992, 'we should have concentrated on French traditional craft instead of purchasing boats in Britain and paying too much for them'. The problem of course was that French traditional craft of that importance had been destroyed or left to rot.

in the open. Trips in the bay were scheduled. Port-Rhu was also to be used as a stopover for historic ships. In short Port-Rhu was transformed into a living museum attractive to a wide-ranging public, from boat specialists to casual visitors. The team which successfully organised the maritime festival 'Brest 92' was given the responsibility for implementing an effective marketing strategy. The museum employed forty-four full-time staff, plus a few young people on employment schemes and some seasonal staff.

To complete the picture, in November 1992, the floating museum launched a new venture called 'A three-masted ship for France'. The aim was to build a clipper, replicating *Paulista*, a forty-eight metre vessel which ran aground and was wrecked in 1865. The launch was due to take place in the year 2000 and the cost of the project was estimated at FF65 million. The timber alone would have cost FF10 million! This grandiose project was due to be financed solely by company sponsorship and private subscription. The huge keel, laid on 23 May 1993 on the small Place de l'Enfer, opposite the Boat Museum, was supposed to ensure the return of visitors, who would regularly check the development of the project, on the understanding that most museum visitors do not want to see the same display twice. Forty thousand acacia dowels to be used in the fastening of the ship's timbers were made available for sale. From the beginning, criticism of the significance and the purpose of the venture was extremely fierce (see Chapter 6). The clipper was also accused of taking over the small square, the building work made too much noise, the construction did not progress fast enough, etc.

Around eight months went by between the opening of the floating harbour in May 1993 and the first articles in the press questioning the financial viability of the venture. From then on, the local press published nearly one article a day, destabilising the venture further.[8] The company running the museum went into receivership in December 1994 and, after months of agony, was pronounced bankrupt on 15 September 1995. The question we must therefore ask ourselves is what made the pack of cards collapse so quickly, especially in a country like France where cultural activities tend to be protected from the harsh reality of market forces thanks to a fairly generous tradition of public funding.

Let us turn our attention first of all to the structure put in place to run the museum, a Public Limited Company in which the town

8. On the intense use of the media by all the parties involved in the venture, see E. De Roux, *Libération*, 31 May 1995, 'Big mouths in Douarnenez are as numerous as the sardines which made the port prosperous in the past'.

council of Douarnenez held a majority of the shares.[9] This structure is not often used in France for running museums, but the model for Port-Rhu was Mystic Seaport, the North American maritime museum created in 1929 in Connecticut, whose four hundred boats attract around 400,000 visitors per year and which does not receive regular subsidies from the authorities. Created by a Communist municipal council, this hybrid structure may seem slightly paradoxical but it was justified by the need to give the floating museum the flexibility of a private company, as well as the normal obligations in terms of public service assigned to any French museum structure. Two persons were in charge of the running of the museum, the president of the company and the curator. Soon the relationship between the two worsened, illustrating the difficulties sometimes associated with tandem leadership. An audit carried out in 1995 at the request of the main partners financially involved in the enterprise emphasised the inherent contradiction at the core of the project: 'a status associated with a profit-making organisation was given to an enterprise with a strong public service mission'. The audit further added: 'the illusion persisted that this organisation could be viable on its own'. Its verdict was unequivocal: the floating museum would never be profitable as a commercial concern. Politicians opposed to the Communist council also commented on this structural and financial aspect of the venture. Ambroise Guellec[10] remarked: 'Douarnenez wanted to act alone and to launch a profitable museum when no museum in Europe is able to balance its books, let alone finance its capital investment'.[11] A hard lesson for Douarnenez but also for all museums at a time when most advanced countries are relentlessly moving away from publicly financed cultural institutions towards new modes of self-financing!

From a financial point of view, a feasibility study loosely based on the number of people visiting the Pointe du Raz and carried out a few years previously, predicted that the museum would

9. The original shareholders of the company were: Douarnenez town council 51 per cent, Compagnie Générale des Eaux 25 per cent, Département du Finistère 10 per cent, CCI de Quimper 5 per cent, Caisse d'Epargne de Bretagne 5 per cent, *Le Chasse-Marée* 2 per cent, GIE Douarnenez 1 per cent, Association Treizour 1 per cent.

10. Ambroise Guellec is a member of the centre-right CDS Party. He was Vice-President of the Conseil Général and local *député* at the time.

11. Other maritime museums in Western Europe have also experienced similar financial problems. The closure of the Boat Museum in Exeter in 1996 and the dispersion of its collection would make an interesting comparative study, although doubtless different in certain important respects.

attract 300,000 visitors per year. All business plans were based on this magic figure, with each visitor spending on average fifty francs per head for the visit. The breakthrough point for the venture was situated around 240,000 visitors per year. With 185,000 visitors in 1993 and 153,000 visitors in 1994, Port-Rhu did become the most visited museum in Brittany but never came close to financial viability. In the words of the president of the company himself, the venture was managed 'in cavalier fashion', with enthusiasm as a driving force. Decisions were rushed through to steal a lead over other competing projects, particularly in La Rochelle. When sources of finance were not completely secured, particularly funds expected from private sponsors and from the European Union, the financial obstacles were brushed aside and ignored.

What is more, maintaining a collection of historical craft – especially if they are afloat – has serious financial implications as regards conservation and restoration. Every five years, paint must be scraped off and boats repainted or varnished; defective parts have to be replaced. To make things worse, it was discovered in November 1995 that the oak landing stages in Port-Rhu were being eaten away by worms. In the budgetary planning of the museum, these maintenance expenses had simply been ignored all together!

The financial outcome was disastrous: losses of FF14 million in less than two years. The town of Douarnenez was liable for the short-term loans of FF14 million and the long-term loans of FF23 million that it had guaranteed. The town council was given the role of running the museum on behalf of the official receiver. The floating museum went back to its previous name, the Boat Museum, and kept running with a budget of FF5.35 million in 1996, less receipts from admission fees. This allowed six members of staff to run the museum, making some of the floating vessels accessible to visitors during the tourist season, and ensuring a minimum of maintenance on the boats. All the craftsmen who had made the port a living museum were declared redundant.

In addition to the financial problem, from the start of the venture the political stakes were high, as the Communist town council wanted to keep a firm grip on the enterprise. Jean-Michel Le Boulanger, president of the company, was also the deputy (*adjoint*) of the very charismatic Communist mayor, Michel Mazéas, who had been regularly re-elected mayor of Douarnenez since 1971. The controversies surrounding the floating museum poisoned municipal life in Douarnenez for many years. Some municipal councillors were radically opposed to the venture such as the GRIL,[12] led by Pascal Boccou, which would have preferred a more radical approach to the economic restructuring of the town, with a greater involvement from local people. There were further irritations; for example Port-Rhu created a serious problem in the matter of town planning. It was impossible to charge entrance fees without cutting off access to the port for local residents who resented having to pay local taxes to finance the venture plus a charge for access to quays which used to be free. The GRIL protested for years about the fact that the free right of way to the port was impeded by the railings surrounding the floating museum. One of the most perverse effects of this revitalising project for the local economy was that it actually stopped access to some of the shops and small businesses in Port-Rhu!

A major political development occured in 1993 when a right-wing assembly was elected and Edouard Balladur became Prime Minister. The government was eager to be seen to counteract the alleged excesses in the funding of French cultural policy followed by its Socialist predecessor, notably in the person of Jack Lang, the high-profile Minister of Culture. This national swing to the right was reinforced by the election of President Jacques Chirac in 1995. In Finistère thus the right came to power with a vengeance and was determined to make the Douarnenez Communist bastion fall at the following municipal elections due to take place in 1996. A journalist put to the mayor of Douarnenez a question that needed no answer: 'A left-wing mayor in a right-wing department, a right-wing region and a right-wing state, is that not a handicap for your town?' When the museum was officially opened in 1993, the absence of leading departmental personalities, notably the President of the Conseil Général du Finistère, M. Charles Miossec, was widely commented on. The Conseil Général had contributed to capital investment but a certain coldness was detectable, contrasting with the enthusiasm generated by other cultural ventures in Finistère.

During the 1996 municipal elections, the failure of the floating museum was used as an excuse to bring out all sorts of skeletons from the bo's'n's locker. In the end the left-wing coalition lost the elections and a right-wing mayor was elected on the strength of a fifty-one vote majority. Suddenly all the proposals put forward by

12. The Groupe de réflexion et d'initiatives locales (GRIL) is a political movement close to the old PSU, i.e., left of the Socialist Party, and close to environmental groups.

the left-wing council in order to save the floating museum started to look more feasible. The defeated mayor however did acknowledge a degree of responsibility for the debacle when admitting that the council had been guilty of 'sinful pride' by refusing to spread the financial risks more widely; for example no other fishing port in the immediate vicinity was given a chance to be associated with the project.

One last observation can be made about the political aspect of the case. The Futuroscope in Poitiers is often quoted nowadays as the standard measure in France of the positive impact that a cultural product can have on regional development. When we compare both initiatives, it is significant that Douarnenez lacked an imposing political figure, with a national profile, i.e., the equivalent of René Monory in Poitou-Charentes.[13]

Another tension at the heart of this enterprise reflects the importance of timing, strategy and good public relations. The prime movers were the local councillors, worried about the decline of the fishing industry and hoping that the economic survival of their town would be ensured by a maritime heritage which could bring in revenue. Yet the local population, which was just as much (if not more) traumatised by the fishing crisis then reaching its peak, was not invited to participate in the process of developing this heritage enterprise. All the decisions concerning the future development of Port-Rhu were made quickly: no time was taken to consult local people or explain how the project was intended to be a recreation of their own past. Throughout the project a sense of exclusion and frustration prevailed among local people. On the day of the opening of the floating museum, fishermen had an opportunity to talk to the press and their comments indicated a marked unease: 'When you think that the local council is spending a fortune to transform our boats into floating museums!'[14] At that exact time the national Mellick Plan was fully operational and offered generous subsidies in order to reduce the size of the French fishing fleet. The plan was very successful in so far as 6,000 fishing boats were still active in France in 1993, compared with 11,243 in 1988. As part of the Mellick Plan, thirty fishing boats were kept afloat in museums or given to various associations instead of being destroyed.

---

13. Ex-Minister, elected President of the French Senate in 1992.
14. F. Boennec, *Le Parisien*, 21 May 1993.

Françoise Péron and Jean Rieucau[15] have suggested that the juxtaposition of a professional culture, based on fishing in this particular case, and a maritime culture based on leisure activities often creates antagonisms in modern coastal societies, usually to the advantage of urban populations with their own specific agenda: a certain idea of the sea, a quest for authenticity, a nostalgia for the past and a level of frustration with the present. With the surge of interest in maritime heritage we are indeed witnessing the triumph of a particular conception of maritime culture, one keener to save traditional craft than the fishing industry, hit very hard by the collapse in fish prices in 1993 and 1994. In Douarnenez, on the day of the opening of the floating museum, subversive posters highlighted this irony in no uncertain terms: 'You've adopted a baby seal, now adopt a fisherman, another disappearing species'.

The sensibilities of that disappearing species did not weigh heavily in the balance when the museum was conceived and developed. Museums are often created to mark the end of a traditional activity in a region and may be perceived as a kiss of death by local populations on the understanding that only what is about to be lost for good needs some kind of protection. This placed the Douarnenez museum in an ambiguous social position. It was indeed displaying traditional methods and activities which had disappeared from the locality, such as local sardine-fishing, but the wider context was one where local people not only did not accept the total disappearance of the present fishing industry but were fighting for its survival. To show that it was not totally indifferent to the fate of local fishermen, the museum dedicated the earnings from its first evening to the 'committee for the survival of fishing'. Created in February 1993, this committee coordinated all the activities undertaken to save the fishing industry during that period of acute crisis. However, this was not sufficient to create an umbilical cord between the museum and local fishermen.

Consigning memories and myths of maritime societies to museums poses a delicate problem, local social history being often rewritten or ignored in the process. Maritime life as experienced by local people is frequently quite different from the idealised image projected by a maritime museum, with its deaths, terrible working conditions, badly built boats, social problems, etc. It is

15. See F. Péron and J. Rieucau, *La maritimité aujourd'hui*, Paris, L'Harmattan, 1996.

therefore difficult at the best of times for fishermen to associate with the cult of maritime heritage. Some late efforts were made in Douarnenez, such as the symptomatic discussion which took place in September 1994, organised by Treizour on the theme 'what can be done to attract fishermen to the museum?' The fact that the museum had given priority to the object (the boat) at the expense of the human being (the fisherman) was acknowledged as a failing. A few solutions were suggested, such as making admission free for all fishermen, and the possibility of fishermen making use of the port facilities for the maintenance of their boats. It is significant however that successful heritage projects in other parts of France have often started with a long phase of associative life and contacts with the population concerned with the heritage process.[16] For the outside observer, it is astonishing how little collaboration took place between the museum and local people. The feeling persisted that Port-Rhu no longer belonged to its inhabitants, and the railings around the site came to acquire a real as well as a symbolic significance.

In December 1996 the newly elected mayor of Douarnenez announced that, after a year of negotiation, an agreement had been signed with the major creditors: the debt had been rescheduled to FF15 million instead of the original FF37 million, as certain banks involved in the financing of the venture wrote off part of their debt. The repayment of the remainder of the debt however led to an increase in local taxes of 10 per cent in Douarnenez itself.

Although the horizon is no longer as threatening as it was, it is clear that the ambitious heritage project employing around fifty people and being used as a flagship for the economic revival of the town failed. The municipal council put the enterprise out to tender in 1997 and was, until June 1999, negotiating with the *Musée Grévin*, Daniel Jouvance and Harmatan group[17], with the aim of granting the total running of the site to this private company. The talks collapsed following a take-over bid by the company running the *Parc Astérix*, near Paris. However, at the time of writing, it looks as if another private partner will be found. Whoever that private partner is, it is clear that the most obvious consequence of

16. The example of the Alsace Museum, which was preceded by forty years of contacts with the local population is often quoted as an example in this context.

17. This group is one of the major names in leisure activities in France: Musée Grévin owns the wax museum in Paris; Daniel Jouvance belongs to the Yves Rocher group; Harmatan is currently designing an interactive museum at the Stade de France, Paris.

this transfer will be a change in the nature of the museum. To use one of the neologisms coined in the 1990s, 'edutainment' is on the agenda with a particular conception of maritime heritage. A storm simulator, a ghost ship and even a miniature train have been mentioned as possible developments on the site. A team including representatives from the private group, the *Direction des musées de France* (DMF) which still maintains the collection of traditional craft, and the elected town council, were still working on an agreement at the end of 1999.

It is likely that tensions will arise again in the future as the result of the conflicting demands created by the cultural rigour required of any museum structure, the interests of the town and its taxpayers, and those of the private partner. On the one hand, the aim of the museum is to collect, preserve and document its collection. In the case of Port-Rhu, the State has recognised the importance of the collection as a unique national resource by doubling its financial contribution to the maintenance and the restoration of the boats. A new curator, Mme Mousset-Pinard,[18] was appointed in 1996 and has declared it her priority to open clear thematic sections and to update the presentation and the museography in order to draw to the museum a variety of social groups while preserving the authenticity of the site. Improving the content of the museum however may clash with the agenda of the private group for whom the museum represents only a short stop in a more comprehensive leisure programme. With attendance in leisure parks on the increase, the aims of the private partner are very clear. In their hands, Port-Rhu will in all probability become a leisure park by the sea. It is noticeable that as soon as the first financial difficulties were experienced by the museum, private companies showed a great interest in taking over the site. Commercial excesses are already very much in evidence during maritime festivals. The risk of being submerged by kitsch activities and of losing the raison d'être of the scheme is undeniable.

As for the local authorities, their priority will be a reduction in the financial burden placed on the town. Generally, in the last twenty years, French towns have preferred investing in the promotion of festival-type activities at the expense of a purely cultural approach. It can even be said that in Douarnenez, the success of huge maritime gatherings, with their large number of participants and their enthusiastic volunteers, has somehow muddied

18. Interviewed in May 1997.

the waters when choosing a coherent strategy for the town and deciding on subsequent financial investment, leading in the end to painful financial readjustments for the whole of the population. 'Brest 96' with its two thousand boats attracted 980,000 paying visitors and was followed immediately by 'Douarnenez 96' with 400,000 visitors, 200,000 of whom paid an admission fee (compared with 78,000 in 1992). The success of these festivals always risks inflating unrealistic expectations. The conviviality of these gatherings with their fiesta atmosphere points to a profound transformation in the relationship between society and culture. In Douarnenez it was thought that the same authenticity, enthusiasm and festive spirit would guarantee the success of the floating museum. However, organising a maritime festival and running a museum on a day-to-day basis are two radically different activities. Every time some kind of festive event is organised in Port-Rhu, crowds flock in. The problem for a floating museum is to keep the enthusiasm of the public going outside these festive periods, especially during the long winter months. As a general tendency, a marked decrease in the number of visitors to museums in the 1990s has been acknowledged and recent projections forecasting holiday preferences for the year 2010[19] are not too encouraging as they predict less interest in cultural activities in the future.

Can a third way, consistent with best practice in managing heritage activities and respectful of maritime authenticity, be developed? Probably not in Port-Rhu, as commercial imperatives may have already triumphed. However, in Douarnenez and elsewhere along the Breton coast, a reappraisal of the role of associations, with their enthusiastic volunteers and the vast amount of competence that they have gathered in the field of maritime culture and heritage, is on the agenda. It is significant that when the audit by L & R was carried out in 1995, it identified as a weakness the fact that the company had turned its back on the valuable contribution that volunteers could make. By going back to grassroots level and to the original enthusiasm for maritime heritage, it might be possible to transform what could after all only be a temporary vogue into a long-lasting love affair with maritime heritage. Heritage activities and living maritime cultures present along the coast need to interact more effectively than they did in Port-Rhu. Heritage activities need to attract visitors from a broader base, espe-

19. P. Krémer, *Le Monde*, 13 May 1998; forecasts made by the *Commissariat général du plan*.

cially young people. Some recent initiatives point the way to the future. In the same way as *Le Chasse-Marée* organised its competition 'Boats of the coast of France' in the context of 'Brest 92', which enabled maritime populations to renew contact with their maritime past by building replicas of eighty traditional local craft, followed by a similar competition 'Heritage of the French coasts and rivers' for 'Brest 96', a new challenge has been devised for the year 2000. Sponsored by Gérard d'Aboville and Eric Tabarly before his tragic death, 'Young Sailors 2000' is a competition aimed at developing good seamanship among young people aged between fifteen and twenty-five. It will focus on traditional seamanship and an enthusiasm for wooden boats and their maintenance. It is probably through such initiatives which embrace an active maritime involvement that a meaningful and lasting interest in maritime culture can be perpetuated, leading the new generation to understand the past and preserve its remains.

Acknowledgement

This study was greatly helped by the fact that the initial exuberance created by the project, the various steps of its implementation quickly followed by a succession of setbacks, attracted intense media attention, especially in the local press. I am particularly indebted to the local newspapers *Ouest-France* and *Le Télégramme de Brest* which followed closely all the different episodes of the saga unfolding in Port-Rhu. National newspapers, such as *Le Monde* and *Libération,* also widely reported events at key moments.

PART IV
CULINARY HERITAGE

9

CULINARY HERITAGE AND *PRODUITS DE TERROIR* IN FRANCE:

Food for Thought

Marion Demossier

The decision taken in 1984 to produce a compilation of the culinary heritage of France, defined as a cultural and economic inventory of traditional and regional food and cuisine,[1] reflects more than just a mere interest in the past. The creation of such an inventory illustrates the various social and economic transformations experienced by French society in recent decades. The crisis in French agriculture and the consequent restructuring of local identities have provided two of the principal driving forces behind these changes. In this context, culinary heritage can be represented as the point at which political, economic and social spheres interact, forming part of the larger heritage movement that has affected contemporary France as a whole. From 1978, the Ministry of Culture deliberately encouraged the promotion of the past as a means 'to follow Ariadne's thread through the labyrinth of the past and thus avoid anguish and sterility'.[2] This state cultural policy, which

1. For a more detailed definition, see the introduction in one of the twenty-two volumes of *L'inventaire du patrimoine culinaire de la France*, published by Albin Michel and the CNAC (National Centre for Culinary Arts) from 1992 to 1996.

2. 'Tirer le fil d'Ariane qui unit le présent, le passé et l'avenir de notre société et qui permet d'échapper à l'angoisse et à la stérilité' quoted by J.-P. Rioux and J.-F. Sirinelli, *Histoire culturelle de la France. Le temps des masses, le vingtième siècle*, Paris, Le Seuil, 1998, p. 358.

was initially spearheaded by Jean-Philippe Lecat in 1978 and after 1981 by Jack Lang, has touched nearly every aspect of French life from small fishing communities to former sites of heavy industry. The success of the celebrations organised to mark the bicentenary of the French Revolution in 1989 provided a classic example of this heritage movement.

Given the importance of culinary heritage in the self-image of French society, it is not surprising that the *Centre National des Arts Culinaires* (National Centre for Culinary Arts, CNAC), an inter-ministerial institution,[3] has been the driving force behind the com-pilation of the culinary inventory. It was in 1984 that the Ministries of Culture and Agriculture entrusted Jean Ferniot, a journalist renowned for his opinions on culinary matters, with the task of formulating a development programme of culinary arts in France. The publication of *L'inventaire du patrimoine culinaire de la France,* for each of the twenty-two regions of France, by Albin Michel and the CNAC was the eventual result. In addition, over one hundred sites throughout France have been classified as *Sites Remarquables du Goût,* that is to say outstanding for their food production. One of the main purposes behind this recognition of quality foodstuffs is the promotion of forgotten or unknown products. The political decentralisation of the early 1980s and the new partnership between the state and the regions have provided the framework for the emergence and definition of this concept of culinary her-itage, during a period of large-scale restructuring of the food pro-duction chain and of French rural society itself (see Chapter 10). At the same time, local economic development, tourism and the con-struction of territorial identities have been based upon the pro-motion of gastronomic heritage, emphasising local cultural produce and regional cuisine. New identities and a positive image of rural society have emerged as a result, a development that has been reinforced by a sympathetic promotion in the media.

This chapter aims to analyse the complex process by which the concept of culinary heritage first emerged in France, and to throw light on culinary changes. Firstly, the historical dimension of the culinary inventory as a genre will be examined; then the social process affecting this heritage movement will be discussed before finally, turning to the new patterns of consumption that have appeared in France.

3. The CNAC was created jointly by the Ministries of Culture, Agriculture, Health, National Education and Tourism in 1990. It is composed of experts in the field (journalists and critics) and professionals.

The history and politics of French culinary heritage

The idea of a regional, geographic and cultural inventory of food-stuffs is not new. Since the eighteenth century at least, there has been an awareness of French culinary diversity, something which favoured the promotion of French regional cooking and a national recognition of local particularities.[4] Soon after the French Revolution, this local diversity, which seemed to be excluded from the new territorial and political order, reappeared in the departmental statistics, published in the form of an inventory and survey of the natural resources and local customs of each province *(Richesses naturelles et coutumes particulières à chaque province).* Thereafter regional specialities and culinary expertise became an important part of this redefinition of the French nation. During the nine-teenth century, a new awareness of regional cooking developed in parallel with both an interest in the natural and artistic inventory of provincial France and the creation of local museums. The old provinces and their people were rediscovered as *lieux de mémoire,* where culinary specialities helped to provide a sense of historical continuity, of common belonging, of heritage.[5]

In many cases, this new consciousness was expressed through culinary literature. Before 1789, recipe books and travellers' accounts were limited to describing regional customs, local prod-ucts and the way they were prepared. However, these publications were largely impressionistic accounts, not scientific inventories. It was not, therefore, until the beginning of the nineteenth century that French gastronomy developed a genuinely literary flavour. Alex Grimod de la Reynière (1803–1812), author of *L 'Almanach des Gourmands* was to the fore in this regard. According to Pascal Ory,[6] within the space of five years, Grimod de la Reynière was respon-sible for inventing the three great types of the culinary genre, namely the *Guide* or *Almanach des Gourmands,* the *Manuel des Amphitryons* and the periodical, the *Journal des Gourmands et des Belles.* His work signalled the arrival on the stage of the gastro-nomic critic with gastronomy acquiring artistic status. In 1808 the first gastronomic inventory by region *Cours gastronomique* was pro-

4. J. Csergo, 'L'émergence des cuisines régionales'. In *Histoire de l'alimentation,* Eds J.-L. Flandrin and M. Montanari, Paris, Fayard, 1996, pp 823–841.

5. J. Csergo, 'L'émergence des cuisines régionales'. In *Histoire de l'alimentation,* Eds J.-L. Flandrin and M. Montanari, Paris, Fayard, 1996, p.187

6. P. Ory, 'La gastronomie'. In P. Nora (ed.) *Les Lieux de mémoire,* Vol. III. Les France, 2. Traditions, Paris, Gallimard, 1992, p.234.

duced by Charles-Louis Cadet de Cassicourt and it was accompanied by a map of *La France Gourmande*. This marked the beginning of what has become a seemingly interminable stream of maps detailing the wines, cheeses and regional delicacies of France. The first books of regional recipes written by professionals, or by *ménagères* (housewives/housekeepers) completed the literary panorama at the end of the nineteenth century. By 1900, almost every French region could claim to possess its own recipes, and its own reasons for sharing in national culinary glory.[7]

During the second half of the nineteenth century, a series of more general works appeared providing recipes and information about regional products together with various accounts and anecdotes of local table manners and customs.[8] These publications were generally penned by local notables [9] and it is hardly an exaggeration to claim that a competition ensued. Nearly every region could point to its own specialities as part of a process of affirming its gastronomic identity. Gastronomy was thus a key factor in defining French regional and national identity. Most of these books looked back to a mythical Old Regime and to so-called 'traditional' cooking.[10] In this context, the culinary speciality was once again defined by the idea of historical continuity, memory and a sentiment of common belonging.

If gastronomy was, in part, a means of affirming regional identities, it was also an aid to those who were anxious to preserve, or rediscover, their provincial roots. One example of this phenomenon is provided by the revival of many gastronomic societies.[11] These societies played a key role in the diffusion of knowledge about regional cuisine. Many were established in Paris by successful migrants from the provinces who created a form of gastronomic sociability that emulated the world of the provincial bourgeoisie. It reinforced a provincial cultural revival then in full sway, which revealed a determination to preserve local customs, language and folklore against the centralising pressure of the

---

7. See for example *Le cuisinier bourguignon* by Alfred Contour, published in 1891.

8. A good example is provided by Charles Gérard, *L'ancienne Alsace à table*, published in 1862.

9. In many cases, they were published locally and their author was seen as an antiques dealer who was protecting and passing on the local memory.

10. J. Csergo, 'L'émergence des cuisines régionales'. In *Histoire de l'alimentation*, Eds J.-L. Flandrin and M. Montanari, Paris, Fayard, 1996, p.830.

11. For more information, see J. Csergo, 'L'émergence des cuisines régionales'. In *Histoire de l'alimentation*, Eds J.-L. Flandrin and M. Montanari, Paris, Fayard, 1996, p.832.

Third Republic. These migrants sought to recreate a supposedly traditional sociability around the sharing of food and local products, allowing them to maintain their distinct identity in Paris. Within the gastronomic societies of the inter-war years, it was also possible to identify a series of networks of social elites such as the liberal professions, independent merchants and businessmen. These social groups were primarily responsible for the revival of *confréries gourmandes* (gastronomic confraternities) that occurred at the same time. The same phenomenon took place in several regions. In Burgundy, for example, regionalism corresponded to the revival of a local gastronomy headed by local elites which was accompanied by various artistic and literary events and the emergence of an efficient promotion of tourism based upon the region's reputation as a gastronomic paradise. [12]

At a more popular level the development of mass tourism, first by rail, subsequently by private car, played a major role in the broadening of culinary consciousness. Gastronomy was promoted alongside national monuments and sites of natural beauty as part of the attractions of France identified by such influential publications as the *Guide Michelin* or the *Guide Bleu*. The period from the beginning of the twentieth century until the Second World War saw a proliferation of works mainly produced in Paris, celebrating the wealth of French culinary heritage and its different social and regional components. The richness of France was emblematised and culinary heritage was culturally promoted to illustrate it. From Reynière to the *Guide Joanne*, these inventories of regional culinary specialities can be interpreted as 'an indication of the status awarded to them in both the imagination and in the symbolic representations of the nation and of national identity'. [13]

The economic expansion and modernisation of France after 1950 struck a blow to the traditional image of *la France gourmande*. The partial triumph of food standardisation in the 1970s, the growth of supermarkets and the transfer of the pleasures of the table from the home to the restaurant under the pressures of urbanisation, as well as the movement of women into paid employment, radically transformed the culinary sphere. These

---

12. G. Laferté, 'Le renouveau contemporain des confréries culinaires: production et usage de traditions'. Unpublished thesis, EHESS, 1999, p.6.

13. '[...]une indication du statut qui leur sera octroyé dans l'imaginaire et dans les représentations symboliques de la nation et de l'identité nationale'. J. Csergo, 'L'émergence des cuisines régionales'. In *Histoire de l'alimentation*, Eds J.-L. Flandrin and M. Montanari, Paris, Fayard, 1996, p.828.

drastic changes and a perceived threat to traditional values were, in part, the inspiration behind the idea of a new culinary inventory, which began in 1980. This project, which is still in progress, encompasses the interests of many different social and economic groups and has contributed to a reinvention of the culinary arts within a national framework, that of French gastronomy with all the sensations and images that it entails. The publication since 1980 of twenty-two volumes dedicated to *produits de terroir* and to the traditional recipes of every French region has contributed greatly to the process of reconstructing a French culinary heritage within a European framework. *Produits de terroir* are defined as local and traditional food products or produce with a unique and identifiable character based upon specific historical, cultural or technical components. The definition includes the accumulation and transmission of savoir-faire (see Chapter 10).

As in earlier periods, this culinary heritage movement has been closely associated with the creation of a national identity based upon the notion of regional and local diversity. With a similar political objective in mind, the CNAC has launched a national programme of sensory awakening in primary schools with the aim of counteracting the supposed homogenisation of tastes represented by, for example, the infamous 'Big Mac'. In 1993, some 20,000 schoolchildren attended lectures by Jacques Puisais, [14] self-appointed *gourou du goût* (guru of taste), and a hundred teachers were trained by gastronomic and culinary professionals.

The culinary inventory of the French regions is also the result of a conscious state policy aimed at both the protection and the promotion of a rural cultural heritage. This approach, which stresses the notion of patrimony, [15] is part of an attempt to produce an integrated policy of economic development, whilst preserving landscapes and managing natural resources. The emergence of *produits de terroir* has played an important role in rural development. In a context of agricultural restructuring where the number of farmers has decreased drastically in France and elsewhere in Europe, *produits de terroir* and the renewed emphasis on the virtues of quality have created new opportunities for French agricultural regions. France today is the world's second largest exporter of agricultural

14. Jacques Puisais (1927–), French oenologist, has researched the development of taste among children. He founded the *Institut Français du goût* (French Institute dedicated to taste).

15. See I. Chiva, *Une politique pour le patrimoine culturel rural*, rapport remis à Jacques Toubon, Ministère de la culture, April 1994.

products, just behind the United States of America, and its reputation is based upon luxury goods and gastronomy. Rural development policies have sought to capitalise upon these strengths in order to create new products with high economic values using tradition and history as the main selling points. At the same time, rural development, and especially tourism is accompanied by a search for roots and authenticity of foodstuffs, and the concept of *goûts du terroir* (tastes of the terroir) have their role to play.

Culinary heritage, economic changes and territorial construction

As with the label of Appellation d'Origine Contrôlée (Controlled Denomination of Origin, hereafter CDO)[16] for French wine, the notion of culinary heritage encompasses a variety of economic interests. Having achieved recognition in the culinary inventory, many producers have subsequently obtained the label of CDO, which is associated with high quality products such as, for example, the cheeses *Camembert de Normandie* or *Epoisses de Bourgogne*. According to Laurence Bérard and Philippe Marchenay (see Chapter Ten), to be included in the inventory is a vital first step in preparing a successful application for official recognition. For the last three years, a group of producers in Normandy has organised various events and meetings centred on regional produce both to safeguard the future of those products already holding a CDO, and to publicise, and hopefully achieve similar recognition for, other forgotten products. In Burgundy, the *Conseil régional* (regional authority) has invested FF110 million in the development of a *Institut de Recherche pour le goût* (Institute of European Research dedicated to taste) with the aim of supporting regional agriculture and food production. Such initiatives have proliferated in the course of the last twenty years as a result of an explosion of consumer demand for so-called 'traditional' products. It is not, therefore, surprising that the *Ministère de l'Agriculture* (Ministry of Agriculture), together with the *Ministère de la Recherche* (Ministry of Research), has launched a vast study of the food trade called *Aliment 2000* (Food 2000), which seeks to boost the relationship between the food industry and the consumer.

16. Created in 1905, the CDO is a major label guaranteeing the quality and origin of 305 wines, 29 cheeses and a dozen food products such as Chasselas de Moissac grapes, le Puy lentils or Bresse poultry.

Central to this process is the use of the concepts of *rural* and *terroir* by a whole variety of social groups, both consumers and producers, including clubs of *gourmands,* chambers of commerce, folklorists, confraternities and associations, retired people, the 'neo-rural' and local political bodies. Heritage can therefore be seen as a resource for local development, and as a means of mobilising these different actors in a cohesive fashion. One good example of this phenomenon is provided by the example of the *Beaufort* cheese in the Northern Alps discussed by Muriel Faure.[17] In her study, she demonstrated how a local campaign for official recognition (CDO status) became the catalyst for the reconstruction of a collective local identity. As Bessière has pointed out,[18] 'Turning to local development as a territorial construction process […], culinary heritage may be used as a means to boost development. Numerous communities have realised that an area may be revived using its cultural value and identity as a starting point by encouraging local actors to promote transmitted skills and expertise'. However as Faure[19] has shown the process needs to be seen as both a product in creating values and as an active force for 'emblematising' objects and meaningful actions. It can therefore be argued that tourism and gastronomy play a regulating role at a local level enabling farmers and rural societies to redefine their identities in the context of the crisis of the nation state.[20]

Rural heritage movements have struck a chord with a large number of middle-class urban French people who have been attracted by 'green tourism' and the search for their roots. In this respect, tourism has contributed to the politics of conservation, with the maintenance of a *national* countryside and cuisine as a deliberate *regional* policy. Gastronomy in this context provides a distinct identity for a region, promotes farm products and meets the needs of both consumers and suppliers of regional tourism. Regions have thus become a term of reference for these new consumers. As one satisfied customer remarked: 'You can eat well in the French provinces, not only because we are close to the place of production, but because the local people are themselves the

17. M. Faure, 'Un produit agricole "affiné" en objet culturel, le fromage de Beaufort dans les Alpes du Nord', *Terrain,* 33, September 1999, pp 81–92.
18. J. Bessière, 'Local development and heritage: traditional food and cuisine as tourist attractions in rural areas', *European Society for Rural Sociology,* 38, 1998, p.31.
19. M. Faure, 'Un produit agricole "affiné" en objet culturel, le fromage de Beaufort dans les Alpes du Nord', *Terrain* 33, September 1999, pp 81–92.
20. J.-P. Poulain, 'Goût du terroir et tourisme vert à l'heure de l'Europe', *Ethnologie française,* 26 (1), 1997, pp18–26.

guardians of a gastronomic heritage, maybe even of a wisdom to which sense and savours are ultimately bound'.[21] Camping on a farm, consuming home produced foodstuffs and cheeses, purchasing wine direct from the wine-grower are all different expressions of this desire to rediscover what is natural, real and authentic in a society characterised by permanent economic and social change. In a series published by *Le Monde* on the future of Languedoc-Roussillon,[22] Guy Julien, in charge of promoting regional tourism, drew attention to the fact that visitors are increasingly motivated by the idea of *terroir* or *pays*. This style of tourism is frequently associated with city dwellers who are looking for an alternative society, detached from the familiar social rhythms, that enables people to develop new forms of sociability.

Consuming France

For the French, food is more than just about eating and drinking. Instead, it encompasses a whole series of practices and rituals with symbolic and representational significance on a number of cultural levels. Rural life, tradition and tourism as well as food are part of these patterns of consumption. Supposedly, traditional products are assumed to possess qualities derived from a transmission of skills and practices acquired over a long period of time, and they form part of the complex process of reinvention that France has experienced. Consumption of *produits de terroir* also bears witness to a quest for identity in a society which, under the pressure of economic change, social mobility and europeanisation has been subject to social and cultural fragmentation. Through a process of standardisation, or what might even be described as democratisation, the modern food industry has made it possible to consume the same product almost anywhere in the world, thus threatening to eliminate regional diversity. Its very success has inspired a powerful but rather disjointed reaction designed to preserve or rediscover local products. Today, the *cuisine du pays* (local cooking) and the seasonal nature of certain products have become highly valued, a source of pride and prestige.

21. 'On mange bien dans les régions françaises non seulement parce qu'on est proche du lieu de production, mais aussi parce que ceux qui y vivent semblent gardiens d'un patrimoine gastronomique, peut-être même d'une sagesse, dans laquelle intimement le sens et les saveurs s'entremêleraient'. J.-P. Poulain, 'Goût du terroir et tourisme vert à l'heure de l'Europe', *Ethnologie française*, 26 (1), 1997, p.19.

22. R. Benguigui and J. Monin, *Le Monde*, 28 February 1998, p.11.

The craze for local traditions indicates a nostalgic quest for collective landmarks in an increasingly fragmented France. For the last thirty years, associations dedicated to the protection of local heritage, museums and markets have grown in number. Rural France and its produce are now at the core of new cultural practices.[23] In 1998, out of eight television programmes devoted to gastronomy, five were focusing on the *terroir*, the countryside, traditions and local recipes. Only three were presenting the recipes of famous chefs or home cooking. All had in common the need to preserve and transmit 'traditional products' and methods of cooking. The success of Jean-Pierre Coffe, an outspoken and controversial partisan of traditional produce and culinary methods, provides a striking illustration of this craze for authenticity, tradition and so-called quality. Rural and local have therefore become two of the major rallying points of the social restructuring of French society. They offer to different social groups a means of expressing new cultural identities and of redefining national identity. As France is now a predominantly urban society, the consumption of rural life in all its diversity forms part of what Claude Fischler[24] has called 'the back-to-nature myth', a counter-tendency to urbanisation.

In the television programme *Aux petits bonheurs la France: les tribulations d'un amateur de vins*,[25] an enthusiast invites us to visit a country where friendship, taste, wine and local specialities dominate. Sociability and the ritual of drinking prevail in his pilgrimage. His quest is about reviving memories of places, people and tastes that are deeply rooted in his own mind. The sociologist Amirou,[26] on the other hand, emphasises what he describes as an *appartenance sociétale*, a feeling of belonging to a social group, and of a common sociability, an original *communitas*, thus an identity. The yearning for a return to the countryside is part of the process of reinvention of a rural and peasant identity, but it is also an expression of a desire for landscape appropriation and a life in communities where togetherness, personal recognition and collective participation are easily combined.

23. See for example J. Menateau, 'Les terroirs se vendent sur le Web', *Le Monde*, 13 May 1999.

24. C. Fischler, *L 'homnivore*, Paris, Odile Jacob, 1990.

25. Television programme on France 3, 6 June 1998.

26. R. Amirou, *Imaginaire touristique et sociabilités du voyage*, Paris, Presses Universitaires de France, 1995.

For tourists, the consumption of a *produit de terroir* offers the prospect of an intimate relationship with a culture that is now separate from their own experience. By eating, they are able to travel and incorporate the other. Gastronomy is a fundamental component of tourism and eating is an integral part of the vacation. The wide range of tastes and culinary sensations on offer provides tourists with an opportunity to travel in time and in space as they reinvent their own relationship with the past, effectively imbibing memories of France. These culinary rovers define their identity in a society where fragmentation combines with modernity. When these gastronomes return from their travels, they bring back some of their discoveries or culinary finds and share them with friends. A particular product or recipe becomes the focus of discussion, exchanges and comments. It provides a way to discover a new area, its cultural and gastronomic heritage and its traditions. It is also a means of symbolically integrating a forgotten culture. In this respect, culinary heritage facilitates the meeting between producer and consumer, and between rural and urban France.

According to Masson and Moscovici,[27] eating in France is still widely seen as a form of collective behaviour. In reality, there have been significant changes in the eating habits of French people, who now cook less at home and are no longer horrified by the idea of the ready cooked meal. Changes have not, however, been simply in the direction of convenience and fast food. The modern eater has built a new culinary culture, a *gastro-anomie* that is defined by a set of very complex habits. While the culinary pick and mix defines his/her taste, meetings with friends and families still offer the main occasions for sharing a meal. However the interesting new aspect of this culture lies in its capacity to combine different spaces, times and ways of eating, for example, a snack on the motorway followed by a gargantuan dinner at a local inn.

In this respect, memory plays a major role, allowing the consumer to anchor his or herself socially and individually. The essential function of food in the construction of cultural identities has been confirmed in various studies. For example, during the post-war rural exodus, people who left the countryside and were obliged to move to Paris and the other major cities in order to find employment were found to be recreating a lost sociability or local identity when they shared a meal or organised social gatherings. As in the nineteenth century, the centre of these festivities was

27. G. Masson and P. Moscovici, *Programme de recherche R94/25* Aliment demain, Ministère de l'Agriculture et de la Recherche, Consommateur et Marché, 1993.

once again food and other products brought back to the capital from rural regions. The memory of food and its taste contributed to the construction of a social space seen as authentic, stable, a-historic, founded on an unchanged tradition, in other words some of the necessary landmarks for the construction of social and cultural identities. Indeed, it is by the medium of cooking and table manners that a fundamental social process operates and that culture transmits and internalises its values. Thus, domestic recipes were transmitted from mother to daughter, from one family to another, from one network to another. Anne Muxel[28] has described the importance of memory and oral history in the transmission of domestic and traditional recipes. She relates that when the question of transmission was discussed, two thirds of her interviewees mentioned the existence of inherited domestic culinary aptitudes. Gestures, tastes, savours are described as having an origin that could be easily traced and that was offered a tie to previous generations. However, the traditional transmission of culinary know-how is gradually breaking down. The loosening of the bonds between generations has seriously affected the process of transmission. Yet culinary skills, methods and products are still passed on according to specific rituals. Food remains a symbol, a sign of communion, a class marker and an emblem that is used by both individuals and social groups.

Conclusion

The sociological, anthropological and historical approaches to regional cooking have all helped to shatter the folkloric view of a stable and traditional cuisine. Rather than regional cooking being fixed, innovations and exchanges have transformed culinary savoir-faire. In the conclusion of their *Histoire de l' alimentation*, J.-L.Flandrin and M. Montanari (see bibliography) have argued that culinary traditions were created, shaped and progressively defined by time and contact between cultures. Thus the creation of culinary heritage questions the nature of these emblematic culinary traditions. How is it possible to protect and authentically restore a domestic and traditional savoir-faire that is passed on by word of mouth and is only given a fixed definition by the relatively recent act of recording? Indeed the institutionalisation of

28. A. Muxel, *Individu et mémoire familiale*, Paris, Nathan, 1996.

produits de terroir in the form of a CDO label operates through the recognition of their authenticity by various state ministries and today from the European Union (see Chapters 10 and 11). Both historical and ethnological approaches have been used in order to legitimise the traditional character of these products and the authenticity of memory has been subject to doubt. In this regard, what is at stake is crucial for economic and social reasons. Social groups, political actors, producers, and local authorities want official recognition because *produits de terroir* are seen as a way of doing something for their region. On the other hand, the state and its representatives, who have created the demands, are in turn asked to participate in the legitimisation of the products. Therefore, culinary heritage seems to be above all a negotiation between experts, producers and political forces or actors. It is part of a process of restructuring new social entities such as *pays* or labelled zones that are crucial to regional and social identities. Thus, culinary heritage has become a political tool for the construction of identity in a context of europeanisation and globalisation. At the beginning of a new century, France seems to be a land of monuments, symbols and memories where visitors, lost in their quest, are looking for collective values and places of solidarity. Gastronomy would appear to offer a key to these promised lands.

10

A MARKET CULTURE:

Produits de terroir or the Selling of Heritage

Laurence Bérard and Philippe Marchenay

There is no better example of the interaction between the heritage movement and the socio-economic interests of modern French agriculture than that of the so-called *produits de terroir*. The term *produits de terroir* itself is notoriously difficult to define, but it is perhaps best described as traditional 'local agricultural products and foodstuffs' (English official rendering) whose qualities cross time and space and are anchored in a specific place and history. Products such as *Epoisses de Bourgogne* or *foie gras* are defined by the fact that they depend on the shared savoir-faire of a given community and its culture. These products, whether of an animal, vegetal or mineral origin, may, or may not have been transformed by human intervention. The production methods involved also vary enormously including everything from domestic scale or cottage industry to industrial manufacture.

The sudden emergence of *produits de terroir* is the result of a variety of social, economic and political factors. The implementation of the European Union's Common Agricultural Policy, the encouragement given to the development of rural micro-economies, the expansion of the heritage movement and the implementation of EU regulations covering geographical protection are some of the reasons why the value of such products has been enhanced and why they appeal to modern consumers.

Perceived as healthier, safer and reassuring in a world where the food industry has been shaken by recent health scares, notably those caused by BSE in cattle and dioxin poisoning in the case of Belgian chicken, these products are now attracting increased attention from producers and consumers alike. The prospect of benefiting from protective measures at both national and European levels is another important reason behind the rise of the *produit de terroir*. Achieving such recognition allows existing cultural values to be supplemented with economic benefits, in a mutually reinforcing and virtuous circle.

Attempts at defining *produits de terroir* have not only raised new questions amongst culinary professionals and consumers, but have also created new expectations within the communities involved in the production process. Due to the intrinsic cultural content contained within any effort to define the specificity of a product, anthropologists in particular have been called upon in order to analyse themes that are central to their discipline such as time, space, savoir-faire and tradition. They are invited to conduct research into a host of cultural projects as well as different production methods. They have also been asked to prepare census data and to analyse the impact of initiatives such as the revival of traditional products, festivals or techniques. What then is the position of those anthropologists who engage in such a study, how can they strike a balance between the pursuit of an original and objective line of research while responding to the questions, even expectations of the organisations who commissioned them?

Between politics, identity and the law: distinction and protection

Of products and landscapes

Amongst the many initiatives undertaken in France during the past ten years, the census of *produits de terroir* begun in 1992 stands out as one of the most significant. It was initiated jointly by the Ministry of Agriculture and the Ministry of Culture, and coordinated by an inter-ministerial committee, the CNAC (National Council of Culinary Arts). The primary objective of the inventory was cultural. It was intended to place on record the traditional culinary knowledge and savoir-faire found in the various regions and *terroirs* of France, to produce an 'état des lieux', that is to say an assessment of the current position of those products, and to make the results available to the public at large. The second objective was economic. By acquiring a better understanding of the food heritage of individual regions, it would then be possible to promote their products, many of which were largely unknown outside their own localities.

These culinary heritage surveys took place within established administrative regions that were responsible for their funding, and their scope was intended to cover the whole spectrum of the agricultural and food sectors.[1] When recording individual products, the aim was also to see the big picture. Amongst others, history, public notoriety and local savoir-faire, were all employed in an effort to help identify factors contributing to the specificity of local agricultural produce or food production. The publication of a series of volumes covering each region by the renowned publishers, Albin Michel, has also added credibility and weight to the exercise, allowing it to reach a wide public.[2] It is likely that by the end of the year 2000 all of the French regions will have their own culinary inventory and list of *produits de terroir*. When a previously unknown product has been mentioned in one of these publications, it has frequently provided the opportunity for an application for formal protection under existing legislation, or the possibility of wider publicity and successful commercialisation.

In parallel with the preparation of these inventories, a project entitled *Sites Remarquables du Goût* (Remarkable Sites of Taste) was launched in 1993. Its aim was to identify and promote one hundred sites of historical and architectural importance, found in unique landscapes identifiable with products belonging to French culinary heritage, or savoir-faire. The aim was to identify entire production systems, whose individual components would themselves be recognised for their contributions to the heritage value of the site as a whole. This magic number of one hundred was not chosen at random, but selection criteria and evaluation procedures were somewhat lax to say the least.

A second, albeit independent scheme was launched by the Ministry of the Environment and the various *Chambres d'Agriculture* under the rather grandiose slogan *Paysages de Reconquête* (Reconquered Landscapes). Once again, the aim was to classify one hundred landscapes recognised for their close connection with local

1. This framework raises a serious question of methodology, i.e., how to deal with cultural boundaries when they do not correspond with administrative boundaries?

2. See bibliography. In addition, a chapter containing 'traditional recipes' is included in each of the volumes published.

products. Those chosen received a label, certifying to the existence of a special relationship between a particular human activity, culture or production and the 'reconquered' landscape. The high point of the entire project was a jamboree organised by the then minister of the Environment in the symbolically resonant venue of the *Jardin des plantes* in Paris. The park was transformed into a vast market for the sale of agricultural produce and the various products associated with the 'reconquered' landscapes. The ministerial invitation to the event trumpeted: 'Come in numbers, with your family or friends, and help save the landscapes of France you love by tasting their products.' The aim was above all to stir public opinion, without worrying unduly about the arid demands of scientific methodology!

If France has been in the vanguard of the heritage movement in the agricultural and culinary sectors, other countries have begun to follow suit. In Italy, systematic surveys into the agricultural and food industries, coordinated by rural sociologists of the *Instituto nazionale di sociologia rurale* (INSOR), have produced a series of important publications. For example, the *Atlante dei prodotti tipici* provide Atlases of regional production including among other things, dairy products, charcuterie, pâtisseries and preserves. Also in Italy, the movement 'Slow Food' was very active in recording such information. In Spain and Portugal, surveys and inventories of food production have also been completed, albeit in a less systematic fashion. Finally, on a European level, member states participated in a project called *Euroterroirs* resulting in the classification of some four thousand products. All of these projects, whether in France or elsewhere, have in common the ability to mobilise large numbers of people, from both the professional and public spheres: ministries of agriculture, tourism and the environment, chambers of commerce and agriculture, administrative and political institutions, farmers, producers and consumers.

Geographical protection

The option of protecting the geographical origin of a product linked to specific manufacturing methods is now well established in Europe, with a formal warrant and a distinctive label issued as protection against imitations. Thus in France, the *Appellation d'Origine Contrôlée* (Controlled Denomination of Origin, CDO) protects a product originating from a well-defined geographical area from imitation. It is a guarantee that it possesses qualities derived from the contribution of 'unique natural or human factors' to its production. This concept was first developed late in the nineteenth century and it was initially applied to wines. Similar schemes existed for cheeses and a small number of other products but the measures were never as formal, nor as rigorously applied as they were with wines.

In 1990 the *Appellation d'Origine Contrôlée* scheme was extended to include the entire agricultural and food sector in an effort to further reinforce and cement the credibility of the concept. The decision inspired the European Community Council to frame an appropriate body of legislation and in July 1992, two regulations were adopted. Regulation 2081/92 dealt with the protection of particular geographical regions or places of origin for agricultural products and foodstuffs, issuing the certificates of 'Protected Denomination of Origin' (PDO) or 'Protected Geographical Indication' (PGI). Regulation 2082/92 certified the specific characteristics of these products. The broad objective behind these regulations is the provision of a legal framework allowing for the formal recognition and protection of the connection between a product and either its place of origin, or the traditions involved in its manufacture. The introduction of these protection measures coincided with the establishment of a common European market designed to remove borders and to allow producers throughout the Community to sell their products without restriction. Paradoxically, this step in the direction of free trade thus started a movement in favour of the protection of the heritage or specificities of various products originating from individual countries within the Union.

To understand these developments we need to remember that they took place within a context favourable towards those products possessing a strong historical tie to a specific geographical area. Indeed, a great deal of effort is currently being expended in this domain as part of regional policies intended to help combat the 'desertification' of rural areas. The impact of these regulatory measures is often significant. The decision to protect one product almost inevitably means the rejection of another. When, for instance, a particular cheese wins protection under the CDO label, the manufacturing of the same product outside of its defined protection area is strictly forbidden. This harsh reality raises difficult questions: what exactly is *tradition*? What is the precise relationship between a product and its *place of origin*? The fact that these pro-

tective measures apply right across Europe adds a further compli-
cation. Concepts and definitions change from one member country
to another. France, and the countries of Southern Europe in general, view their foods and culinary production as an important part
of their heritage, with a crucial social and cultural dimension.

A re-examination of anthropological themes and values

At present, tradition is invoked in all quarters and is mentioned in
all kinds of contexts, and the world of food is no exception. Even
if current European regulations do not specifically mention the
word *tradition* when defining the geographical limits of production zones, it clearly underlies some elements of the legislation.
The same applies to time, to the connection between a product
and its place of origin and to the status of local knowledge and
practices. These are all major themes at the core of post-modern
anthropology and they almost inevitably recur during any investigation of *produits de terroir*.

Time

In defining a *produit de terroir,* time presents itself under several
guises. This is revealed most obviously in the form of the past
defined simply as a precedent or historical record. History in its
classical form is based upon archival research into written documents. Yet the archives are frequently silent when it comes to *produits de terroir* and references to them are fleeting at best. As a
result, oral history, derived from interviews conducted in the field,
is the best tool available for the collection of information. Time is
thus defined by collective memory handed down orally which, by
definition, is selective.

When examining *produits de terroir*, time is also measured by its
length or duration. The time needed for the production of a commodity is an integral element of a product's identity – particularly
where maturation and aging are involved. It is also an essential step
in the maturation or fattening of livestock. Its importance is further
reinforced by the fact that many products were preserved for later
consumption, an essential process in ensuring a steady food supply
in days gone by. For modern consumers food and delayed con-

sumption is no longer an obligation, it is a choice, and the cultural dimension of the process is thus accentuated. Finally, the seasonal cycle offers another point of chronological reference. It too is no longer something to be endured as in the past, but instead offers reference points allowing products to be situated in relation to time.

Place of origin

One of the characteristics of any local product is by definition its attachment to a particular place. Yet such a self-evident statement hides the more complex question of the precise nature of the relationship between the product and its place of origin. Environmental conditions have a major influence on all agricultural production, but it is particularly relevant in the case of fruit and vegetables, which are so susceptible to climatic and pedological conditions. However, these physical factors alone do not explain what creates the specificity of a product. It is human intervention, through technical knowledge and savoir-faire, social organisation and representation which makes sense of this notion of *lien au lieu* (tie to a place), allowing these physical factors to express themselves. It is, however, possible to talk of regions that are physically *predisposed* to produce products under the influence of human activities. In Abondance (French Alps), it is the management of the Alpine high country, and more specifically of its pastures – as well as the breeding of the local cattle of the same name – which are the cornerstones of the entire production system. In traditional arboriculture, the choice of fruit varieties and the subsequent grafting, pruning and harvesting methods are all essential elements in producing a fruit whose characteristics are much more than a simple expression of the physical attributes of a regional climate and soil. The link between a product and its place of origin becomes even more difficult to define when it comes to manufactured products. What about *charcuterie* for example? In this instance, specific practical knowledge is an integral element not only of the link between a product and its place of origin, but also of its actual composition.

Savoir-faire

An examination of local knowledge and savoir-faire raises a multitude of questions about the nature of *produits de terroir*. The role, for example, of a vital stage in the production process, or the contribution of a key ingredient are subjects worthy of investigation in their own right. Similarly dietary habits and the way food is both prepared and consumed play an important part further down the production chain. This, in itself, begs a number of other questions in connection with shared technical culture. How does this culture evolve? How does it become diversified and how is it passed on? These questions become particularly relevant in attempting to explain, for example, the subtle variations found in a product within a single production area. Finally, there are instances of local products where aesthetic criteria and style are an integral part of either their production process or their presentation. Although such an additional dimension is not always officially recognised, it is nevertheless realistic to suggest that talent, combined to style and aesthetic requirements may lead to a product acquiring a reputation for excellence.

Naming products

The names of products have their roots in local culture and history and are often the result of evolution and adaptations, and they may even reflect specific claims. The subtle variations found in manufactured products often have an impact on their nomenclature. Food products within their own production areas, on the other hand, are often nameless because they are such a familiar part of the daily lives of local people. There are many examples of such products. In a number of French regions, local cheeses are described simply as 'the cheese', without any further qualification or even mention of the actual place they come from. The cheese now known as *Tome des Bauges* [3] was only given the name of one of the mountain ranges in the Savoie region when a concerted promotional campaign was launched. Before that it was a local staple and was simply called 'la tome'. In Italy, numerous cheeses are simply referred to as '*nostrale*' – 'ours' – without anyone thinking it necessary to be more specific. A similar pattern can be observed in Catalonia in Spain where a local vegetable was christened the 'Castellfollit Bean' once producers decided to promote it commer-

3. In this instance, 'tome' is spelt with one 'm' only, contrary to the usual spelling of 'tomme' used generically. This difference could be interpreted as a subtle marketing ploy adopted to distinguish the product from its namesakes. This cheese is presently under consideration to be given Controlled Denomination of Origin.

cially. Until then, it was simply 'the bean', the only one cultivated locally. It is therefore the commercialisation, consumption and ultimately recognition of a product beyond its own production area that leads to the adoption of a name, often as part of an attempt to tie a product to a given geographical area.

The growing notoriety of a product can lead both to confusion and conflict about the way products are named. An attempt by a reputable perfume maker to market a fragrance under the name *Champagne* soon came to grief after legal threats from the highly sensitive winemakers of that region, but even less glamorous products can run into difficulty. The name of *Rosette*, for example, refers to a type of *charcuterie* that is both well-known and widely distributed. In the area around the city of Lyon, it is called 'Rosette de Lyon'. Yet, the reference to the city, which boasts a formidable gastronomic reputation for, amongst other things, *charcuterie*, is not the result of any specific manufacturing method, technical process, or even ingredient. The example of the 'Rosette de Lyon' raises serious questions about how rigorously definitions of *produits de terroir* are applied when products are named.

Heritage and the immaterial

Produits de terroir possess a unique identity that plays a major role in their recognition and economic success. Yet that identity is far from fixed or stable and is a reflection of the organisation of the societies in which they are produced and the status that those societies accord them. Indeed, the majority of *produits de terroir* have already outgrown their original role as local domestic produce to become the focus of artisanal or even industrial production. Yet no matter how far they may have drifted away from the societies where they originated, their roots remain.

This notion of identity is crucial to the transition of a product into a form of heritage. Indeed, vast numbers of products are now claimed to possess a value as 'heritage' under the pressure of many different social actors, but principally their producers. This dynamic process conjures up a link between time, whether past, present or future, between men and women sharing images, stories, memories and space. It is an integral part of collective representations of social reproduction. *Produits de terroir* can therefore be described as part of an 'evolving' heritage, directly influenced and 'constructed' by humans through their social activities. This form of heritage also reveals the ability of modern societies to act collectively, projecting themselves into the future through a sense of shared identity derived from the *terroir* and its products.[4] Its success depends upon the full participation of the groups and individuals involved, and requires a sense of togetherness on their part. This notion of heritage is selective and it is constantly changing, which in a sense is paradoxical. On the one hand, these products are deeply rooted in their past, in their traditions and their respective *terroirs:* they are steeped in their own history. On the other hand, they are also 'modern' products fulfilling a purpose connected to the status and significance that are attributed to them. For the producers and the other professionals involved in the world of *produits de terroir,* it is difficult to get to grips with this paradox because they are conscious of the role heritage has to play, while being aware of the potential consequences of tampering with it. The effect of this awareness can be detected on what are, for example, considered to be accepted practices, or in the way raw materials are handled which, in turn, is a reflection of the way these same groups approach the problem of heritage.

What is it that makes heritage? What are valid criteria for defining heritage and for whose benefit is heritage produced? In terms of the food industry, the idea of heritage depends upon a number of perceptions that are likely to vary according to the position of the social actors involved. Consumers in particular would appear to be crucial, but with the exception of local people or connoisseurs, they are frequently ill-informed of the methods involved in agricultural or food production, and this is especially true of *produits de terroir.* When acquiring recognition as a *produit de terroir,* the status of a product changes and may even be completely 'turned on its head'. It is not unusual for a product previously considered to be a part of the staple diet of a rural community to become an exceptional product in the eyes of distant urban consumers.

Groups of producers are not the only ones to claim the tradition and heritage of *produits de terroir* for their own. Politicians, agricultural and cultural bodies, the food industry and all manner of local groups and organisations stake their own claims. The economic consolidation of a number of these products is taking place under our very eyes: the various actors position themselves, trading circles are formed and commercial links and networks are established.

4. For further information on this particular subject, see M. Rautenberg, *Evaluation et mise en valeur des patrimoines de l'agriculture dans les projets de développement: quels patrimoines pour quel développement ?* Ardèche, Le Pradel, 1997.

Thus, contrary to what one might expect, products that are often associated with the past and unchanging traditions are in fact surprisingly dynamic. They are regularly confronted with the reality of technical development and innovation and they must position themselves in the market, particularly when they are the focus of vigorous revival or publicity campaigns that may be connected to the issue of official protection. As a group, *produits de terroir* show great diversity as much for the status they acquire as for the commercial activity they generate or the actions that accompany them.

Anthropology to the rescue

Social scientists are increasingly called upon to answer the many questions of concern to modern societies relative to agricultural and food activities. The opinions of anthropologists in particular have been especially sought after since the promulgation of the European Union's regulatory framework relating to local agricultural foods and foodstuffs. These regulations had major repercussions on the national systems of protection of these local products within individual states. The demands upon anthropologists are doubly sensitive because of their economic and cultural significance. The protection of a product, including the savoir-faire, and the restriction of its zone of production to a specific geographical area, obliges the producers to define just what is unique about their product and to provide adequate historical proofs to legitimise their claims.

There is no doubt that anthropologists are particularly well qualified to understand the specificity of such products by identifying their unique characteristics. Those products that can fulfil the criteria required to obtain the status of *produit de terroir* have a certain form of cultural coherence that is easily recognised by an ethnologist whose craft is to interpret the reality of local cultures. The formal description of a product and its manufacturing processes calls upon the particular expertise of the discipline. In addition, such a description must include those factors and those characteristics that define its specificity and its identity. However, as experience shows, the application of a scientific approach is not always straightforward. It requires the deployment of comparative analysis as well as prior knowledge and understanding of technical practices and of comparable products.

The knowledge and information acquired in the course of ethnological fieldwork can easily be transferred to the socio-economic sphere where it can be appropriated by a whole series of different interests. Whenever possible the aim is to identify certain essential criteria that permit a simple definition of these products, thus preventing them from being lumped together in the category *'fourre-tout'* in which so many imitations of *produits de terroir* in France currently flourish. The same principle applies to research work undertaken with the aim of defining the geographical, historical or other factors which allow producers to claim protection for their products. The current French legislation requires them to prove a historical link and geographical basis as well as a 'traditional' dimension to the production process. As producers who happen to fall outside the proposed zone of protection may suffer serious economic consequences, as they may no longer be able to use the name and notoriety of a product to market their produce, it is vital for those submitting a case for geographical protection to do so with the utmost thoroughness. Yet on what criteria should claims for historical justification be based? How can claims for geographical exclusivity, the so-called *lien au lieu* (tie to a place) be judged? Similar questions can be asked in the technical field. Which technical traits should be emphasised in the specifications defining the conditions of production? How should processing variations within the same category of product be dealt with? These are all extremely difficult questions confronting not only those groups applying for protection, but also the ethnologists and other professionals responsible for the assessment of their claims. Nor is it easy to agree upon a valid methodology when assessing those demands.

The classic historical approach has problems coping with the relationship between *produits de terroir* and basic chronology. Written sources may help in providing the wider historical context, explaining how and why products were produced or accorded status, but they are frequently silent on many aspects of their manufacture. Oral history is therefore helpful not only in filling gaps in the historical record, but even providing the basic information needed for an informed decision. Personal accounts allow us to evaluate the reality of the social and economic changes associated with traditional manufacturing processes and to gather information about the recent past, extending up to a maximum period of approximately one hundred years. Moreover the evidence obtained from oral history offers a useful insight into the validity of claims for the 'local' nature of a product. The anthropological method also offers an opportunity to assess the scientific value of the oral evidence used in studying these products. Until recently such methods had been largely ignored by those responsible for assessing applications for the status of *produit de terroir*. The institutional apparatus and most of the parties involved remained wedded to the notion that the only legitimate way to submit evidence was in the form of a written document which could stand the test of being subjected to rigorous scrutiny. Only slowly is that attitude beginning to change.

The proof of the existence of a link between time, place and product remains a major preoccupation for some departments within the French Ministry of Agriculture which are not yet accustomed to dealing with the evidence supplied by researchers in the human and social sciences. The debate is also intense within the National Institute for Denominations of Origin,[5] which has traditionally favoured claims for recognition based upon pedoclimatic and more broadly, environmental data when identifying a *terroir* and according it protected status. However, technical practices or food customs can be just as effectively located within a specific geographical area as a particular soil type or a pattern of flora and fauna.

The practice of anthropology tends to generate a seemingly inevitable sense of frustration, that is, in part, due to the methods and nature of the discipline: there is never enough time and work is seemingly left unfinished. Nevertheless, it remains the case that an ethnological approach to this type of problem raises interesting questions about contemporary issues, for example, the diversity of production practices, the status of products, the integration of the recent history and the consequences of winning or losing the right to official recognition of a *lien au lieu*. Furthermore, the considerable volume of evidence collected in the course of ethnological field-work enriches future studies and stimulates new hypotheses in the process. It is also true that such research, by concentrating upon a product inside its place of production prior to any official recognition or attempt at commercialisation, helps to raise questions about product specificity, giving all the actors involved the means to better understand and appreciate the problem in hand. It is for them to make any subsequent decisions with full knowledge of the facts.

The ultimately complementary relationship between theoretical and applied research now becomes clear. The material gathered in the course of commissioned fieldwork feeds data directly into the hands of those engaged in research of a theoretical nature. These

5. The official body specifically dealing with Controlled Denominations of Origin.

exchanges are essential for the intellectual health of the discipline, allowing the constant analysis and interpretation of new material. As we have seen, the process by which, for example, a product, animal breed, cultivated variety or landscape becomes an object of heritage, frequently involves a change in its cultural status. It is precisely because of the social and cultural process involved in such a transformation that anthropologists are called upon, although what is expected of them is frequently ill defined. When the anthropologists present their results, the scientific objectivity that they strive for does not always match the hopes and expectations of those who had sought their intervention. Finally, a researcher's deliberate choice to work on specific themes or objects makes him/her de facto a social actor, with the choices made leading almost inevitably to a degree of social involvement. This is certainly the case with *produits de terroir*, which raise questions related to the depth and meaning of their roots in local cultures, to cultural diversity and to the role and function of heritage in modern societies.

Conclusion

When addressing the issues of local food and agricultural produce, the current debate oscillates between unrealistic expectations and the conviction that nothing traditional exists anymore and that such objects already belong to a world we have lost. The results of ethnological fieldwork suggest that the reality on the ground is more complex. A cultural approach offers a new strategic tool for understanding and promoting *produits de terroir*, and their social anthropological dimension has never been so widely appreciated. The advantage of ethnography is that it enables us to understand how societies function in fine detail. From that starting point, it contributes theoretical concepts and questions that acquire a new dimension from the interaction with the reality and competing interests of society. Thus the material collected and analysed leads to a re-examination of perspectives in relation to social, technical and economic realities. An outsider's theoretical gaze remains more than ever necessary in studies of local agricultural products at a time when new national and European regulations are both fixing new boundaries and raising expectations. Between the management of an image and the establishment of legitimacy, our aim must be to study the manner in which a modern society with vested commercial interests confronts its own culture and its past.

11

PRODUITS DE TERROIR:
Between Local Identity and Heritage

François Portet

The regional ethnologist and the making of heritage

In the course of the last twenty-five years, the conception and practice of both French heritage and culture have been transformed. The 1970s were marked by the proliferation of cultural activities touching on regional identity, languages, traditions, trades and the individual culture of specific professions. In 1978 the creation of a *Direction du Patrimoine* (Department of Heritage) within the Ministry of Culture opened the way for new objects to be studied, protected and preserved. 1980 was declared 'Heritage Year', and events associated with it helped to legitimise new forms of heritage especially in the industrial and rural sectors. The approach adopted at the time by the Ministry of Culture was to bring more recent initiatives together with a number of long-existing cultural functions and services. Some of these had been established decades ago or even earlier. The *Service Régional de l'Inventaire* (Regional Inventory Service) for example had been founded in 1959 to study and catalogue 'the riches' of France, while the *Service de conservation des Monuments Historiques* (Service for the Conservation of Historical Monuments), under the *Direction des Antiquités* (Department of Antiquities), had been functioning for more than a century. It was hoped that the creation of a Department of Heritage within the Ministry of Culture would allow experimental work of research and collection to be undertaken by new groups such as the Mission into photographic or ethnological heritage.

According to the Committee on Ethnological Heritage,[1] which met in 1979 under the auspices of the Minister of Culture, Jean-Philippe Lecat, a series of trends could be identified in French public attitudes towards heritage. They noted a growing public interest in and desire to understand 'the various old and original building blocks of French society', something that was affecting collective identities. One of the most significant features of this changing public attitude was a greater willingness on the part of both individuals and communities to become involved in neighbourhood activities and cultural affairs, a development that was interpreted as 'an important trump card favouring an ethnological approach'.

The committee went on to advocate the establishment of appropriate public entities to encourage the emergence and supervision of relevant heritage projects. At national level, the *Conseil du Patrimoine Ethnologique* (Anthropological Heritage Advisory Panel) would be formed under the Department of Heritage in order to assess the value of new research projects, and it was to be assisted in this task by the *Mission du Patrimoine Ethnologique* (Anthropological Heritage Mission). Without going into too much detail, anthropological heritage can be defined as the recognition of a growing number of objects as individual elements forming part of a heritage memory. Alongside monuments and other symbolic objects – held as 'the artistic and monumental heritage through which the nation identifies itself'– there emerges 'a steadily growing collection of daily artefacts, influenced by the passage of time and changing fashions that are representative of lifestyles that have either disappeared or are in the process of disappearing.'[2]

1. 'Un intérêt public très marqué, populaire même, se manifeste aujourd'hui pour la connaissance des composantes anciennes et originales de la société française. (...) il révèle une prise de conscience collective des problèmes d'identité et de patrimoine culturels, où le sentiment de la différence préservée ou retrouvée joue un rôle central jusque dans l'aménagement quotidien de la vie d'aujourd'hui. (...)volonté de prise en charge de sa propre histoire traduit, (...) un désir toujours plus grand de participation à la gestion de la communauté de voisinage. A cet égard, la réforme tendant à accroître la responsabilité des collectivités locales constituera un atout important pour la politique de l'ethnologie.' *L'ethnologie de la France, besoins et projets,* Paris, Ministère de la Culture et de la Communication, 1979, p. 13.

2. Next to 'L'héritage artistique et monumental dans lequel la nation peut se reconnaître' emerges 'une collection d'artefacts quotidiens, représentatifs de genres de vie qui ont disparu ou disparaissent... collection qui s'alourdit avec le temps qui passe et les modes'. P. Bonnain and D. Chevalier, *Une politique pour le patrimoine culturel rural,* Paris, Ministère de la Culture, 1995, p.21.

The committee also proposed that, in parallel with these two central bodies, other entities would be established, and funded accordingly, to coordinate activities at a regional level. These proposals were welcomed by the Ministry of Culture and the new institutions were established in the course of the 1980s.

As a logical development of these earlier measures, a number of *conseillers à l'ethnologie* (advisers for ethnology) have been appointed within the *Directions régionales aux affaires culturelles,* Regional Directorates of Cultural Affairs (DRAC). The advisers are charged by the Ministry of Culture with the task of assessing the anthropological heritage of individual French regions; he/she is also responsible for its promotion and management. In addition, an adviser may contribute to and encourage the development of current cultural practices, as a close observer of the cultural scene. The creation of these posts was followed by a gradual administrative decentralisation giving both the advisers and the directorates greater decision-making, management and funding power. This was accompanied by the appointment of *Commissions régionales du patrimoine historique archéologique et ethnologique,* COREPHAE (Regional Commissions for Historical, Archaeological and Ethnological Heritage). These commissions were charged with initiating additional measures to protect the country's heritage as defined in the broader sense, not just the conventional realm of historical monuments.

Despite these measures, the process did not yield a homogeneous administrative structure as a number of Regional Directorates of Cultural Affairs are still without an ethnological adviser. In addition, the increasingly decentralised political and administrative structure of France has encouraged regional diversification. As a result of its proactive policy, the Ministry of Culture had anticipated that local communities, and their regional councils in particular, would develop centres for the study and promotion of their own ethnological heritage, under the responsibility of appointed ethnologists. This did occur in the Lorraine, Champagne-Ardennes, Lower Normandy and Poitou-Charentes regions. Elsewhere, however, these appointments were made under the direct aegis of the Ministry for Culture. Moreover, the stated ambition to create a sufficient number of posts to cover the entire country was only partially fulfilled, with regions where the influence of universities or other tertiary institutions was particularly in evidence being accommodated first.

Thus by the middle of the 1980s, France had a more decentralised but far from uniform structure for the development of its national heritage policy. By looking in detail at the case of Burgundy and its gastronomic production, this chapter will explore the relationship between the state, regional culture and the often ambiguous role of the ethnologist.

Heritage and food ethnology

In 1985 the Regional Directorate of Cultural Affairs of Burgundy was accorded a post of adviser for ethnology, which I held until 1999. As a result of the Report on the Ethnology of France (1979), which recommended the conscious recognition and the broad study of 'the matters of identity and cultural heritage [...] going as far as the daily management of day-to-day life',[3] a number of topics had been identified, and were already the subject of specific research and study activities by museums or other centres of learning. These projects included the study of amongst others the evolution of rural habitats and landscapes, industrial production zones, and endangered techniques and trades such as professional fishing or canal shipping.

It was within this context that the idea of an investigation into 'gastronomic heritage' was first launched. In the autumn of 1988, I participated in round-table discussions, which brought together the Regional Directorate of Cultural Affairs, historians and geographers in order to consider three major themes: the relationship between food and its live components, food transformation chains and the link between tastes and food types. The results of these discussions were published the following year,[4] and in the introduction to the report, our preoccupations at the time are easily identifiable. The first few lines of the introduction refer to the food production of Burgundy and the demands of various cultural institutions, especially museums, for a specific focus on an ethnological study of techniques. As an adviser for ethnology, I was in the difficult position of being both a researcher and a consultant acting as cultural agent and working with local institutions. This required me to focus on the broad needs of *all* those involved, in-

3. 'des problèmes d'identité et de patrimoine culturels (...) jusque dans l'aménagement quotidien de la vie d'aujourd'hui'. *L'ethnologie de la France, besoins et projets*, Ministère de la Culture et de la Communication, Paris, 1979, p.13.

4. *Du sauvage, du vivant et du cru*, proceedings of the round-table on Food Ethnology, Dijon, 1989.

line with the duties and responsibilities of the position as envisaged by the Ministry of Culture.

During the round-table discussions, two key themes had come to the fore. They were the relationship between food and its living components and secondly, the question of identities, particularly with reference to non-French food traditions, such as those of Chinese and the Portuguese immigrants in Paris. These studies served as a springboard for a broader research project concerning the relationship between any social group and its consumption preferences or taboos. In this wider context, societal attitudes towards living organisms for human consumption took centre stage, especially with regard to harvesting (hunt and kill or animal production and slaughter), food preparation and the transformation and consumption of meat.

These questions were revisited in a series of research programmes carried out in Burgundy. Indeed, I was particularly anxious to develop an anthropological approach, using as a foundation the important ethnological work that had already been carried out in the village of Minot in the Côte d'Or region.[5]

Burgundy and its culinary customs

At the beginning of the 1980s, a number of books and papers were published about the work undertaken in Minot by the Laboratory of Social Anthropology at the Collège de France. Some time later, Yvonne Verdier, one of the ethnologists involved, published a work entitled *Façons de dire, façons de faire* (Ways of saying, ways of doing). In it, Verdier confers a central role within the rural community she had observed in Minot to three female characters in charge of what at first appeared to be mundane tasks: the seamstress, the cook and the woman who had assumed the role of midwife. She argues that, through these three functions which were vital to the life of the village, these women were 'making' local customs as each one played an essential role in the community. The first 'made the bride and the bridesmaids' by sewing her wedding dress and their gowns. The second 'made the marriage' by

5. Amongst the numerous papers and works published as a direct outcome of this research, the following should be mentioned: M.-C. Pingaud, *Paysans en Bourgogne, les gens de Minot*, Paris, Flammarion, 1978. Y. Verdier, *Façons de dire, façons de faire, la laveuse, la couturière, la cuisinière*, Paris, Gallimard, 1979. F. Zonabend, *La mémoire longue, temps et histoire au village*, Presses Universitaires de France, Paris, 1982.

cooking for the wedding banquet and the third 'made babies and the dead' by cutting the umbilical cord of the newborn and laying out the deceased.

For our purposes, greater attention will be placed on the role of the cook and on culinary traditions. It was customary in the rural society of Burgundy for the custodian of these traditions not to be a member of the family and to be called upon to prepare festive meals for christenings, confirmations and wedding banquets. At such banquets, this person was in fact an essential mediator between the two families who were being joined together through marriage. The preparation of special dishes and the way they were circulated in the course of such meals were as important as the exchange of goods and chattels between the parties. It is the recurring expression *porter à la noce* – literally translated as 'bringing to the wedding' – that Verdier links with the accomplishment of a custom:

> Custom thus brings together the entire village community in the atmosphere of bustling merriment which precedes a wedding (...) Let us imagine young girls, a basket or a plate in their hands, cautiously walking towards the bride's own home (...) The gift of food creates a state of broad reciprocity within a circle going well beyond the boundaries of the two uniting families: it encompasses the whole countryside.[6]

In an extension of Claude Levi-Strauss' argument, Verdier demonstrated the intrinsic social role of cooking and of the transition of raw and wild matter into cooked food through feminine intervention. In Burgundy, cooking for weddings included the traditional preparation of three meat dishes and the making of wine sauces. From an anthropological perspective, wine and meat are, of course, two ingredients strongly linked to Burgundian culture. In outlining the role of the cook, Verdier admitted that this 'way of creating' custom in a rural society was rapidly coming to an end. The seamstress and the woman 'who helps' had already disappeared. Meanwhile the cook, called on from house to house to prepare meals on special occasions, was gradually being replaced

6. 'La coutume met donc en scène la communauté villageoise toute entière dans cette atmosphère de joie affairée, mouvementée qui précède la noce (…). Qu'on imagine les processions de petites filles, le panier ou l'assiette à la main se dirigeant précautionneusement vers la maison de la mariée (…). Le présent de nourriture met donc ici en oeuvre un principe de générosité généralisée, et la sphère de l'échange dépasse de beaucoup la sphère des deux familles qui s'allient: elle inclut tout le pays'. Y. Verdier, *Façons de dire, façons de faire, la laveuse, la couturière, la cuisinière*, Paris, Gallimard, 1979, p.285.

by professionals who no longer visited homes, but asked families to eat at the communal hall or in a restaurant dining room instead.

This traditional society was, in part, undermined by the introduction of 'finer' foods to the village which caused the breakdown of custom. Villagers gradually began to ask the traditional cook to prepare the more complex dishes that they had tasted while dining out, before turning directly to restaurateurs for such 'exotic' specialities:

> Not only does the field of reciprocity shrink, it breaks down completely. Gifts of traditional food dishes are no longer exchanged. As Brillat-Savarin had reflected, the language of menus reflects an irreversible breakdown through the use of borrowed or even 'stolen' words and names. They bring to the table food from far away which can never be given back in return. [7]

This subtle analysis draws our attention to what ethnologists describe as sets of opposites. The first traditional opposition is provided by the contrast between a daily menu marked by poverty, which relies upon basic staples such as bread and potatoes, with that employed for festive occasions, using rare or expensive ingredients that become the object of a ceremonial cuisine. The second opposition occurs between the local community and the outside world. The inhabitants of Minot gradually adopted new 'foreign products', new ways of 'doing' things from outside, while outsiders, whether tourists or gourmands, wanted to taste 'local specialities'.

Cuisine, gastronomy and *produits de terroir*

A few years after the completion of the collective work on the village of Minot, the break with tradition was complete. The food products of Burgundy, originally reserved for festive occasions, have long since been borrowed by gastronomes who have carefully recorded the way they were prepared and have adapted and served them in cities, in the same way that local elites originally contributed to the reputation of the region's great wines. The very name Burgundy not only conjures up images of its great wines,

7. 'Il y a non seulement rétrécissement du champ de la réciprocité mais surtout rupture, rupture de l'échange qui se traduit dans la langue des menus par sa négation même: ces emprunts, ces vols – de mots – qui, comme l'indique Brillat-Savarin, possèdent la vertu de ne pas être "sujets à restitution" et amènent sur ces tables ces provisions lointaines qui ne seront jamais rendues'. Y. Verdier, *Façons de dire, façons de faire, la laveuse, la couturière, la cuisinière*, Paris, Gallimard, 1979, pp286–7.

but also of its many gastronomic products and dishes. One should not, however, ignore the existence of the popular movement which is seeking to claim back some of the dishes 'taken away' by gastronomes. A particularly good example is provided by a large popular festival that has been held in Bresse in recent years, which is organised around the consumption of the *poulet de Bresse* (Bresse chicken) at a large communal banquet. The festival can be seen as the source of a new custom, defined by the festive consumption of a luxury product traditionally enjoyed by a few gastronomes only.

Yet those products used in the preparation of festive meals, and so prized by gastronomes, remain at the margins of agricultural production. Recent estimates suggest that products enjoying the label of *Appellation d 'Origine Contrôlée* (Controlled Denomination of Origin, hereafter CDO) account for only ten to eleven per cent of the total food market in France, providing a livelihood for some 180,000 farmers. This label, established by specific legislation enacted on 30 July 1935, guarantees the geographical origin of the product and certifies that it has been produced by traditional methods. By examining a number of agricultural products that have become emblematic of their region, it is possible to demonstrate the importance of the *lien au lieu* (tie to a place) in conferring authenticity on Burgundian foodstuffs.

During the last fifteen years, a number of young researchers, working in various institutions and supported by the Regional Directorate of Cultural Affairs, have produced more than ten ethnological monographs on the professional, cultural and social world of Burgundian agriculture and its food industry. The *Ecomusée de la Bresse bourguignonne* (Ecomuseum of Burgundian Bresse) has published part of this work in a collection aimed at the general public. Other studies, funded by the Ministry of Culture, produced a series of unpublished reports, and three films examining agricultural production. In addition, two theses based on ethnological research in the region have been completed. Finally, a number of meetings have been held with regional partners at the instigation of the Anthropological Heritage Mission.[8] These regular exchanges provided an opportunity to compare the results of earlier research with work currently in progress. In the area of agricultural food products and production, four major fields were examined: livestock production (which constitutes the most widely studied field,

8. See the following publications: *Atelier sur le paysage*, Mission du Patrimoine ethnologique, Ecomusée du Creusot, 1991; *Les communautés viti-vinicoles*, Die, 1992; *Cultures de la viande*, ENESAD, DRAC de Bourgogne.

including publications covering poultry and pig production and ethnographical films produced with the participation of beef producers); viticulture, especially in relation to Marion Demossier's doctoral thesis; cheese and its production; finally, Anne-Marie Guenin's thesis on the producers of fruit and vegetable produce.

Through a comparative review of these studies, and especially those connected to livestock production, notably the poultry of Bresse and the cattle of the Charolais, it is possible to examine how the systems of representation within rural societies can be reinterpreted through the eyes of an urban society. [9] We shall then consider the example of cheese production, the process of fermentation and the transformation of foodstuffs *avant la cuisine*.

The art of fattening livestock for the production of meat

At the outset, it must be noted that the quality of Charolais beef and poultry from Bresse has long been recognised in urban markets well beyond their individual production areas. Like the wines of Burgundy, both products carry the name of their respective region of origin. Since at least the eighteenth century, Charolais cattle had been driven to Lyon from the Brionnais; subsequently farmers began to provision Paris from the Nivernais region as their production expanded. The fine poultry from Bresse had similarly found its way to the market stalls of major urban centers. Both became the focus of careful selective breeding, a process initiated by the local aristocracy. For Charolais cattle, the process took on an official form in 1864 with the creation of a Charolais beef herdbook in Nevers, and this was closely followed by competitions such as the National Charolais Breeding Championship in Vichy and, since 1870, the Paris All-Breed Championship.

A similar pattern is detectable in the case of the poultry of Bresse, with breeding standards becoming recognised through competitions starting in 1862. In 1904 Joseph Donat founded the Bresse Club whose primary objective was the preservation of the breed. However, unlike the Charolais herdbook which defined one single stan-

9. The detailed description of Charolais beef and Bresse poultry productions which follows relies heavily on the following works. S. Urbano-Frossard, *La Volaille de Bresse. L'évolution d'un savoir-faire*, Pierre-de-Bresse, Ecomusée de la Bresse Bourguignonne, 1992 and P. Pellegrini, *La volaille de Bresse, un terroir et des hommes*, Bourg-en-Bresse, Musée des Pays de l'Ain, 1992.

dard, the Bresse Club recognised three varieties: the so-called 'black bird' variety of Louhans (the capital of the Louhans Bresse), the Bourg Grey (capital of the Ain region) and the Beny White (from the village of Beny in the Ain). In 1957 the recognition of these three breeds was brought into question when only the White Beny was accepted for the purpose of commercialising the poultry of Bresse under the official CDO label. Although the poultry of Bresse was the first food product to be granted CDO status, which until then had only applied to quality wines, this decision was in total contrast to the position of local notables who, as early as 1914, had shown a much greater awareness of the realities at the production end of the market. It was as if the market had imposed a single identifiable variety which could easily be related to its region of origin, to the detriment of the other two which were still recognised locally as formal breeds. The White Beny which had been chosen for the CDO label, had all the right marketing characteristics, even its comparison with the French national colours, with its blue feet, white plumage and uniformly red crest! Breeders' competitions gradually institutionalised the connection between a single variety and a specific production area, a link formally enshrined in the official charter conferring its CDO status. In competitions, the slaughtered birds are exhibited with a necklace of white feathers left unplucked and with their feet, crest and wattles well in evidence. European Community regulations attempting to forbid their exhibition with the traditional necklace of white feathers are vehemently criticised: 'the Community is determined to mutilate this queen of poultry.'[10]

In order to pursue the comparative analysis of what has become of these two livestock productions, one must reflect on cultural standards which, while varying over time, are nevertheless specific to breeders or to consumers, and even on occasions to both. In particular, we shall concentrate upon two factors that can be interpreted in terms of opposition, namely large- and small-scale farming or fat and lean meat.

Small- and large-scale animal farming

Poultry farming, which obviously belongs to the category of small-scale animal farming, was the traditional preserve of women who reared chicks, fed chickens with farm products,

10. 'La Communauté européenne veut mutiler la Reine des volailles', P. Pellegrini, *La volaille de Bresse, un terroir et des hommes*, Bourg-en-Bresse, 1992.

sweetcorn in particular, carried out force feeding and castrated capons earmarked for fattening. They would then sell their produce on the market and keep the income. This scenario changed significantly with the introduction of the CDO. Official protection encouraged a much higher degree of specialisation in these small enterprises, with men taking control of their management. The production chain, which consisted of only two entities, breeders and wholesalers, has now expanded with the advent of separate hatching centres supplying chicks to farmers and through the development of slaughtering facilities.

In contrast, specialisation in cattle production is much older, better developed and is connected with the needs of the production of lean and fat meat. Since the commercialisation of meat production first began, some cattle breeders, called in the trade *emboucheurs* because of their position at the end of the production chain, were already fattening beasts of burden on their pastures. By taking advantage of their rich pastures and the proximity of the market in Lyon, peasants from the Brionnais area were to the fore in this type of production as early as the eighteenth century. Later, they expanded their activities to the farms of the Nivernais, opening the way to the Parisian market. Cattle raising for the specific purpose of meat production has gradually spread beyond the boundaries of the Charolais and Brionnais regions. Before the Second World War, in hilly regions like the Morvan where mixed farming was still practiced, cattle were used for farm work before being sent away from the area for fattening. The natural distribution of richer and poorer *terroirs* within agricultural regions has preserved the differentiation between calf producers, growers and finishers.

Lean and fat meat

Traditionally the key to cattle raising was to finish the beasts on green pastures.[11] The Brionnais farmers only kept their lean cattle for a few months before selling them fattened on the meat market. After the Second World War, the internationalisation of meat markets offered new openings for animals at various growth stages of their life, pushing specialisation even further. The best stock would be purchased from producers specialising

---

11. B. Lizet, 'L'herbe violente, enquête botanique en pays Brionnais', *Etudes rurales*, 1993, vol.129, p.130.

in selective breeding; new markets opened for younger cattle, which were sent in large numbers either to the west of France or to Italy to be fattened by intensive farming. These new opportunities triggered profound changes in production methods and precipitated the disappearance of the traditional *emboucheurs*. During the 1970s, the Charolais country – which spreads over most of Burgundy, in a green belt including the Nivernais, Morvan, Charolais-Brionnais and the Auxois regions – produced lean beasts that were fattened outside the region, even if some breeders continued here and there to finish their own product to satisfy local demand. At the same time, producers who concentrated specifically on raising cattle for meat had developed new livestock breeds which could be fattened in their own stables and slaughtered at a younger age. The virtual disappearance of traditional fattened cattle was more in-line with the new ways of eating adopted by an increasingly urbanised society in quest of a 'purer' lifestyle. However, this last decade has been marked by overproduction and, when coupled with the recent BSE scare, this has caused a number of producers in the Auxois, Charolais and Morvan regions to reorganise in order to finish their own cattle, and even to slaughter and sell the meat themselves. In a related development meat can now be found with, for example, labels certifying its production under natural conditions or in accordance with traditional techniques. Finally, some producers are attempting to obtain the CDO label for cattle raised under specifically regulated conditions in the restricted Charolais region where the breed supposedly originated. These new measures aim to bring back a more 'traditional' line of cattle to the consumer, which would appear closer to the original breed: a beast with finely marbled meat, finished with a layer of fat when ready for consumption.

In the case of poultry farming, producers never lost control of the production chain. As a result, the techniques for raising fattened birds did not change, notably the method of preparing capons and chickens from Bresse specifically protected under the CDO label. The empirical selection process was started by the women who traditionally raised the Bresse varieties, and it resulted in a gradual increase in the meat to bone ratio of these birds, a trait further reinforced by the lack of limestone in the local soil: 'The perfect object is the capon, cylindrical in shape and whose flesh is enhanced by fat and whose firmness can be assessed by touch and sight, by checking the vein found under the wing which must be white from the fat.'[12] It is an ideal product that is easily recognised and appreciated by its producers: 'one feels like caressing it because the skin is so beautiful, the pigmentation is so sharp and the colour of the fat so clear.'[13] The perfect produce is the result of a meticulous transformation process calling on specific techniques: the bird is first raised, then finished by overfeeding in a process called *en épinette*. Slaughtering takes place on the premises because presentation is of such importance. It is first wrapped in strong cloth which is then sewn before being rolled to give the sought after shape of a cylinder of meat and fat, an image that is reinforced by the criteria used by judges at breeders competitions.

The image of a fattened animal is, in part, a reminder of the symbolic link between meat and times of plenty in rural societies. In a similar way, fat is associated with festivals and other special occasions. This latter association leads one's thoughts to the southwest of France where geese and ducks are fattened by force feeding for the preparation of *foie gras*. It must be pointed out that such feeding practices are strongly anchored in rural mentalities in contrast to those of city dwellers who not only frown on fatty foods but also view such feeding methods as a form of cruelty to animals. Regardless of these opinions, capons from Bresse or the *foie gras* from the southwest remain sought after by these same city dwellers as delicacies for special occasions.

The animal products examined above reveal the distance between the views and perceptions held by rural producers and those of urban consumers with regard to such a staple product as meat. We have also noted the manner in which the ties to a specific region can be manipulated, both in relation to varieties of animals and in terms of defining the zone of production. Raising animals for human consumption may be seen as an extension of basic animal care and husbandry, starting at the time of reproduction, continuing through the animal's development and ending with the various stages of fattening, slaughtering and, finally, the ageing of

12. 'C'est le chapon, cylindrique dont la chair est mise en valeur par la graisse dont on évalue la consistance au toucher et au regard par cette veine, sous l'aile qui doit être blanche de graisse'. S. Frossard-Urbano, *La volaille de Bresse,l'évolution d'un savoir-faire*, Pierre-de-Bresse, Ecomusée de la Bresse Bourguignonne, 1992.

13. 'Vous avez envie de le caresser parce que la peau est belle, la pigmentation de la peau est belle, la couleur du gras est belle'. S. Frossard-Urbano, *La volaille de Bresse, l'évolution d'un savoir-faire*, Pierre-de-Bresse, Ecomusée de la Bresse Bourguignonne, 1992.

meat. These stages have the ultimate purpose of progressively transforming animals into objects of consumption and promote a transition from the wild to the domestic.

By analysing the methods used by the Brionnais *emboucheurs*, for example, Lizet[14] demonstrates how rearing animals creates a link between the wild and the domestic. She shows that, in the mind of these growers, only an animal sufficiently domesticated – a mature beast – can handle the pastures' harshness, which would in fact kill younger and less domesticated animals. In another context, Frossard-Urbano[15] argues that feeding and fattening chickens with cooked gruel is another step in the process of domestication.

The BSE scare exposed to a bewildered public the fact that animal domestication through feeding had been corrupted by the actions of the food industry which thought nothing of mixing meat residues with the feed given to animals destined for human consumption. It is only a lack of public knowledge of so-called intensive production systems which allowed the transgression of one of society's taboos. Apart from certain hunting practices where wild species acquire a special kudos, the idea of eating carnivores or carrion-eaters is nearly as horrific as cooking the family pet.

The manufacture of 'live' food products

Among the emblematic foods of Burgundy, fermented products hold a prime position alongside its meats and wines. For these particular products, especially cheeses, the close connection to their place of origin is reinforced in two ways. Firstly by the specificity of the fermentation process itself and secondly by the fact that the manufacturing savoir-faire does not seem to be transferable from one *terroir* to another.

There is no doubt that cheese traditionally had a particular function when compared with other foods, often acting as a substitute on meatless days. Cows milk cheeses from the north of Burgundy took the names of small towns like Epoisses from the Auxois, or of villages, such as Saint Florentin or Soumaintrain in the Yonne. *Epoisses* is a soft cheese which has its rind washed with a Burgundy grape brandy (*marc de Bourgogne*). The process gives it a red colour

14. B. Lizet, 'L'herbe violente, enquête botanique en pays Brionnais', *Etudes rurales*, 1993, vol.129, p.146.

15. S. Frossard-Urbano, *La volaille de Bresse, l'évolution d'un savoir-faire*, Pierre-de-Bresse, Ecomusée de la Bresse Bourguignonne, 1992.

caused by the red ferment. Saint Florentin, manufactured in the North of the Yonne, belongs to a family of *Chaource* cheeses, earlier called cheeses of Troyes. *Soumaintrain* is a Saint-Florentin cheese which has been washed and matured like the *Epoisses*.

It is likely that most of these products were originally sold on local markets by the women who made them, in much the same way as the poultry of Bresse. These farm cheeses were subsequently produced and aged in small regional manufacturing plants. In their work, C. Delfosse and M.-T. Lestablier[16] describe this manufacturing transition from the initial dual combination of cheese maker and cheese processor to a single manufacturing stream entirely controlled by industrial cheese makers. Prior to industrialisation, processors would purchase fresh cheese at the end of the summer and age it until the beginning of winter. The particular feature of these cheeses washed in *marc de Bourgogne* is to be found in a double fermentation process: fermentation of the cheese followed by the fermentation of the 'red' crust. The second fermentation is induced by locally occurring yeast, which is a process sometimes difficult to reproduce elsewhere. The broad question of the cultivation of locally occurring fermenting agents and the actual mastering of the fermenting process is at the heart of the product's identity. One of Epoisses' main cheese makers, personally involved in applying for the official CDO status of this particular cheese (1994), readily tells of his own unfortunate experience: his brand new manufacturing plant had to be destroyed because it could not provide the right environment for the cultivation of a 'good ferment'. The same manufacturer sometimes relies on cheeses produced on small farms as a source of working yeasts.

Natural fermentation induced by man transforms an insipid product into a tasty cheese in a process akin to cooking. However, it is no longer part of the world of domestic activities controlled by women, it has now shifted to become an industrial process in the same way as the poultry production described earlier. Goats cheese produced in Les Monts de Charolais and the Mâconnais in the Saône and Loire and then sold on the markets of the regions' small towns are another example. These cheeses were initially manufactured by women on their farms, and were then sold on to other women who finished the product before reselling it in cities like Mâcon or even Lyon. It is only very recently, since these cheeses

16. C. Delfosse and M.-T. Lestablier, *Le transport des savoirs traditionnels dans l'univers industriel*, Research Report, Centre d'Etudes de l'Emploi, Noisy-le-Grand, 1994.

have acquired a name outside their own areas of production, that men have become involved, establishing goat farms and finishing the product themselves. Due to its strong taste, goats cheese belonged to a class of foods usually eaten during lean times. This explains why it has had difficulty in joining the ranks of the *produits de terroir* and why its gastronomical status is a recent phenomenon.

The investigation of food production based on living matter has led to the examination of endogenous examples and practices as the actual building blocks of broader production systems. Behind this research focusing on customs associated with better times, times of plenty and rich tastes, one can still sense the underlying fear of food shortages and penury reminiscent of the more common lean times. All these activities, where man actually manipulates living creatures, in the first instance animals or animal products such as milk as well as vegetable materials, call upon concepts and a range of practices which have become foreign to most city dwellers. Their only contact with animals is with pets and, for an increasing proportion of the urban population, the act of slaughtering has become almost criminal. They strive for pure food, and are often terrified of contamination. Yet cooking meat dishes presupposes, in a broad sense, the slaughtering of animals with the separation of edible from inedible parts and, for living matter in general, different preparation techniques like the process of fermentation exist to control the transformation process of this same matter. Cooking, brining, or the use of fat to facilitate the maturation or preservation of foods are all ways of doing these things based on customary culture. Despite such contradictions, these animal products have long been sought after and consumed by an elite living in cities, made up of aristocrats and a wealthy middle class who, one or two centuries earlier, were the very people who started the gastronomical elevation of Charolais beef and Bresse poultry. Today, the taste for *produits de terroir* has spread. Through their consumption, urban consumers make an attempt to assimilate some of their properties – to 'acquire' a small corner of the countryside. As Marion Demossier[17] has shown, wine consumption represents the ultimate in such a process. Wine buffs will go as far as to identify the plot of land which produced the vintage wine they are tasting: *Romanée Conti, Romanée Saint Vivant* or *Les Caillerets*.

---

17. M. Demossier, *Hommes et Vins, une anthropologie du vignoble bourguignon,* Dijon, Editions universitaires de Dijon, 1999.

So, life has turned full circle. Twenty years have passed since Yvonne Verdier was asking herself about the search for 'exotic dishes' and subtle preparations, signs of modern times for the people of Minot who wanted to escape from meats cooked in wine sauces. Now, *produits de terroir* rank very high on the menu of three-star restaurants, a trend already being copied by the majority of more modest eating establishments.

PART V

URBAN CULTURES
AND NEW EXPRESSIONS

12

FAST FORWARD TO THE FUTURE?

Cultural Policies and the Definition of Urban
Identities in the Era of De-industrialisation[1]

Susan Milner

Obviously, we have a duty to remember, but we also need to reject
an identity-based culture which cuts us off from the rest of the
world. Collecting lamps, turning mines into museums, keeping up
the memory of the heroic past – all very well, but it doesn't move
things forward.[2]

Industry, post-industrialism and urban identities

The task of defining urban identities seems to be more necessary
than ever at a time of massive socio-economic upheaval and residential mobility, and as the relationship between the local, national
(itself undergoing redefinition) and international is changing.
There are important political, economic and social reasons for
defining specific urban identities. The political reasons relate to
successive urban regeneration initiatives since the early 1980s as
well as decentralisation laws dating from the same period. Eco-

1. The ideas for this chapter are based on two research projects, one carried out in
1994–1995 in Vénissieux (Rhône-Alpes) and financed by the University of Bath, the
other (ongoing) in Lille and the surrounding area, financed by the British Academy.
2. Bruno Bonduelle, director of Bonduelle Foods and chair of various development agencies for Lille and Nord-Pas-de-Calais: B. Bonduelle, *Nord et Pas-de-Calais.
L'impossible tête-à-tête*, Lille, La Voix du Nord, 1998, p.68.

nomic regeneration has a marked regional and local aspect, particularly since decentralisation, as mayors compete for business location and state funding on the basis of local attractiveness or need. Social reasons involve the need to rebuild communities shattered by economic change and residential mobility. In each of these dimensions, cultural policy has featured heavily among the instruments used by the central state and by local authorities.

How are urban identities defined? For sociologist Martine Segalen, 'A town's identity is given to it by its inhabitants, its built environment and the images it projects.'[3] Segalen's definition stresses not only the sociological element of identity, but political will (expressed in urban development and in self-promotion). Similarly, Monique Fourdin, drawing on definitions of regional identity, stresses self-image and the role of political and other elites in the creation of local identity: 'Local identity is the specific image which the actors of a particular town have built for themselves'.[4] Clearly the past has a part to play in this task, in some cases as a problem to be overcome, in others as the key to a clearly defined image and successful marketing. Segalen uses Freud's analogy with the soul, marked by previous deeds and misdeeds. For many observers, towns are above all *lieux de mémoire*, and critics of the 1950s and 1960s modernist urban planning (notably the architect Roland Castro) stress the psychological as well as social effects of uniform, characterless and historyless architecture. However, there is some contradiction between the successful management of heritage and the need to project an image as forward-looking, not to say futuristic. This is nowhere as evident as in former industrial towns and city suburbs: the 'rustbelt' or industrial wasteland (*friche industrielle*), which are aesthetically offensive to some, and today associated with decline, low social status and unemployment. Media images tend to reproduce and aggravate negative images of such towns and cities. Thus, a 1995 television programme on 'survivors' (people making ends meet) featuring a young Saint-Etienne worker showed a town full of old people, and the commentary spoken against a shot of the emblematic Couriot mines (today a museum) evoked a town without hope and without a future. Local leaders in northern France bemoan the stereotype of 'a sad and dreary city outskirts, sur-

3. M. Segalen, *Nanterriens. Les familles dans la ville: une ethnologie de l'identité*, Toulouse, Presses Universitaires du Mirail, 1990, p.25.
4. M. Fourdin, 'Communication urbaine: l'apport des représentations sociales', *Sciences de la Société*, 30, 1993, p.152.

rounded by an industrial belt such as may be found in the North, in Arras or Lens'.[5]

Images of such urban areas create a sense of unease about France's recent industrial past. France is not alone in finding it difficult to come to terms with this past: British films like The Full Monty and Brassed Off express the anguish of local communities and their enthusiastic reception in France suggests disquiet as well as sympathy. However, there may be specific identity problems in a France which has never felt particularly comfortable with industrialisation in its self-image. This is commented on explicitly, with reference to the Ardèche, in an exhibition housed in the Couriot mine in Saint-Etienne, which lays claim to the title of France's oldest industrial city: at the 1937 International Exhibition in Paris, the bustling industrial town was presented only as the counterpoint to the prevailing, peaceful agriculture of the surrounding Forez-Vivarais region. Similarly, paintings of the town in the mid-nineteenth century play down its industrial aspect, with the mines watching over a peaceful and well-ordered chequerboard of roofs like birds on the hill. In this example, industry and its concomitant social order are equated with unrest. As historian Louis Chevalier has shown, concerns about the 'pathological state' of urban living – more specifically, bourgeois fear of a dispossessed proletariat and underclass – have long been a hallmark of literary representations of urban life in France.[6]

On the other hand, the weakening of local folk memory through economic regeneration (new 'poles of activity') can also create problems for local populations. As Segalen notes for Nanterre, whose proximity to Paris has made it impossible for local inhabitants to create attachments to the past and thereby to their local environment; their self-identity is confused.[7] In both cases, residential mobility makes it difficult for local inhabitants, or at least certain sections of the population, to make an 'affective investment' in their town. This can lead to a completely negative view of the local environment, especially where residential mobility is more or less forced, as for example in the case of a 45-year-old cleaner interviewed in a 1995 study of *Front national* (FN)

5. Cited in Bonduelle, *Nord et Pas-de-Calais. L'impossible tête-à-tête*, Lille, La Voix du Nord, 1998, p.91.

6. L. Chevalier, *Laboring classes and dangerous classes in Paris in the first half of the nineteenth century*, Princeton, New Jersey, Princeton University Press, 1981.

7. M. Segalen, *Nanterriens. Les familles dans la ville: une ethnologie de l'identité*, Toulouse, Presses Universitaires du Mirail, 1990, p.10.

voters in Vénissieux: 'I was put here because I wasn't wanted elsewhere'.[8]

A sense of rejection by an outside world which has a negative view of the town further contributes to a spiral of low self-esteem which can find expression in political 'exit' (abstention or voting for the FN) and anti-social behaviour. The constant message from young people living in *la banlieue* is that outsiders only want to see the bad side. The construction of cohesion through a negative self-image is obviously fraught with problems, as documented by anthropologist Colette Pétonnet in the case of inhabitants of a housing project she called *'La Halle'*:

> Lumped together under the same scorn and sadly surprised by the names they are called, the residents of La Halle have no alternative but to recognise themselves as the group they form in relation to the outside world. They quickly define the territory belonging to them and refer to themselves as 'we in La Halle'. The children fight any outside group.[9]

Other anthropological studies confirm the importance of aggressive defence of the project for local children.[10] As one 17-year-old rapper from Ozoir-la Ferrière told journalists: 'When you've nothing to hold on to, you hold on to the honour of the project. You make sure the project gets respect'.[11] Similarly, mayor and local MP André Gerin notes that Vénissians' identity as an industrial town was constructed out of adversity,[12] and local historian Maurice Corbel records the way this adversity was transformed into defiance (*Vénissieux la rebelle*) as the town identified itself politically with the left and a series of Communist mayors.[13] Even the heroic age of the *banlieue rouge* represented historically a 'space of rejection'.[14] In the case of Saint-Etienne, too, the combination of industrial ('black city') and Communist ('red

---

8. 'La SOFRES analyse et décortique le vote Front National à Vénissieux', Supplement to *L'Humanité*, 26 October 1995, p.7.

9. C. Pétonnet, *Those people: the subculture of a housing project*, London and Greenport, Connecticut, Greenwood Press, 1973, pp.xxi–xxii.

10. See, for example, D. Lepoutre, *Coeur de banlieue. Codes, rites et langages*, Paris, Editions Odile Jacob, 1997.

11. M.-P. Subtil, 'Une semaine dans la vie des jeunes d'un quartier HLM', *Le Monde*, 3 June, 1998, pp.16–17.

12. A. Gerin, *Minguettes. Challenge pour une ville*, Paris, Messidor, 1988, p.35.

13. M. Corbel, *Vénissieux la rebelle*, Paris, Cercles d'Art, 1997.

14. See J. Menanteau, *Les banlieues*, Paris, Le Monde Editions/Marabout, 1994, pp.36–40.

city') pasts has proved a heavy burden for those seeking to attract inward investment.[15]

In such circumstances, the past can be psychologically repressed as a source of negative self-images, but it may then serve to stigmatise local inhabitants in the eyes of the outside world. The past may also intrude by creating a nostalgically rosy view of a past which is the mirror image of everything seen as problematic today, reflecting the loss of community roots. In a context of social uprooting, concern with the past as an expression of local identity may indicate 'fears, psychological repressions which are not always healthy'.[16] As historian Richard Kuisel notes, the disappearance of peasant society created a sense of loss and vulnerability; French national identity seemed under threat, and the past became attractive as a 'warm memory', standing for social certainties and economic well-being.[17] A similar argument could be made for the disappearance of older industries, with the exception that the spatial concentration of such industries meant that the communities affected felt cut off and victimised, exacerbating social rivalries and envy. In this context, the desire to cling to a threatened community based on shared adversity, as a means of regaining control over one's own life, risks generating further social exclusion along racial lines.

For most of the twentieth century, urban identities in France have been inextricably linked with social class. Whilst the same is true of all industrialised countries, in France the link between industrial towns or city suburbs and a stable and hermetic working class was amplified by the dominant role of the French Communist Party (PCF) and the particular configurations of capitalism *à la française*, with dominant heavy industrial firms requiring a dependent local working class. In the post-war period, many of these firms were owned by the state and encouraged to grow as 'national champions': coal and steel production in the north-east and the south, shipyards in the north-west, aerospace construction in key industrial sites around Paris and the south-east, motor vehicle production around the capital and in the north-east. Even

15. E. Sabot, 'Traitement d'espaces, traitement d'image; de la difficulté d'être et d'avoir été: le cas de Saint-Étienne', *Modern and Contemporary France*, NS5/4, 1997.

16. P. Nora, 'On ne peut faire de la France le musée de la France', interview, *Le Monde*, 29 November 1994, p.2.

17. R. Kuisel, 'The France we have lost. Social, economic and cultural disconti- nuities'. In *Remaking the Hexagon: the new France in the new Europe*. Ed G. Flynn, Oxford and Boulder, Colorado, Westview Press, 1995, pp.31–48.

today, the major employers in most French regions are either state-owned industrial companies, or firms newly privatised in the 1980s and 1990s; however, their share of total employment has fallen dramatically as they too have downsized, contracted out and rationalised. Unemployment in these urban industrial centres rocketed in the 1980s and 1990s.

According to official thinking in the regional planning agency *Délégation à l'Aménagement du Territoire et à l'Action Régionale* (DATAR), the problem is not so much the move from an industrial to a post-industrial economy, since industry remains central to economic life. Rather, since industry has lost its links with natural resources (coal, water, minerals), it has cast off its space-specificity and become more mobile: 'Problems of industrial location now arise in terms of the match between skill levels and pay levels, of access to markets, logistical centres and management services – all obviously at international level.'[18] Consequently, the race to attract the right skills mix – particularly highly qualified technical and professional personnel – has become a central feature of local development strategies, to the extent that the national statistical institute (INSEE) produces league tables classifying and ranking cities according to their ability to attract skilled professions. Surveys show that attractiveness depends on general 'quality of life' indices, particularly for inhabitants of large cities, for whom the environment is 'people rather than nature'.

Population censuses carried out in 1984 and 1990 showed striking shifts in the social composition of France's major towns and cities in the 1980s. In major cities like Lyon and Dijon as well as nearby Villeurbanne and Besançon, the proportion of working-class residents had dropped considerably, whereas numbers of managerial and technical employees had increased by between 30 per cent and 42 per cent. In such cases, demographic dynamism formed part of a virtuous circle of economic prosperity. In other urban centres, particularly in the south-east and Alsace, relatively sizeable working-class populations remained but had been joined by a new influx of scientific and technical staff, often as a result of conscious high-tech industrialisation programmes (as in Montpellier, the best-known case of *technopole* development, or Grenoble). The southern and eastern outskirts of Paris represented something of an anomaly, with no new skilled groups to replace working-class populations lost through commercial redevelopment of land

18. F. Damette, *La France en villes*, Paris, La Documentation Française, 1994, p.11.

to create extra office space. In this race to attract highly skilled residents, rustbelt cities and towns situated in declining regions – those with working-class populations already above the national average – found themselves at a disadvantage. As shown by the persistence of such trends in the preliminary findings from the 1999 census, the past becomes either a burden or an asset, determining present and future attractiveness. Thus, for example, a study of Calais' attempts to promote itself to investors continually fell foul of the city's image which 'although changing, is still one of nineteenth-century industrialisation'.[19] Indeed, a study of economic regeneration projects in a range of towns and cities undergoing economic recession found preoccupation with external image to be universal. The very fact of being classified as needing regeneration assistance seemed to indicate 'a dying town'. As well as the problems associated with industry (belonging to the past, polluted) or with industrial working classes (troublemaking) alluded to above, the study found that towns founded on industrial values of hard work and discretion had cultural difficulties in adapting to a new competitive environment where self-confidence and external marketing provided the key to success.[20]

Nevertheless, some cities had managed to break free of such path-dependency. In Vénissieux, for example, the proportion of top management, liberal professionals and technical staff increased considerably in the 1980s. The main reason cited by DATAR for this case of demographic renewal was proximity to Lyon-based financial centres, in other words access to an expanding work catchment area; investment in further and higher education establishments providing another possible explanation. DATAR's studies suggest that broader quality-of-life indices are also relevant, and these are certainly taken seriously in local development strategies.

Such strategies cover an increasingly wide area. Towns are becoming more flexible in performing various functions as the delocalisation of production weakens the historic ties between certain cities and types of production.[21] In the move towards a 'knowledge' society or 'informationalism', 'there is a specially

19. P.J. Reid, 'Calais "The Red City": its position in economic development in Nord Pas-de-Calais', *Modern and Contemporary France* NS1/4, pp.397–408.

20. C. Beslay, *La construction des politiques locales. Reconversions locales et systèmes locaux d'action publique*, Paris, L'Harmattan, 1998.

21. N. García Canclini, 'Urban cultures at the end of the century: the anthropological perspective', *International Social Science Journal*, 153, 1997, pp.345–356.

close linkage between culture and productive forces, between spirit and matter'.[22] The emergence of new forms of social interaction and social control takes place through the medium of culture, hence the politicisation of culture[23] and the growing importance of cultural policies. Not only can cultural policies play a mediating role between economic regeneration strategies aimed at the outside world and local cohesion programmes (with a view to the creation or maintenance of political clientèles), we might expect them to become increasingly central to economic policy-making as attention shifts towards human capital. In all senses, cultural policies become an integral part of identity building. As policy analyst Guy Saez remarks, 'Towns exist through their cultural policies, too.'[24]

Political decentralisation and urban cultural policies

Cultural policy is further defined by Saez as 'comprehensive and coherent interventions which are clearly defined and justified by the elected officials, which are backed by financial resources, staffing and an administrative framework'. According to this definition, many towns, small and medium sized especially, do not have cultural policies, but an increasing number do. The eminent media administrator and government advisor Jacques Rigaud, who in the 1970s bemoaned the lack of local cultural activity, referred in 1995 to the now undisputable visibility and emergence of towns' cultural policies.[25] Originally, however, local-level interventions preceded state cultural policies. If the French Revolution gave birth to both the first municipal institutions and the first institutions for managing heritage, the nineteenth century saw cultural policies become a major part of municipal identity, particularly in drama and sculpture (statue building). Thus, Dijon in 1835 presented itself as 'la Petite Athènes' (city of arts and learning). In the early twentieth century, municipal cultural policies

22. M. Castells, *The Rise of the Network Society*, Vol. I: The Information Age: Economy, Society and Culture, Oxford, Blackwell, 1996.

23. S. Wright, 'The politicization of "culture"', *Anthropology Today*, 14 (1), 1998, pp.7–15.

24. G. Saez, 'Villes et culture: un gouvernement par la coopération', *Pouvoirs*, 73, 1995, p.109.

25. Quoted by P. Poirrier, 'L'histoire des politiques culturelles des villes', *Vingtième Siècle*, 53, 1997, p.129.

formed an important part of the identity of PCF 'red towns' (Le Havre from 1956) or of experiments in municipal socialism, as in Saint-Etienne 1900–1908.[26] Thus, early cultural projects were directly associated with the rise of industrial society and the political expression of working-class solidarities.

In the early years of the Fifth Republic, culture became a major part of government policy under the stewardship of André Malraux, with the twin objectives of redressing regional imbalances (*aménagement du territoire*) and widening access across social groups. This policy, known as *action culturelle*, saw the state involved in contractual relationships with regional and local decision-makers, mediated and controlled through a network of government agents in the departments (prefects and associated technical services). The paradigm of democratisation took hold in the 1970s and became official discourse of the Culture Ministry. As a result, French people came to expect heavy state involvement in the arts.[27]

Deconcentration of the state's cultural policy provision took place largely through regional coordinating bodies, the *Directions Régionales des Affaires Culturelles* (DRAC) from 1972 onwards. The state continued to hold the purse strings and define broad policy objectives, but increasingly the regional bodies decided on the way the money would be spent. The decentralisation laws of 1982–1983 did not give specific new powers to municipalities or regions in the sphere of cultural policy. However, in broader terms the new division of powers between the four levels altered the framework for cultural policy. Mayors, whose status had already been enhanced by direct election since 1977, emerged as the biggest winners from the changes, particularly those in the largest cities whose municipal budgets rivalled those of state departments. The 1980s also saw the development of *la politique de la ville*, an urban regeneration programme with the broad aim of combating social exclusion, which transferred money from the state to local authorities within the framework of 'urban con-

26. P. Poirrier, 'L'histoire des politiques culturelles des villes, *Vingtième Siècle*, 53, 1997.
27. A top-level commission set up by Minister for Culture Philippe Douste-Blazy and chaired by Jacques Rigaud reported in 1997 that, despite the state's budgetary crisis, 90 per cent of French people surveyed wanted continued state involvement in the arts, and 14 per cent called for more substantial investment. See N. Bentolila, interview with Jacques Rigaud, 'Donner mauvaise conscience à l'Etat', *Cassandre*, 10, 1997 (http://wwwusers.imaginet.fr/~cassan.revue/10/rigaud.htm).

tracts'. In 1982 and 1983 the Ministry of Culture signed cultural development agreements with as many as ninety-one towns and cities throughout France.[28] Municipal cultural expenditure rose strongly in the 1978–1984 period, as a proportion of local spending.[29] Cities which already prioritised cultural spending were able to use the new political environment to their advantage. Grenoble stands out as the forerunner of this model, under the Dubedout administration from 1971 and then Alain Carignon in the late 1980s. The socialist *député* and mayor Hubert Dubedout successfully used cultural policy as part of a radical urban development strategy, based on investment in education and research to attract and sustain high-tech industry on one hand, and experiments in social housing and urban architecture on the other. As a result, Grenoble is one of only two municipal administrations (with Rennes: see below) cited by political scientist Patrick Le Galès as having demonstrated the capacity to counter the trends of economic globalism in the 1970s and 1980s.[30] Grenoble still has the highest expenditure in the arts, in terms of the proportion of its municipal budget (around 16 per cent compared with an average of 10.2 per cent in 1993), and the highest cultural spending per capita. In this sense, the new cultural role of municipal councils preceded political decentralisation and may be seen as helping to prepare for it. Indeed, in broader policy terms it is acknowledged that the contractualisation of public policies was introduced progressively 'by the back door' in the 1970s and that the decentralisation laws confirmed a trend which was already firmly based in reality.[31]

The new polycentric nature of decision-making has encouraged professionalisation of local cultural policies and the development of multi-level policy networks.[32] Rather than direct from the centre, the state has entered into contractual relationships with local councils, at the same time as it has disengaged financially: the proportion of state funding dropped very slightly in the 1980s to the

28. J. Forbes, 'Cultural policy: the soul of man under socialism. In *Mitterrand's France*. Eds S. Mazey and M. Newman, London, Croom Helm, 1987, pp.131–165.

29. C. Lephay-Merlin, 'Les dépenses culturelles des communes en 1993'. In *Données Urbaines*, Eds D. Pumain and F. Godard, Paris, Economica, 1996, pp.17–24.

30. P. Le Galès, 'Du gouvernement des villes à la gouvernance urbaine', *Revue Française de Science Politique*, 45 (1), 1995, p.88.

31. On this, see J.-P. Gaudin, 'Politiques urbaines et négociations territoriales. Quelle légitimité pour les réseaux de politiques publiques?', *Revue Française de Science Politique*, 45 (1), 1995, pp.31–56.

32. G. Saez, 'Villes et culture: un gouvernement par la coopération', *Pouvoirs*, 73, 1995.

early 1990s from over 22 per cent to under 22per cent (half of this devoted to Paris alone), whilst local authority financing rose from under 50 per cent to over 60 per cent of the cultural budget (over 40 per cent of this by municipalities). Cultural spending represented 0.91 per cent of the state budget, 2.4 per cent of the regional budget, 2.7 per cent of the departmental budget, and 10.2 per cent of the municipal budget (in towns with over 10,000 inhabitants). Cities with over 150,000 inhabitants spend an average 13.3 per cent of their budget and 15.5 per cent of their running expenditure on culture (see Table 1).

Table 1: *Cultural expenditure by different levels of administration, 1984–1993 (billion francs)*

	1984	1987	1990	1993
Culture Ministry	10,67	10,40	11,31	14,50
Local authorities	24,33	29,08	31,98	36,90
Communes	21,35	24,92	26,34	30,00
Departments	2,28	3,20	4,39	5,40
Regions	0,70	0,95	1,25	1,50
Total	35,00	239,48	43,29	51,40

Source: French Culture Ministry[33]

The deconcentration and decentralisation of cultural policy depends on close cooperation between the four levels of administration and between public authorities and all actors concerned in cultural production, particularly in the absence of a clear division of tasks in the decentralisation laws.[34] Cities must cooperate with each other in regional networks, as well as with the regional and departmental councils which also have cultural responsibilities. At the same time, cities compete with each other for state funding and for private business investment. Cultural policy thus provides a good example of the ways in which the relationship between the central state and local authorities has been modified in the 1980s and 1990s. The traditional (rural) model of centre-periphery relations, based on a hierarchical relationship between central state

33. See in particular the Ministry's bulletin *Développement culturel*, 113, July 1996 (*Les dépenses culturelles des collectivités locales en 1993*).

34. G. Saez, 'Villes et culture: un gouvernement par la coopération', *Pouvoirs*, 73, 1995; Lephay-Merlin, 'Les dépenses culturelles des communes en 1993' In *Données Urbaines*, Eds D. Pumain and F. Godard, Paris, Economica, 1996. For a case study of a cooperative network, see R. Rizzardo, 'Action culturelle et réseau de villes en Rhône-Alpes', *Cadmos*, 56, pp.63–71.

and local notables, has given way to a more complex and fragmented situation, in the largest cities (regional capitals) at least. These new forms of 'urban governance'[35] rest on a multi-layered set of relationships, often with apparently conflicting objectives: '[Cooperation] is first and foremost the capacity of local authorities to mobilise actors from outside the locality and persuade them to collaborate in the development of institutions which only have meaning in urban life. [...] Towns' capacity to create such urban regimes of co-operation is a good indicator of performance.'[36]

This analysis chimes with DATAR thinking on economic development, which stresses the importance of inter-urban relations within the regional framework for the performance of individual towns and cities. In the case of Grenoble, close proximity and good infrastructure links with other cities in the same area (principally Lyon and Saint-Etienne) create a positive setting for attracting the right professional mix and inward investment, whilst competition with neighbouring cities spurs Grenoble city council to maintain its high cultural profile. Elsewhere, regional imbalances combined with poor relations between city management and regional deciders tend to hamper attempts to promote cultural policies. Thus, in the case of Lille, the imbalance between the regional capital and the myriad smaller towns around has at times created resentment and incoherence in cultural production, which is stretched between Lille, Roubaix, Tourcoing.[37] Since inhabitants of large cities tend to be bigger consumers of cultural production, tensions between urban and rural cultural practices may result in clashes within regional councils over the allocation of budget expenditure.

Differences may also arise between the goals of regional economic development and local development strategies, particu-

35. The term 'urban governance' was first developed to describe local administration and policy networks in the United States of America. It has been modified to help conceptualise local administration in France and Great Britain, where the central state plays a much bigger role than in the U.S.A. and where private business interests are conversely less well organised and less influential. Despite this difference, commentators see local government in Europe as becoming more like the American model in the sense that local policy networks are more diverse and fragmented than in the past. For a more detailed discussion, see Le Galès, 'Du gouvernement des villes à la gouvernance urbaine', *Revue Française de Science Politique*, 45 (1), 1995.

36. G. Saez, 'Villes et culture: un gouvernement par la coopération', *Pouvoirs*, 73, 1995, p.113.

37. B. Bonduelle, *Nord et Pas-de-Calais. L'impossible tête-à-tête*, Lille, La Voix du Nord, 1998, p.60; L. Desbenoit, 'Les combats dans Lille', *Télérama*, 2280, 22 September 1993, pp.16–20.

larly when high-profile mayors adopt an entrepreneurial strategy which is explicitly focused on the city rather than the region (as, for example, in Montpellier's campaign for recognition as a 'Eurocity' rather than a regional capital).[38] At a time when mayors too are beginning to experience the effects of a 'crisis of representation' as they seek to satisfy increasing demands from a number of different local constituencies, their relationship with voters crucially depends on their ability to project a positive image of the city within and to the outside world. There is thus potential for conflict between methods and styles which may occur between different levels of government or between the needs of different local groups: for example, an aggressive 'communication' strategy aimed at attracting businesses through the promotion of a forward-looking image will tend to use highly personalised mayoral strategies relying on public relations specialists and high-profile events (such as festivals or architectural projects), whereas community-based groups may prefer a more participative method involving small-scale projects and systematic consultation of residents.[39] The state, for its part, will tend to focus on more technocratic methods and long-range planning of broad economic objectives (see Table 2). In fact, whilst state and regional initiatives fall mainly in the 'strategic' column of the analytical grid shown below, local government uses a mixture of methods, depending on local circumstances and the political project of the mayor and his/her team. Competition between cities tends to favour the 'communicative' method, at the expense of participative methods which local socio-economic conditions might call for. Such tensions arise inevitably in a system of shared tasks, since they reflect conflicts between different political clientèles, and local urban self-images and identities do not always coincide with regional identities. Decentralisation has thus reinforced both interdependence and competition, with actors at different levels involved as 'associated rivals.[40] Cultural policies are an expression of territorial politics and as such become caught up in power struggles at local level and between different levels of local government.

---

38. For an account of mayor Georges Frèche's communication strategy for Montpellier, and his resulting clashes with the regional council, see G. Parker, 'Montpellier ou la maïeutique mercatique – from ideality to reality. The art of wishful thinking', *Modern and Contemporary France*, NS1/4, pp.385–396.

39. J.-P. Lacaze, *La ville et l'urbanisme*, Paris, Flammarion, 1995.

40. A. Mabileau, *Le système local*, Paris, Montchrestien, 1991.

Table 2: *Analytical grid of urban planning methods*
(developed by Jean-Paul Lacaze)[41]

Type of method	Strategic	Social Engineering	Participative	Managerial	Communicative
Objective	Modify structures	Create new zones	Improve daily life of residents	Improve quality of services	Attract businesses
Priority aspect	Economy	Construction	Social relations	Service networks	Global image
Frame of reference	Efficiency return	Esthetics Culture	Use values	Demand Cost-efficiency ratios	External reputation
Technical back-up	Engineers Economists	Architects Planners	Sociologists 'Animateurs'	Managers	Architects Communication/public relations experts
Mode of decision-making	Technocratic	Autocratic	Democratic	Managerial	Personalised

The politicisation of culture was amply demonstrated in a series of well-publicised cases involving a handful of large towns in southern France which elected *Front National* mayors in 1995. In-line with anthropologist Susan Wright's observation that culture has become a code word for far-right policies on race, in France the FN focused on cultural spending. Subsidies to local theatre groups and café-bars were cut not only to spare the burden on local tax-payers but as a deliberate act of revenge on liberal opposition to the FN, whilst simultaneously the party emphasised regional cultural traditions as part of its campaign for the 1997 regional elections. The FN's reworking of local cultural policies emphasised a partic-ular type of culture, based on ancient traditions and residential sta-bility ('roots, tradition, identity'), in order to exclude non-white immigrants and anti-FN liberals (presented as Parisian newcomers to the south). The local council and in some cases, the departmen-tal level of government, joined the fray, as in the Var where the president of the departmental council decided to double the cul-tural budget in an attempt to redeem the department's 'detestable' image after several years of battle with the FN mayor of Toulon,

41. Adapted from J.-P. Lacaze, *La ville et l'urbanisme*, Paris, Flammarion, 1995, p.110.

Jean-Marie Le Chevallier.[42] Cultural associations were also at the forefront of a massive anti-FN movement which sprang up in response to the election of several mainstream right-wing politicians at the head of regional councils, thanks to the support of FN councillors, following the 1998 regional elections.[43] The FN cases demonstrated not just an interrelationship between culture, politics and identity, but the instrumentalisation of culture and identity for political ends. Perhaps what they revealed above all is the extent to which cultural policies normally benefit from a political consensus among elites, which operates despite local disputes about expenditure levels for any particular project.

Cultural policy and urban regeneration: the integration of culture and economy

The existence of a broad political consensus on local cultural policies reflects a shared belief in the need for urban regeneration, based at the lowest level on a fear of the consequences of new or growing spatial inequalities. Decentralisation is a feature of the attempts of countries belonging to the Organization for Economic Cooperation and Development (OECD) to regenerate mature industrial areas which are the worst affected by structural economic change:

> The actual and potential roles of local institutions in the active design and implementation of economic regeneration programmes are under scrutiny. As a result, the relationship among national, regional and local economic policies is undergoing and will continue to undergo marked changes.[44]

France's partnership approach involves the twenty-two regional governments as chief partners with central government for economic development. The main feature of the multi-tiered structure is the Planning Contract (*Contrat de Plan*). Resources are channelled through the Urban Development Fund (*Fonds Social Urbain*) via regional councils to urban areas with social problems, in particular for housing and the redevelopment of city centres.

42. C. Bédarida, 'En Rhône-Alpes, la résistance culturelle à l'extrême-droite', *Le Monde*, 10 June 1988.

43. J. Lenzini, 'Le Var va doubler le budget de la culture', *Le Monde*, 21 July 1998.

44. J. Fox-Przeworski, in J. Fox-Przeworski, J. Goddard and M. de Jong, *Urban regeneration in a changing economy: an international perspective*, Oxford, Clarendon Press, 1991, p.119.

Looking at the subject from the viewpoint of the state's top-down approach, France's urban regeneration policies have been criticised for being unwieldy and inconsistent.[45] The number of urban areas classified as being in difficulty and therefore in need of help has increased dramatically from fourteen in 1984 to 744 in 1996, whilst financing has remained inadequate and unequally spread.

From the local viewpoint, urban centres in need of help for economic regeneration can appeal in the first instance to the region and to the state's services in the department, and can then use these services to apply for European funding. A study of economic regeneration programmes in a variety of urban and semi-rural areas (mainly in southern France) identified a great variety of actors and different clusters of actors in different settings, according to the 'local system of public action': state, regional council, urban communities bringing together neighbouring municipal councils, local councils, and to a lesser extent private interests (local companies, particularly where these were the dominant employer). Gaps between local actors' conviction that the crisis would not last, and the alarm raised by external actors, were particularly evident in localities with strong working-class traditions (Tarbes with its heavy industry, the mining town of Carmaux) or whose local identity rested on the company or activity affected by economic crisis (Michelin in Clermont-Ferrand).[46] Overall, the researchers found that mobilisation against industrial decline tended to be slow and sometimes even needed the impetus of experts brought in from the outside (the region or the central state). However, once regeneration projects were launched they followed three main approaches: aid to the activity affected, including subcontractors, in order to diversify production; the development of companies not affected by the recession, and measures to attract new businesses, including start-up help for small businesses; improving infrastructures; initiatives to make the area more attractive, by improving infrastructures and improving the local image. Where local actors analysed the crisis as resting on a particular company or industry, strategies focused on the first two, whilst the third approach was more prevalent where the crisis was seen as a wider territorial crisis (usually marked by demographic flight as well as high unemployment).[47]

45.For an official evaluation, see J.-P. Sueur, *Demain, la ville. Rapport présenté au ministre de l'emploi et de la solidarité*, Vol.I, Paris: La Documentation Française, 1998.

46. C. Beslay, *La construction des politiques locales*, Paris, L'Harmattan, 1998, pp.99–100.

47. C. Beslay, *La construction des politiques locales*, Paris, L'Harmattan, 1998, pp.116–117.

Difficulties of local mobilisation and an initial reluctance to believe the scale of the problem help to explain why, to begin with, economic development paid relatively little attention to cultural policies, although 'in the rest of Europe many city decision-makers saw the development of cultural policies as a valuable tool in diversifying the local economic base and achieving greater social cohesion. They paid new attention to expanding economic sectors like leisure, tourism, the media and other "cultural industries" including fashion and design, in an attempt to compensate for jobs lost in traditional industrial sectors'.[48] However, according to Patrick Le Galès, France's relatively high – but unevenly spread – levels of local cultural spending resulted more from the dynamics of national-local political relationships and inter-urban competition than from a concern with urban regeneration.[49]

Le Galès notes optimistically that most French cities were economically buoyant in the 1980s and that economic development reflected innovation. In the case of Rennes, cultural policy formed an essential component of transformation from 'a rather boring provincial capital' to one of the most successful and dynamic urban areas in France. Rennes City Council's urban development strategy, backed by the new decentralisation laws and state subsidies, prioritised artistic creativity through sponsorship of a dance theatre (the *Théâtre Chorégraphique de Rennes*), youth theatre companies throughout the city, opera and the establishment of a regional symphony orchestra, and new exhibitions in visual arts. A network of professional associations was supported through the provision of premises and equipment in theatre, popular music, film and video. Part of the strategy involved support for traditional regional culture (including the creation of a museum and an eco-museum). The creation of a prestigious image in national and international terms meant moving beyond local (in this case, regional) culture to embrace cultural exchange and less territorially specific production.

In an attempt to change its image and attract a new local population, Poitiers was one of the first cities to appeal to marketing specialists in the early 1970s. The marketing consultants interviewed Parisian industrialists and managerial staff to ascertain

48. F. Bianchini, 'Culture and the remaking of European cities' in F. Bianchini and M. Parkinson (eds), *Cultural policy and urban regeneration. The West European experience*, Manchester and New York, Manchester University Press, 1993, p.6.

49. P. Le Galès, 'Rennes: Catholic humanism and urban entrepreneurialism', in Bianchini and Parkinson *Cultural policy and urban regeneration. The West European experience*, Manchester and New York, Manchester University Press, 1993, pp.178–198.

the factors which might encourage them to move out of Paris, and found that as well as material factors, psychological aspects of the local environment helped to encourage relocation: housing, leisure and cultural facilities, children's education and the presence of higher education establishments.[50] Today the importance of the sociocultural environment is well known and has helped fuel a competition among France's regional centres.

Unfortunately, inter-urban competition has worked to the advantage of those cities initially in a stronger position thanks to their more diversified economic structures, such as Grenoble or Montpellier, to the detriment of older industrial centres. France has begun to catch up with its European neighbours in promoting cultural policies as a tool of urban regeneration, as cities like Saint-Etienne and neighbouring Givors, as well as Limoges, Valenciennes and Nantes reinvent their image through new architectural and artistic projects (such as the Museum of Modern Art in Saint-Etienne). Some observers, however, note that the new interest in cultural policies and heritage coincides with a budgetary squeeze which requires more creative use of public spending and the search for 'softer and more subtle recipes for growth and development'.[51] State disengagement thus parallels the effect of inter-urban competition, working against the avowed objectives of redistribution and equalisation (*aménagement du territoire*).

The local industrial heritage can form an important plank of tourist development strategies (as in the example of Carmaux, which has promoted its mines as a *lieu de mémoire*). Industrial centres such as Saint-Etienne have also been able to exploit a historical reputation for innovation and know-how. In such cases, the past can provide a powerful motor of development if allied with investment strategies aimed at boosting research and development, along the American model, or policies to attract and support small businesses within a local culture of artisanal skill and production. It has been found however that concentration on industrial tourism (which is difficult to sustain as a principal activity) diverts local councils away from tackling long-term economic regeneration.[52] In many cases the past is simply seen as a burden

50. C. André, 'Changer l'image d'une ville', *Revue Politiques et Management Public*, 5 (4), pp.51–64.

51. F. Grosrichard and M. Valo, 'La culture en vitrine', *Le Monde Dossiers et Documents*, no.227, December 1994 (*L'avenir des régions*), p.3.

52. See C. Beslay, *La construction des politiques locales*, Paris, L'Harmattan, 1998, pp.64–65, on Aubin.

for economic regeneration, as Bertrand Tavernier caustically observed in his caricature of the northern Communist mayor in his 1999 film *Ça commence aujourd'hui* (It all starts today). Local leaders in Lille certainly saw overcoming the industrial past and 'finding what was there before' as a necessary part of their strategy aimed at attracting visitors and businesses to the city and the region.[53]

Cultural policy as community-building

In France, small-scale community projects have aimed above all at building social cohesion and social capital (social networks and values of social trust and solidarity). Urban Contracts (within the framework of urban regeneration programmes) between central and local government usually stipulate involvement of local residents and subsidies to local associations. Increasingly in the 1990s, such contracts focused on cultural policies in various forms: 'artists in residence, subsidies to new companies, support for amateur production through associations or facilities, new venues for contemporary music, transformation of urban wastelands into cultural spaces, intercultural festivals'.[54] 'Neighbourhood cultural projects' or *projets culturels de quartiers* involved sixty sites classified as disadvantaged in 1996–1997. Close relationships between public and private actors were also fostered by the economic climate of the 1990s, which required the state to withdraw from full funding and/or administration of cultural provision and to contract out services to non-profit organisations. The non-profit sector consequently expanded in terms of employment and voluntary activity. The proportion of French people involved in cultural and leisure associations rose markedly in the 1980s and 1990s, from 12 per cent in 1979–81 to 20 per cent in 1996–97, almost as many as took part in sporting associations (21 per cent).[55]

Voluntary associations are seen as central to the construction of social capital, as they promote inter-personal trust and indicate the possible benefits of social integration (through the provision of facilities and encouragement of group activities, or simply as a

53. Interview with Annick Lesschaeve, Cultural Affairs Department, Lille Municipal Council, September 1999.

54. J.-P. Saez, 'Que peuvent les politiques culturelles pour le lien social?', in *L'État de la France 1999–2000*, Paris, La Découverte, 1999, p.163.

55. G. Hatchuel, and J.-P. Loisel, 'La vie associative: participer, mais pas militer', in INSEE, *Données Sociales*, Paris, INSEE, 1999, pp.359–365.

means of having a good time). At an individual level, participation in group activities can give a sense of self-esteem and value, as in the case of young participants in a Saint-Etienne cultural festival: 'Here I find the affection I was missing in my life, and I learn self-control'; 'The human warmth we find here breaks down solitude and gives us confidence.'[56] Cultural associations, like sporting associations, also help to cement explicit group identities (local or regional cultures, ethnic or racial traditions). In addition, they may serve as 'gatekeepers' to the local community, allowing access for politicians and other local leaders. For example, when Bertrand and Nils Tavernier went to make a documentary about life in a housing project in Montreuil, they had no success in finding residents willing to talk to them until they won the trust of a local dance group; a rap group was also prominent in early meetings.[57]

Social cohesion can also be encouraged through cultural projects which give local people a voice and a chance to give their views on their relationship with the local environment. An example of one such programme, financed by the *Direction Régionale des Affaires Culturelles* of the Rhône-Alpes region, was the *Paroles Urbaines* literacy project carried out in several sites from the mid-1990s. For example, in the socially disadvantaged districts of Bron, writers met local residents in everyday places such as the supermarket or unemployment office, whilst residents were encouraged to write down their own thoughts, some of which were later published or used in drama productions. In other towns, emphasis was placed on cultural exchanges reflecting the ethnic mix of the local population. In all cases, the type of project reflected specific local problems or local ways of defining identity, many revolving around youth experiences.

Of course, such projects receive only small amounts of funding and reach only a small fraction of the population, but they can help to promote networks which have longer-term effects, particularly among the young. Other problems have also been identified: many associations fear manipulation and capture by electorally-minded local elites.[58] The danger exists that cultural

56. See http://www.culture.fr/rhone-alpes/dossier/culturqu/pages/projunid.htm.

57. De l'autre côté du périph', (On the far side of the ringroad), film made in 1996 and broadcast in December 1997.

58. P.-D. Tchetche-Apea, interviewed (with M. Wievorka) by P. Bernard and N. Herzberg, 'Un sociologue et un militant associatif débattent sur la politique de la ville', *Le Monde*, 10 February 1998, p.18.

programmes may be seen as too 'artistic' by community organisations and too 'social' by cultural groups.[59] Finally, the stigma of poverty and exclusion attached to community cultural projects may lead to resentment, particularly where outside policy-makers fail to consult local populations, as in the case of murals painted on walls in a low-income district on the southern outskirts of Lyon.[60] In this case, the top-down approach of the project, coming directly from the national Ministry of Culture, exacerbated the divide. Nevertheless, the meeting-point between cultural producers and providers on one hand, and new audiences on the other, is generally seen as both culturally and socially beneficial, as long as a bottom-up, participative approach is adopted.

Question marks remain at a more general level. Despite local successes, and despite the undisputed value of culture as a referential value 'helping [the individual] to control his or her relationship with the world', the sheer scale of problems associated with unemployment and crime put them beyond the reach of cultural policies alone.[61] If urban culture is above all associated with hip-hop and the more disadvantaged sections of youth, it expresses a profound sense of rejection and otherness which cultural policies can help to transform into pride and social solidarity; but they cannot necessarily address the root causes of feelings of rejection.

Conclusion

Conflicts between artists and community groups, within the context of anti-exclusion projects, are an example of the tensions which may arise from cultural policies with a specific objective and aimed at a specific audience. In this sense, the trend towards greater professionalisation of cultural provision, which is widely identified by observers, should be seen as part of a wider movement towards fragmentation. More generally, cultural policies are carried out in a contested terrain. Conflicts may arise between different segments of the local population: for example, policies

59. C. Bédarida, 'Banlieues d'Europe fédère les projets créés et encouragés à la lisière des villes', *Le Monde*, 17 March 1998.

60. P. Bavoux, J.-M. Berthet, P. Dupont, and B. Minet, 'Art public et identité urbaine', research report for the *Mission du Patrimoine Ethnologique*, May 1993, cited in A. Morel, 'Des identités exemplaires. La ville avant les habitants', *Terrain*, 23, October 1994, pp.151–160.

61. J.-P. Saez, 'Que peuvent les politiques culturelles pour le lien social', in *L'État de la France 1999–2000*, Paris, La Découverte, 1999, p.164.

aimed at attracting highly-educated social groups may alienate long-standing residents, as in the case of the Amiens district of Saint-Lieu, whose past was bound up in small-scale industrial production. The arrival of a sizeable middle-class population disrupted the dynamics of local identity.[62] In this case, cultural policies could only create new identities by destroying old ones, with consequent social confusion and resentment. The process of identity formation, whether artificial (that is, through deliberate cultural or architectural projects) or not, is inevitably conflictual.[63]

Further conflicts arise between different levels of local, regional and central government, as new forms of urban governance emerge alongside more traditional patterns. We have seen that cultural policies became more important in the 1980s and 1990s as an expression of various, broadly converging political objectives: competition between cities, fuelled by new powers for mayors and a battle for increasingly scarce resources; orthodox thinking on economic development which identifies a need to restructure local populations and identities; a diagnosis of territorial crisis which encourages decision-makers to look beyond aid to specific industries and focus on image-building. At the same time, large-scale economic change has created territorial imbalances which cultural policies must face and help to overcome. Cultural policies seem torn between prestige and participation, between past and future.

The way local communities deal with their industrial past, through which their identities were developed and sustained, depends on many factors, not least the ability of local leaders to attract new economic opportunities and new social groups, and then to integrate them and mediate between different social groups. In this context, cultural policies will work best if local leaders can successfully bridge communicative and participative strategies. More and more municipal councils – on the centre-right as well as the socialist and communist left – are moving away from high-risk, high-status showcase projects to experiments in local democracy. Concern with the past, as reflected in present concerns about economic survival and social integration, may well prove to be an indispensable transitional phase for industrial society.

62. C. Bidou, 'Les enjeux identitaires dans la production d'un quartier rénové de centre historique', research report for the *Mission du Patrimoine Ethnologique*, 1992, cited in A. Morel, 'Des identités exemplaires. La ville avant les habitants', *Terrain*, 23, October 1994.

63. A. Morel, 'Des identités exemplaires. La ville avant les habitants', *Terrain*, 23, October 1994, p.160.

13

PUBLIC POLICY AND URBAN CULTURES IN FRANCE

François Ménard

Three-quarters of the French population live in urban areas, and yet urban cultures have only recently begun to take their place in cultural policy. While it is true that the state does now finance operations or organisations which are defined by a specifically urban frame of reference (*Projets culturels de quartiers* – Neighbourhood Cultural Projects, *Rencontres des cultures urbaines* – The Festival of Urban Cultural Expression, *Maîtrise d'oeuvre urbaine et culturelle* – contracts for the construction of cultural projects in urban areas), the involvement of the public authorities is often ambivalent. This means that the operation can fit rather uncomfortably with the specific urban site, target audience or the notion of urban culture in general. In order to understand why this discrepancy exists and what is at stake when public policy tries to take urban cultures on board, it is necessary to examine the main developments in this field and to offer an analysis of those moments when the two sides meet. First, we need to establish exactly what is meant by 'urban cultures'.

Urban culture, urban cultures: the new kids on the block

No clear definition of 'urban cultures' exists. Indeed, the term has only recently become current in France. Since the 1930s and especially since the Second World War, the political debate about the role of culture in France has tended to be polarised around either the advocacy of 'popular' culture or the defence of 'high' culture, thus excluding any other categorisation. As an anthropological phenomenon, urban cultures are taken to mean contemporary patterns of behaviour or new practices found in modern towns and cities. As such, they have rarely received any more attention than the pop counter-culture and rock events of the 1960s. Consequently, right up to the end of the 1980s, 'urban cultures' – understood in both a normative and anthropological sense – have rarely featured in the drafting of cultural or social policies in France.[1] However, the expression is now more common, as public-sector decision-makers and cultural mediators turn their attention to hitherto disregarded forms of cultural expression.

Today, it is paradoxical that the term 'urban cultures' has come to refer to a rather limited group of activities – those associated with hip-hop (rap, break-dancing, tagging, graffiti, etc.) – attached to the world of youth of the *banlieue* (outer-city estates), especially those of the problematical *grandes cités* (housing estates).[2] The paradox is that this definition is in itself exclusive – the *bal musette* and rock music are both urban cultures, after all – as if the radically urban nature of hip-hop gave it a specific status, despite its 'imported' and highly mediatised status. In fact, hip-hop and the practices which have grown up around it do undoubtedly bear the mark of their urban background[3] more than others, in so far as they are readily identifiable with those places which give substance to the urban phenomenon in its most critical social and spacial sites: the street and the ghetto (or in the French context, the housing estates of the *banlieue*). The dances developed around the

1. In fact when they do appear, they are usually linked to very specific or short-lived initiatives: the exhibition '*Graffiti et société*' at the Pompidou Centre in Paris in 1981; an exhibition of the work of American graffiti artists put on by the RATP (Greater Paris transport authority) in 1984; the inclusion of rap and DJ-ing on Radio 7, a state-owned channel. A variety of music festivals in the working-class *banlieue* were created or given financial backing: *Banlieues Bleues* in Seine Saint Denis; *Fêtes et Forts* in the several districts at the edge of Paris which have a military fort (Aubervilliers, Ivry, etc.), *Y-a de la banlieue dans l'air* in Bondy. There appears to be a definite distinction being made between making up for a lack of general cultural activity in peripheral urban zones on the one hand and opening up cultural space to new urban cultural expressions on the other.

2. *Cité* is used here to mean an estate of social housing, usually of blocks of flats, being part of a distinct architectural plan which sets it apart from other neighbouring housing estates or the surrounding urban environment.

3. The expression is used here to identify 'that which is associated with urban life' rather than to characterise any supervised structure of social relationships.

hip-hop phenomenon were first seen on the streets and in the squares of these housing estates, or sometimes in underground *métro* stations, but never in dance halls. Tags covered walls unsuitable for commercial advertising hoardings and were scrawled on the carriages of underground and suburban trains. This shows the extent to which established public areas were being shunned and, in the case of the underground, can be seen as symbolic of the social tensions in the Paris region. The underground network, cutting a swathe through the very diverse urban landscape, highlights the social differences of the areas it crosses and its trajectory marks it out as one of the few remaining spaces where different social groups collide. In choosing the underground as one of their main targets, the taggers send out a message which is interpreted in two different ways. To some, their tags are seen to represent some kind of menace to society, warning against the urban integration of poorer peripheral areas with Paris. To others, they are signs of the result of the 'relegation' of whole communities to exile in marginal districts.[4] Rap arrived in France as the vernacular expression of the American black ghetto and was quickly adopted by *banlieue* youth who not only identified with the sentiment of the lyrics, but who also recognised they shared a common social and geographical origin with the black American rappers.[5]

When looked at in this setting, recognising the existence of urban cultures means by extension recognising a specific sector of the population responsible for its production: that is young people from the *quartiers en crise* (deprived estates), above all those of ethnic minority origin. Hip-hop has, in any case, come to epitomise new urban cultures in France,[6] to the extent of dominating the field and masking the historical roots which place it in a continuum and discontinuum of past practices. In the specialist press[7] and programmes of cultural events produced by the public sector, the cultural practices inspired by hip-hop are not presented as an

---

4. The terms 'relegation' and 'exile' are taken from the titles of two works, *Banlieues en difficulté: La relégation* (Paris, Styros) written in 1991 by J.-M. Delarue, former head of the Inter-Ministerial Taskforce for the City and *Quartiers d'Exil* (Paris, Le Seuil) written by two sociologists, F. Dubet and D. Lapeyronnies, in 1992.

5. This is certainly the case for the most emblematic French rap groups, including NTM, IAM, Assassins.

6. The *Rencontres des cultures urbaines de la Villette*, which will now be held annually and financed in part by the Ministry of Culture, is a major example of this.

7. Here I am thinking of French language magazines specifically targetting a hip-hop audience, *Radikal, l'Affiche, Groove.*

up-dating of urban culture, nor are they seen as new forms of expression which have taken over from others: rather they are described as urban cultures, full stop. The use of the plural here might suggest that other activities could come under this umbrella, but hip-hop remains both point of reference and overall matrix for the youth cultures of the outer-city estates. However the recognition accorded to hip-hop as *the* form of urban culture is fraught with difficulty. It is linked to a long history of French public policy-makers being wary of using popular culture in the formulation of social or cultural policies. It also has to be considered against the more recent reluctance to acknowledge the role of collective identities in forming social dynamics, when putting together the *politique de la ville*[8] (urban regeneration policy) for problem areas.

To try to understand the complexity of the French situation, we need to look back at past initiatives, accepting the hypothesis that urban culture did not begin with hip-hop, even in the field of public policy initiatives.

1960s to the 1980s: cultural institutions and cultural policy respond to new urban cultures

It was in the 1960s, and in rather specific circumstances, that urban cultures first came to the attention of public policy makers.[9] As France emerged from the Algerian war in the early 1960s, two parallel problems came to the fore, which were to radically change the way in which urban culture was perceived: *grands ensembles* (high-rise estates) and *blousons noirs* (rockers/teddy boys).

The *grands ensembles* can be characterised as estates of social housing made up of tower blocks and flats, usually conforming to

8. In France, this *politique de la ville* has nothing to do with urban planning. It is a transversal policy initiated by central government in the early 1980s which aims to address the urgent social and specifically urban problems of deprived areas. It brings together city, regional and central government agencies in a *contrat de plan* (Planning Contract) and has been extended to an ever-growing number of areas. It is characterised by its concentration on a specific area which tends to be small (a *quartier* or district of a town) but which is extending to take in whole towns or built-up areas; by the contractual nature of its implementation and by its non-sectoral approach which covers employment, social and urban issues, as well as education and culture.

9. Here I shall not look at criminological approaches which predate this period, notably the phenomena of 'the underworld' (*la pègre, le milieu*) and hooliganism (*les Apaches*) particular to Paris at the beginning of the twentieth century.

the same design, built to house the urban influx of population or to re-house communities during the slum-clearance programmes of post-Liberation reconstruction.[10] These spaces attracted much criticism as they were impersonal, isolated from city centres and lacking basic facilities.[11] The problems of coping with life in these high-rise estates coined a new phrase: *Sarcellite* (Sarcellitus), after the name of a small town which became synonymous with these new developments.[12]

At the same time, more and more young people were catching on to the American imports of rock music and the twist. The more rebellious aspects of these cultures, seen at the time as deviant, appear today to have been seen more as a symptom of social dislocation than as an emerging new cultural form in itself.[13] The mass mediation of youth culture was equally worrying, given that it inspired behaviour perceived as marginal and that it mobilised growing numbers of young people, already increasingly visible on the streets. After giving a concert to a crowd of 150,000 in the Place de la Nation in Paris in 1962, the singer Johnny Hallyday declared that '*Nous sommes plus forts qu'un parti politique*' (We are more powerful than a political party).

Attempts to deal with these phenomena were mainly social: the building of neighbourhood community centres (*équipements sociaux et culturels*) on the model of the existing MJC youth clubs (*Maisons de Jeunes et de la Culture*) and Social and Cultural centres (*Centres sociaux et socio-culturels*).[14] *Clubs de prévention* also appeared, these being centres staffed by community youth workers employed to keep young people off the streets and thus prevent juvenile delinquency. Most of these centres were created at the behest of the government, but generally they were run and managed by the main associations of the workers' educational movement. Their ideas, strongly imbued with the social ethic of the politics of the immediate post-war period, dominated the sector: education as a force for enlightenment; training young people

10. It is important to note that it was only in 1945 that the urban population of France equalled that reached by Britain a century earlier.

11. C. Bachmann, *Violences urbaines: ascension et déclin des classes moyennes à travers 50 ans de politiques de la ville*, Paris, Fayard, 1996.

12. F. Ménard, 'L'histoire du logement à travers la revue Informations Sociales de 45 à 90' in *Informations Sociales*, no.53, 1996, pp81–94.

13. F. Dubet, *La Galère: jeunes en survie*, Paris, Fayard, 1987.

14. G. Saez, 'L'éducation populaire de la Libération aux années 60: entre le modèle républicain et la tentation communautaire' in *La République des Jeunes – Actes du Colloque du 17 et 18 décembre 1994*, Paris, FFMJC, 1996, pp133–146.

who, in turn, will become trainers themselves; the quest for leisure pursuits which can have an accompanying social utility. Essentially an urban phenomenon, these clubs and centres gave rise to a new, hybrid field of intervention, that of socially conscious culture: *le socio-culturel*. This employed a wide range of consciousness-raising activities centred on an introduction to the arts in order to encourage personal development and motivation. Initially, urban cultures had no significant place in this philosophy, which concentrated on the cultural activities traditionally associated with the youth and workers' educational movements. Right up to the end of the 1960s, rock and pop music were dismissed as signs of the 'americanisation' of culture. They were certainly not seen as a new form of cultural expression capable of translating new social aspirations.

In the 1970s, these values and practices continued to be marginalised within the programme of the MJC and other centres: they were still identified as manifestations of a youth counter-culture, and not as a distinct culture of new urban spaces. The move to the mainstream came about with the arrival of fresh young community workers rather than any concerted public policy. Belonging to the generation of post-war baby-boomers and influenced by the spirit of May 1968, they widened the scope of the programmes on offer in community and youth centres. These transformations highlight the institutional struggle going on at this time between the state and the youth and workers' educational associations which were running the centres.

It is important to note that throughout this period, two distinct cultural policies were emerging. On the one hand we have the official Ministry of Culture policy which encouraged artistic production and dissemination based essentially on an elitist definition of culture (masterpieces of universal importance). This policy gave priority to widening access to cultural works, rather than to widening the notion of what constituted cultural activity. On the other hand we have the Ministry for Youth Affairs and Sport which took over responsibility for workers' education initiatives in the mid-1960s. Their policy was to encourage sociocultural activity of all kinds, giving associations free rein to develop initiatives, whilst at the same time establishing a regulatory framework for the sector. This was based on an all-embracing, anthropological definition of culture, in which any practice can be seen as culturally inspired.

This model was challenged in the late 1970s and early 1980s, for several reasons. Firstly, the crisis of the Welfare State (*Etat Provi-*

dence) led to fewer provisions for the associations which were running youth activities, leaving the sector in a vulnerable position. Secondly, as part of the new responsibilities given to local, departmental and regional authorities (*collectivités territoriales*) under the decentralisation laws, the associations came under the direct control of local councillors. These local politicians tended to contest the role played by the associations in defining the course and organisation of local life, and sought either to exploit them for political gain, or attempted to limit their intervention to that of service providers. At the same time, many of these *collectivités territoriales* began to develop their own cultural policies, despite the fact that, in their early days, the decentralisation laws made little provision for the cultural sector.[15]

With youth unemployment on the increase, the sociocultural approach seemed rather ineffectual. New approaches focused more on vocational training and job opportunities – economic replacing cultural integration. Cross-sector policies also began to gain ground, notably the *politique de la ville*. These changes of priority relegated sociocultural and cultural concerns in general to a very minor position, even though the existing clubs and centres were used to run these new initiatives. Another challenge to the sociocultural model was the coming of age of the young people who had frequented the centres. As they grew up and became upwardly mobile socially, their leisure time was spent in more consumerist pursuits such as attending rock concerts. For whatever reason, the activities on offer were increasingly considered obsolete or 'dated'. Sarcastic comments levelled at the urban sociocultural activites charged them with being too *néo-rural* – with their pseudo-rustic crafts – pottery, macramé, etc.[16] During this period new cultural practices came to the fore. They were resolutely anchored in an urban frame of reference (notably hip-hop

15. P. Moulinier, *Politique culturelle et décentralisation,* Paris, Editions du CNFPT, 1995. The considerable sums spent on culture by towns and cities in France in recent years, which far outweighs their statutory obligations towards the cultural sector, bears witness to the importance of culture in contemporary local politics. Medium-sized towns are leading the way as key political players become increasingly aware of the positive benefits of raising the cultural profile of their municipality, not only in terms of 'corporate image' and identity, but also in terms of making the town more attractive for inward economic investment.

16. It should be noted that the anti-establishment counter-culture of the 1960s and 1970s strongly rejected, in France at least, urban spaces and patterns of community. A rather idealised model based on rural social structure was seen as the preferred alternative.

with tagging and break dance, followed by rap) and often the domain of young people from immigrant – mainly Maghrebi – communities. These new cultures 'spoke' to these youngsters and provided them with a unique means of expressing their discontent and feelings of marginalisation within French society, in a language which was not that of their parents or of mainstream society. Hip-hop provided an off-the-peg identity which encompassed the individual (performance), the collective (the 'posse') and founding myths and community values.[17]

Sporadic outbreaks of violence in the *banlieue*, although not quite on the scale of those which marked this period in Great Britain, saw young people from working-class areas and under-privileged neighbourhoods in running battle with the police. In some cases, it was the neighbourhood sociocultural clubs themselves which were targeted,[18] demonstrating the gulf now separating the community youth workers from their young audience.

Missed opportunities for the integration of working class and ethnic minority youth in the 1980s and 1990s

The beginning of the 1980s was marked by these violent episodes in the *banlieue*, often sparked off by confrontations with the police (for example the *'été chaud'* on the Minguettes estate in Vénissieux near Lyon). In a reaction to the absence of job prospects, reinforced by a feeling of both social and cultural exclusion, many young people – especially those of Maghrebi immigrant descent – formed loose associations. France witnessed the rise of an informal movement led by these young second-generation Maghrebi immigrants, termed 'the Beur generation'. The movement mixed demands for social change and cultural advancement with political consciousness raising. This movement might have had a specific ethnic

17. For details of the development and diversity of hip-hop in France, see H. Bazin, *La Culture Hip-hop*, Paris, Desclée de Brouwer, 1995. For the importance of hip-hop to young people from immigrant and marginal communities, see C. Warne, 'Articulating identity from the margins: le Mouv' and the rise of hip-hop and ragga in France'. In *Voices of France: social, political and cultural identity*. Eds S. Perry and M. Cross, London, Cassell, 1997. For the significance of tagging and new urban myths in French society, see A. Vulbeau, *Du tag au tag*, Paris, Desclée de Brouwer, 1992.

18. See C. Bachmann, *Violences urbaines: ascension et déclin des classes moyennes à travers 50 ans de politiques de la ville*, Paris, Fayard, 1996 and F. Dubet, *La Galère: jeunes en survie*, Paris, Fayard, 1987.

focus, but it did not follow the existing community structures. That is to say, its relational and cultural practices differed from those put in place by specific ethnic communities. Indeed, the main manifestations of this movement, the 'March for Equality' in 1983 which first brought it to public attention and *Convergence 1984*, were founded on the desire for equal treatment rather than for the recognition of any distinct community agenda. The accent was on highlighting the situation of young immigrants in France in general, rather than the promotion of any specific community or inherited identities. As a result, a distinct hybrid Franco-immigrant identity began to emerge whereas prior to this, only two administrative categories had been recognised: French or foreigner.

Even though the leaders of the March for Equality were invited to the Elysée Palace by President Mitterrand, public authorities very quickly dismissed these new voices as too disparate and rather 'untrustworthy'. They preferred instead to deal with the organisation *SOS Racisme*, created in 1984 and which reflected the emerging awareness in urban middle-class youth of anti-racist and universalist issues, in the face of the rise of the National Front. This strategic choice was also politically motivated. Public authorities favoured centralised negotiations with this media-friendly national organisation which highlighted its altruism (i.e., of the native-born vis à vis immigrants)[19] rather than cooperating with locally-based associations. The latter were often short-lived and found it difficult to federate, making negotiations conflictual and less media-worthy. Local councillors seemed to have focused their efforts on identifying potential leaders who could represent the communities and youth from peripheral housing estates, rather than attempting to work alongside the existing cultural or socio-cultural associations which were condemned as no longer being representative of their community.

The young populations on the estates, especially those of immigrant descent, found themselves in deadlock. With their internecine quarrels, the reticence of the public authorities, and lack of common ground or message, the movements of the early 1980s failed both to organise themselves into a coherent Beur cultural movement and to find a mouthpiece for the articulation of their social demands. It is this which can be understood as a 'missed opportunity'. A period of repressed anger ensued, which

19. The movement's slogan *'Touche pas à mon pote'* (Hands off my mate), bears witness to this stance.

sometimes bubbled up to the surface with destructive consequences. It was at this time that François Dubet and his team
undertook the research published under the emblematic title 'La
Galère' (punishment).[20] It was also during the late 1980s that hip-
hop first made it onto French television, along with some of the
youngsters from the estates themselves. This was only a fleeting
appearance on a programme which lasted for under a year, but the
effect was catalytic.[21]

Hip-hop: an ambiguous recognition

The late 1980s saw the spread of hip-hop culture in France, with its
different components taking their turn to come to the fore: DJ-ing,
dance, tagging, rap, etc. This wider diffusion of hip-hop culture
was accompanied by a new public recognition which took it far
beyond its usual audience and sphere of influence. From its beginnings as the latest imported fad, it was by now the symbolic cultural expression representing the banlieue, and was even
considered as an art form in its own right. 'Street culture: in
France, the only art that matters'; so wrote Newsweek of French
hip-hop, almost a decade later.[22]

This period was marked by a parallel extension of the concept of
culture itself on the part of the state, to take in new urban cultural
practices. This move was anticipated by the Minister of Culture
himself, as Jack Lang pushed publicly for the recognition of hip-
hop. Tags and graffiti found their way into art galleries and museums, and the recognition of hip-hop culture became a means of
showing that youth aspirations were not being ignored. The
implicit aim of this extension of state cultural policy was to promote
political and social integration of banlieue and immigrant youth.

Thus cultural recognition was the instrument of social integration. However, this recognition was inconsistent and not backed

20. F. Dubet, La Galère: jeunes en survie, Paris, Fayard, 1987.
21. This was a programme fronted by Sydney (who had previously broadcast on
the aforementioned Radio 7) who went on to present a TFI television programme
called HIP-HOP between 1984 and 1985. This show centred on dance, above all acting as a showcase for dance demonstrations by youngsters from the banlieue
estates.
22. Newsweek, 26 February 1996. The cover of the European edition carried a shot
of MC Solaar got up in a gangsta rap look for the occasion – a 'hard' image not normally associated with him – pictured against the Louvre pyramid.

by clear, comprehensive policy initiatives. Therefore they had little effect. The selective nature of this recognition, allowing some street artists to display in museums or to accede to the contemporary art scene, was always either part of a logic of absolute cultural relativism, or part of the cultural establishment's dalliance with popular culture.[23] In both cases, the subversive energy of these new forms was neutralised. In the first case, it was lost in the total lack of distinction between cultural practices, works of art and consumer objects. In the second, it evaporated as its creators were suddenly elevated to the status of artist, detached from the environment which had informed their work and given it its sense. Similarly, no genuine public policy destined to help fund production or diffusion was forthcoming. Rather, a few one-off, short-term initiatives were supported here and there: help in setting up an event or funding given to a specific creative group. A large majority of community workers and managers in neighbourhood centres, coming from the rock generation themselves, were to take several years to open up their space to these new forms of cultural expression. The possibilities for dialogue remained few and far between.[24]

Given the situation related above, it is necessary to reflect upon the nature of this recognition of urban cultures and the way in which those responsible for social and cultural policies sought to legitimise practices in order to aid the social and cultural integration of the populations which had generated them. For the inept application of the initiatives shows how these decision-makers often found it difficult to move beyond the ethnocentric logic in which they were bound. This incapacity sometimes had negative results for their targeted audience.[25] Museums ran exhibitions of tags, street art and graffiti, hip-hop dancers were invited to perform at contemporary dance festivals (the *Biennale de la Danse* in Lyon, *Montpellier Danse*, the Chateauvallon Festival or *Suresnes*

23. See the analysis of V. Bubois, with reference to tagging, particularly 'Action culturelle / action sociale – Les limites d'une frontière', *Revue Française des Affaires Sociales*, no.2, 48th year, April–June 1994.

24. I am thinking mainly of the *Maisons des Jeunes et de la Culture* (MJC) or more recent ventures such as *cafés-musiques*. The way in which these centres are run and programme their events, as well as the cultural background of the staff, means that they find it difficult to cope with the unruly and irregular nature of these emerging new urban cultural practices.

25. V. Dubois, 'Action culturelle / action sociale – Les limites d'une frontière', *Revue Française des Affaires Sociales*, no.2, 48th year, April–June 1994.

Cité Danse) and rap was seized upon by cultural commentators even before it had moved into the mainstream of French society.[26]

The social impact and the cultural significance of these initiatives need to be called into question. One could conclude that they amount to forced attempts to legitimise these social practices by making them fit into the traditional categories of legitimisation, which are assigned to popular or foreign culture by the state or the dominant social classes. Of course, it is very affirming for young people who are looking for a way out of the non-spaces (*non-lieux*) they generally have to occupy to be given access to galleries and to the contemporary cultural scene. This confers professionalism upon them, if one can call such a precarious activity a profession. In addition to this, the acculturation which results from confronting those outside their culture all plays its part in turning the young people involved into autonomous subjects, rather in the manner of the *tiers-instruit* described by Michel Serres.[27] On the other hand, this process of integration and *adobement* ('be-knighting')[28] as established by the agencies of state policy, effectively removes the cultural practices from the context which produced them and for which they represented a new form of social expression.

In the case of young hip-hop dancers, the elevation to the world of professional modern dance led to difficulties in finding their own niche: such a trajectory could lead to them leaving hip-hop behind and re-positioning themselves as part of a new cultural and professional perspective. However, it could also lead to a loss of bearings and of dynamic, as they lost sight of their initial motive of social commitment. Some of the young practitioners held back from mainstream cultural recognition, probably not because they were afraid of 'selling their souls', rather because they feared losing the respect of their peers. Moving into the mainstream also meant adopting a certain acclutured language: often, the strictures of producing a dance piece for general consumption meant having to work within a new choreographical language, which, even if the hip-hop alphabet was still present, could be incomprehensible to its original audience. If the original audience

26. Althought dealing mainly with the scene in America, G. Lapassade's remarkable book, *Le Rap ou la fureur de dire*, Paris, Loris Talmart, 1990, written with P. Rousselot, does outline the adoption of French rap by intellectuals.

27. M. Serres, *Le Tiers-Instruit*, Paris, François Bourin Editeur, 1991.

28. V. Dubois, 'Action culturelle/action sociale – Les limites d'une frontière', *Revue Française des Affaires Sociales*, no.2, 48th year, April–June 1994.

cannot relate to the work, can the dancer still claim to represent hip-hop and street culture?[29]

Once its artists and creations became an integral part of a general promotional policy, urban culture became the focus of media attention and at the same time lost its voice. Even if rap established itself in the media as being 'without political connotations' and 'without local origins', very little was done, in return, to help these diverse forms of expression to establish themselves at local level with a legitimate discourse, or to provide the means for them to reach an audience who would be able to identify their own aspirations with those of the performers. For some, recognition *was* to be found in the media success of rappers, for example, or by being asked to set up dance classes in community and educational centres, which was to bring the role of the state and local authorities back into play. Teaching dance in these centres was a sign of adult, institutional recognition which probably would not have been afforded elsewhere. This recognition was sometimes seen by the dancers as compensation for the inertia they believed (rightly or wrongly) to characterise the attitude of the community centres and their workers, with whom they often felt they were in competition. It was also a sign of continued – or renewed – links with the younger population of the neighbourhood, who had sometimes been left out of developments. It showed a desire to put something back into local community life. It also showed increased professionalisation, for the dancer him/herself controlled part or all of the performance content. One constraint was that in taking on the role of teacher, the dancer had to stand alone and break with the informal collective relationships of the street. Some of them managed to do this, but others found it hard to function without the other members of their group or their friends, who joined the classes on the sly or might be found acting as teaching assistants from time to time. Another limitation was the lack of space or financial means given to those who organised the classes. For some, being given inadequate back rooms in which to operate was interpreted as a sign of the half-heartedness of the local authorities, rather than as a first step towards recognition. Being given space in neighbourhood community halls and drop-in centres was looked on as marginalisation rather than acceptance.

29. As a result, some companies such as *Käfig* or *Les Accro rap* always stress that they belong to the hip-hop movement, even though their choreography is not that of the street. However, the contemporary dance scene sees these companies as nothing other than hip-hop dancers.

We can see how the recognition of hip-hop was strictly controlled and highly ambiguous. It is against this back-drop, with urban cultures being in a vulnerable position, that the Ministry of Culture and its regional directorates, as well as local, departmental and regional authorities, have begun to think up experimental projects which take the urban space as their frame of reference.

Les projets culturels de quartier: recognition at last for new urban cultures?

After a period when it looked as if sociocultural projects had lost ground at local level, cultural projects with a social focus are today back in use on the large housing estates. One such example is the *projets culturels de quartier* (neighbourhood cultural projects), financed in part by the Ministry of Culture. Other examples followed in the wake of the *politique de la ville* such as the *'MOUC'* – *Maîtrises d'Oeuvre Urbaines et Culturelles* (contracts for the construction of cultural projects in urban areas) inspired by the *'MOUS'* – *Maîtrises d'Oeuvre Urbaines et Sociales* (social projects). In most cases, the set-up includes a variety of public partners who finance all or part of the project, and a range of service providers working together (artist / trainers, trainers / performers, etc.).[30] These projects are generally all motivated by the same objectives, explicitly or implicitly. They fall into two main categories: firstly, those which combine the goals of cultural production and the social integration of the participants. Secondly, those aiming solely to reinforce or encourage social cohesion at a local level.

Both of these types can themselves be classified according to three distinct approaches. For projects focused on cultural production and social integration, we find firstly a category having the professional mobilisation and social reinsertion of the participants as objectives. These participants generally have no secure employment or are marginalised in some way: unqualified school-leavers, those receiving supplementary benefit (*'RMIstes'*), or the long-term unemployed. In these cases, the cultural or artistic activity offered is merely a medium or pretext, often used in con-

30. This could be the preparation of an event bringing together professional artists and young unemployed, or the creation of artists' residencies, whereby a professional artist will work for several weeks training youngsters towards an event which will show off their newly-learnt talents. In most cases, music, drama or dance are the focus of these events, rather than an exhibition of artwork.

nection with a specific social operation (back-to-work or job-seeker training) run by another agency. Secondly, there is a category of projects leading to the participants gaining new qualifications in the field of the performance arts, which could open up secure employment. In these cases, the cultural or artistic nature of the project is an integral part of the training process, which may or may not be run by an outside agency. The participants probably do not have any specific qualifications at the outset, but are motivated to attend due to their interest in the specific training on offer. Thirdly, we can distinguish activities enabling the participants to gain a professional qualification in a particular artistic or cultural domain, or to reinforce any professional qualification they may already have. In these cases, the training is an integral part of the artistic process. Those attending might not have yet secured full-time employment, but will have basic qualifications at the outset.

For projects focused on encouraging social cohesion at a local level, there are firstly programmes aimed at promoting or revitalising local social activity. In these cases, the local population is both an actor in and a target audience for any artistic or cultural project. The reasoning here is that this will stimulate networking, dialogue and social exchanges. Secondly there are programmes aimed at promoting local amateur activities (be they new urban cultures or not). The aim here is to 'showcase' a specific social group (young people, women, immigrant communities, etc.). Finally, other programmes aim to encourage local social and cultural development by establishing permanent networks or pilot bodies. Here the aim is to bring together a variety of different actors (associations, local councils, the regional cultural affairs directorate or any other sponsors).[31]

It is rare for any of these programmes to receive long-term financial backing as most are set up on an experimental basis. It is therefore difficult to evaluate their impact, and those evaluations which have been undertaken have been very half-hearted. Looking at the list of events which have received backing and the few serious evaluations undertaken,[32] it is apparent that for the most

31. This is my own typology, based on an analysis of projects listed by the *Direction du développement et de la formation* (Training and Development Directorate) of the Ministry of Culture in 1997.

32. Notably F. Darty, *Evaluation de l'action culturelle pour l' insertion et le développement du lien social mise en oeuvre par le Centre Culturel l'ESPAL, au Mans*, working document, FORS Recherche Sociale, 1996.

part cultural leverage is used to promote social insertion and cohesion, rather than for the support and legitimisation of urban culture. This approach has engendered some promising programmes which mix various artistic and cultural activities, but they remain few and far between: there have only been a few projects directly inspired by hip-hop culture, while others blend theatrical arts and circus skills to limited effect and do not give rise to new cultural practices. Moreover, even though local communities may well be involved in cultural productions as actor and audience, more often than not, they will be invited to work to an imposed theme, rather than to set the agenda themselves. Local areas are rarely apprehended in their community dimension or as the arena for the articulation of a specific urban culture, be this hip-hop or any other form of expression. Here one could mention the widespread use of street furniture inspired by contemporary art which bears little relation to the specific urban space.

However, by working at a neighbourhood level, state-inspired cultural initiatives can give rise to new interactions which are both cultural and social. Yet so far it would appear that the institutionalised cultural action has done nothing more than find a new space to legitimise its own initiatives. It invests itself with a social function without questioning the pertinence of this role, without thinking about the form and method which would best allow new urban groups – the young, those on the margins – to participate on their own terms. With projects which turn districts in on themselves rather than towards larger horizons, and with a cultural remit which neutralises initiative just as much as legitimising it, the scope of public initiatives aimed at urban cultures appears to be very limited indeed. At present it would seem that there is no will to widen this scope: the dominant cultural institutions' infatuation with hip-hop appears to have been short-lived, and there seems to be no initiative to revisit the question of urban cultures.

Today, market forces rule in this whole area. The music industry has seen what money there is to be made from the rap scene, but it is not certain that the young rappers will necessarily benefit. What is quite clear is that insofar as urban cultures are concerned, public cultural institutions have now been written out of the equation. Rap has become a consumer product, with *le street wear* beloved of rappers now appearing in all the high-street stores and so-called rap magazines, which are little more than advertising opportunities, running into double figures. This is without doubt a kind of recognition, but one devoid of the underlying social dynamic of urban cultures and which sidelines their questioning of the ownership of urban public space. Only dance has managed to avoid this fate through the backing it has been given by the public sector, but even here the initial dynamic is faltering and younger generations of dancers are not being produced. One can but wonder whether public sector cultural policies at national or local level will ever again turn their attention to urban cultures. If they do, it will probably be once the industry has lost interest in the current generation of rappers and when hip-hop dance has lost its edge, but will this not be too little, too late?

14

THE MEAN(ING OF THE) STREETS:

Reading Urban Cultures in Contemporary France

Chris Warne

Cities, and capital cities in particular, are clearly the central focus for national memory. At the centre of such memory is the manner in which the city space is captured in the shorthand of symbol or mental representation. For example, the city of Paris is most easily represented by certain of the monuments that define its central space, or possibly by less monumental buildings that nonetheless capture the flavour and atmosphere of a particular quarter or *arrondissement* (administrative district), made familiar to the intended target of that representation by repeated itineraries and wanderings. Yet this double vision of the city, whether it be the structured monumental centre to inspire awe and civic pride in visitors or inhabitants, or the sort of village-in-a-town local community, sustained by rooted networks of human interaction is, essentially, a nineteenth-century vision of the city. It neglects, perhaps deliberately, both recent and long-term developments in the pattern of the city's mutation. Without question, the major modification of Paris and France's major urban centres since at least the 1930s has not been the erection of impressive monuments or the rehabilitation for the benefit of the heritage industry of once derelict inner city areas, but the massive and phenomenal growth of its suburbs and 'periurban' areas. Such developments would at first sight seem only to reinforce the importance of the monumental elements of the urban landscape: an immediate relationship is created between city and suburbs of periphery and centre, the latter becoming the hub of all journeys, even of those displacements where the centre is not the eventual destination. The structure of public transport routes in France reflects this essentially centrifugal pattern. However, as the peripheral sprawl continues to grow, this balance of dominant centre and subordinate periphery comes increasingly into question. Indeed, some observers contend that this model of suburban, peripheral development has now been extended to the whole of France. The national landscape itself has been transformed. Where once could be found the clustered local communities of *la France profonde* (timeless, rural France), a more transitory and transitional space exists. To quote the historian Dominique Borne in his assessment of France at the end of the twentieth century:

> La géographie de la France elle-même, dans sa variante up to date, ne décrit plus la 'personnalité des terroirs', comme au temps de Vidal de la Blache, mais les flux, la circulation des hommes, des marchandises, voire des capitaux. Entre les zones urbaines ou péri-urbaines, où, au recensement de 1990, habitent 85% des Français, ne subsistent que des espaces de transit. (France's geography itself, in its up to date version, no longer reflects the varied personality of a locality, as in Vidal de la Blache's time, but rather the flows, the movement of people, goods and indeed, capital. Between the urban and suburban areas where, according to the 1990 census, 85% of the French live, there exists only transitory spaces.)[1]

As a consequence of such changes, more and more the question arises of just what it is that fills these in-between spaces, these lines of transit that link traditional centres of human commerce and interaction. Are they a mere void, blank canvases, ignored and overlooked by town planners and architects in their concern to maximise the circulation of people and goods? If nature abhors a vacuum, what of human society: would it tolerate the presence of such voids?

If the physical landscape of contemporary France has been marked by the appearance of in-between, transitory space, then it is possible to observe an analogous process taking place in the lives of its citizens. In this case, the transitory is experienced by increasing numbers of the young as they make the prolonged move from adolescence to adulthood. Sociologists of youth such as Olivier Galland[2]

1. D. Borne, *Histoire de la société française depuis 1945*, Paris, Armand Colin, 3rd ed., 1993, p.176.
2. O. Galland's extensive work on this phenomenon includes 'Un nouvel âge de la vie', *Devenir adulte, Revue française de sociologie*. XXXI, 4, oct–dec. 1990, pp529–51; *Sociologie de la jeunesse: l'entrée dans la vie*. Paris, Armand Colin, 1991; 'La jeunesse en France, un nouvel âge de la vie'. In *L'Allongement de la jeunesse*. Eds A. Cavalli and O. Galland, Poitiers, Actes Sud, 1993, pp19–39.

and Jean-Claude Chamboredon [3] describe an increasing *allongement de la jeunesse* (prolonging of youth). If socialisation is conceived of as a process of establishing long-term and autonomous identities both in the private sphere of family and domestic relationships, and in the public sphere of work or civic duties, then several factors are combining to produce a relatively new experience of extended transition from the dependence of childhood to the independence of adulthood: the extension of education, both to a greater number, and in terms of the time spent being educated; the extension of a period of trial and error in sexual and social relationships, before settling on a longer term partnership that might lead to the founding of a new family; the growing tendency of the young to respond to high structural unemployment and a devaluation of their hard-won qualifications by the strategy of staying longer in the parental home; the disappearance of traditional, settled work patterns particularly associated with forms of industrial labour that once guaranteed a job for life; the modifications in the roles ascribed to the sexes and the changes in expectation and ambition associated with this, particularly for younger women; the growing number of young people unable or unwilling to emulate the professional trajectories of their parents. All these various factors have produced a significantly different context that allows us to distinguish the experience of a generation of young people from that of their predecessors. For some, with the cultural and financial capital of their social background, this prolonged transitional experience is a time to experiment socially and professionally, an opportunity to travel more widely, or maybe to retrain or re-enter education. For those lacking in such resources, the experience may be more endured than enjoyed, a perpetuation into the public realm of the dependencies experienced in a disadvantaged upbringing. In either case, situations can arise where a certain virtue is made out of necessity. Rather than settling immediately into the established patterns of adulthood, the young are increasingly exploiting this transitional phase as an opportunity to establish new cultural and social modes of behaviour, thus further enhancing the generational distinction drawn above. [4] It is at this

---

3. For Chamboredon's slightly different perspective, see his 'Adolescence et post-adolescence: la "juvénisation". Remarques sur les transformations récentes des limites de la définition sociale de la jeunesse'. In *Adolescence terminée, adolescence interminable*. Eds A. M. Alléon, O. Morvan and S. Lebovici , Paris, Presses Universitaires de France, 1985, pp13–28.

4. The existence of this generational distinction should not be taken as a sign that youth can be read as a simple homogenous social category. While the context of the move from adolescence to adulthood may be similar, clearly, the different social

point that the in-between spaces of the city intersect with the transitional phases of biographical trajectory. In her study of young people and their social interactions in Lyons, the sociologist Laurence Roulleau-Berger[5] has observed a process whereby far from responding passively to a situation where the established social fabric seems to be eroding, certain groups are actively reinvesting the urban landscape with new patterns of use, culture and contact. For Roulleau-Berger, these groups, and particularly those who invest their time in sociocultural projects (the creation of an art collective, the founding of an independent bookshop or record store, the publication of a local magazine or newspaper, the organisation of concerts, club nights and festivals) are embracing the experience of what she calls *la ville intervalle* (the in-between city). Frequently, the site of such activity is precisely those spaces evacuated by the disappearing organisations that apparently gave such permanence to the perpetuation of social structures across the generations (abandoned warehouses or industrial quarters, empty churches or civic buildings), areas she defines as *espaces de transition culturels* (spaces of cultural transition).[6] Having been obliged to occupy the in-between spaces, both physical and temporal, the young are responding with the development of cultures that both make sense of and give positive value to the intersticial, the transitory, the suburban.

resources and cultural capital available to groups and individuals will tend to maintain, perhaps even exacerbate existing social, economic and gender differences within this new context. In that regard, it remains the norm for French sociologists to talk of *les jeunesses* (youth in the plural), rather than *la jeunesse* (youth in the singular), e.g., R. Boyer and C. Coridian (eds), *Jeunesses d'en France*. Condé-sur-Noireau, Panoramiques-Corlet, 1994; F. Dubet, 'Jeunesses et marginalités', *Regards sur l'actualité*, 172, juillet 1991, pp3–9; C. Baudelot and G. Mauger (eds), *Jeunesses populaires: les générations de la crise*, Paris, L'Harmattan, 1994. This heterogeneity of youth is also observable when it comes to the analysis of youth cultures, which in France at least, have increasingly reflected this diversity and plurality, both in their geographical and their social variation. In this respect, hip-hop represents just one of many French youth cultures. Indeed, given the prolonging of youth described by sociologists such as Chamboredon and Galland, where the clearly defined boundary between adolescence and young adulthood is becoming increasingly blurred, it is perhaps more appropriate to discuss hip-hop as one of many *urban* cultures, maintaining a long-term presence in the contemporary city, rather than as an age-specific culture that passes when its adherents cease to be young.

5. See her: 'Des microcultures et des jeunesses au centre et à la périphérie de l'espace urbain'. In *La Culture des jeunes de banlieues*, Document de l'INJ (4), October 1989, pp33–9; *La Ville intervalle: jeunes entre centre et banlieue*, Paris, Méridiens-Klincksieck, 1991; 'Cultures et danses urbaines'. In *Danse ville danse*, Vénissieux, Préfecture de la Région Rhône-Alpes, Éditions Paroles d'Aube, 1992, pp8–9.

6. L. Rouleau-Berger, *La Ville intervalle: jeunes entre centre et banlieue*, Paris, Méridiens-Klincksieck, 1991, p.12.

Given this fundamental change in the geographical and bio-graphical space in which France's younger citizens move, it is therefore not so surprising that the last two decades have seen the emergence of a form of urban culture that not only bears a direct relationship to the in-between spaces described above, but seeks to actively invest them with presence, meaning and activity. In this regard, the development of a distinctive and vibrant hip-hop scene in France has been perhaps one of the major features of suburban culture in the period, an importance testified to by the increasing interest shown in hip-hop by sociologists, social animators and official cultural bodies (see François Ménard's account of this growing interest in Chapter 11). As an urban culture, it encom-passes a variety of social and artistic practices, each with their own highly developed styles and codes: specific and stylised forms of dance (break, body-popping, electric boogie); elaborate and eye-catching wall and fresco art; the practice of repeatedly marking a personalised signature or logo on walls, and blank spaces of pub-lic transport vehicles (tagging); and rap, the part of hip-hop culture that has perhaps received the most attention, a form of verbal declamation against a rhythmical and musical soundtrack pro-vided by a DJ, enhanced by the techniques of mixing, scratching and cutting together different sound sources and events.

Now clearly, the recent emergence of hip-hop in France has much to do with the commercial processes of pop culture and the multinational music industry.[7] It has also been welcomed by some

---

7. The more recent sustained commercial success since the mid-1990s of French hip-hop, and of certain rap groups and artists in particular, brings this question of French rap as a market commodity to the fore. Of central interest is the question of hip-hop's relationship to a wider audience, the majority of which certainly finds itself a long way from the socially excluded suburbs that constituted the principal (but not exclusive) origins of hip-hop culture in France. How does this newer, wider audience relate to, or consume hip-hop? Is part of its appeal to do with the con-sumption of exotic difference, a perhaps facile identification with the revolt of a dis-affected youthful underclass? Or is it the more acceptable aspects of French hip-hop (its stress on education, its anti-racist, anti-drugs outlook, its commitment to mutual support within a close-knit social group) which have secured its spread to the main-stream of French pop culture? While I would not deny the pertinence of such ques-tions, my focus for the purposes of this chapter is on the origins of hip-hop culture in France, which have shaped its fundamental character, especially in its particular relationship to a shifting urban context. At the centre of these origins is what might be termed an active minority, for whom hip-hop and its various practices have rep-resented a distinct social outlook and a distinct set of social possibilities. The role of this group in the shaping of hip-hop in France is such that any consideration of it extends beyond questions of consumer choice in the marketplace.

in official circles as a potential reinvigoration of France's beleaguered traditions of chanson, or as a means of assuring the continued flowering of Francophonie. However, hip-hop in France is
more than just the sum of its relationship to either the influences
of commerce or those of the state. There was undoubtedly during
the early 1980s an initial period of fashionable focus on hip-hop,
and on the forms of hip-hop dance in particular, referred to in
France as *la vague smurf* (the smurf wave) and inspired by a curios-
ity for the latest in a succession of pop cultures to emerge from
America in general and New York in particular.[8] This interest was
sustained by an ultimately unsuccessful tour in 1984 of leading
American hip-hop practitioners (graffiti artists, rappers, break-
dancers), and by a weekly Sunday broadcast on the national television station TF1, hosted by the club DJ Sydney, which featured
both home-grown and American talent. By means of the competitions and talent contests that featured on this programme, many
French artists gained their first taste of exposure to a wider audience. However, the replacement of this programme within a year
by a broader based music magazine, indicates that for many
working in the media, hip-hop had been no more than a fad, interesting enough, but short lived nonetheless. This was however, to
underestimate the impact of Sydney's broadcasts on a certain constituency that was to prove vital in the emergence of an indigenous French hip-hop culture, and this for two reasons. Firstly, the
broadcast itself provided a medium for young dancers, artists and
musicians: while it ran, the studios at TF1 on a Sunday morning
became the meeting place where contacts were made, ideas
exchanged, projects planned and links established between previously unconnected parts of the Paris suburbs. Secondly, the programme acted as an important means of identification for a social
group previously under-represented in the French media. Numerous movers on the current hip-hop scene refer to the revelation
that Sydney's broadcast represented for them. For the first time,
they were seeing themselves, or people very much like themselves, on television. The impact that this had on a young, multi-
ethnic population growing up in France's suburbs should not be
underestimated. It signified a whole new range of possibilities,
but above all that movement out of the restraints of the local quarter or housing estate was possible, particularly when articulated

8. S. Cannon, 'Paname City Rapping: B-boys in the banlieues and beyond'. In
Post-Colonial Cultures in France. Eds A. G. Hargreaves and M. McKinney, London
and New York, Routledge, 1997, p.152.

by this new and exciting culture. If by the mid-1980s, the media outlets of television, music press and radio were now closed to hip-hop, a network of inspired and committed individuals had been created. Thus for a crucial period in its development, French hip-hop has grown at the edges of media and institutional space. While initially introduced 'from above' and 'from outside', the most vital period of its growth has been 'from below'.

Given that the conventional public spaces of media or national institutions were closed to French hip-hop, it is not surprising that in its growth and development it should occupy the only other spaces left to it. In other words, French hip-hop has insinuated itself into those very same in-between spaces that have been the striking feature of urban development in this century. Such insinuation is symbolised by certain sites that have become central in the mythology of French hip-hop, particularly in Paris. Referred to significantly as *terrains vagues* (wasteground, but literally 'indistinct areas'), these are derelict patches of the city, such as that at the Porte de La Chapelle or near the bus station at Stalingrad, bordered by criss-crossing metro and RER lines.[9] Empty walls or arches provided the perfect canvas for graffiti art and tags. The concrete floors of ex-warehouses could be turned into dance floors by the simple expediency of laying down flattened-out cardboard boxes. Even the electricity needed to power turntables and a PA system could be pirated from nearby lighting junction boxes. Above all, if only initially, these places existed beyond the inquisitive gaze of the forces of law and order. In the cases where the police did show an interest in stopping the perceived threat to public order posed by the impromptu gathering of in-comers from the suburbs (the RATP was by the late 1980s spending significant sums on anti-graffiti operations, and tagging had been identified by Chirac in his capacity as mayor of Paris as a considerable social menace),[10] such territories by their very lack of distinct borders, offered several ideal escape routes.

If certain specific sites have become central in the mythology and collective memory of French hip-hop, as the culture has developed its particular form in France, there has emerged a more generalised meaning ascribed to the in-between spaces of the con-

9. O. Cachin, *L'Offensive rap*, Paris, Gallimard, 1996, p.68.

10. F. Chenoune and J.-F. Poirier, 'Rap et tag: l'esthétique des banlieues sur la place publique' in Encyclopaedia Universalis, *Universalia 1993*, Paris, Encyclopaedia Universalis, 1993, p.349; A. Vulbeau, *Du Tag au tag*, Paris, Desclée de Brouwer, 1992, pp46–9.

temporary urban landscape. In other words, the physical spaces and sites that saw the development of localised hip-hop practices (Parisian youngsters emulating what they knew of the American scene in general, and the New York one in particular), became slowly transformed into a social space, even a sociological one. A self-designated, nation-wide collective (referred to by its members as *Le Mouv'*, short for *Le Mouvement* (The Movement)) began to coalesce around the identification with a certain set of social practices (rap, tag, graff, dance), each having a specific relationship to the urban environment in which they are exercised. This transition from physical to sociological space is vital in that it allowed individuals who identified with the expanding group to participate in the memory attached to specific sites, without necessarily having been there 'back in the day', or even having ever been to the location at all.

At the heart of this identification with an emerging sociological space is the use of *la rue* (the street) as the bearer of a certain set of values, as an explanation for the origins of the culture, and as an indicator of the destiny and purposes of hip-hop. Running through the discourses of French hip-hop is what the sociologist Hugues Bazin has called a 'meta-street',[11] a kind of guiding narrative or framework that gives shape and significance to an otherwise potentially random life-experience. In representing what is essentially a transitional and interstitial space, this 'meta-street' is itself transitory, even unstable, uncertain as a bearer of meaning. While clearly metonymical in the sense that one street appears to stand both for the whole of a culture and for all streets in all cities everywhere, 'the street' is also polyvalent. Its flexibility lies in the fact that it has immediate and common meaning for those involved in the culture, it becomes the shorthand for things which can remain unspoken, and yet it also permits the insertion of highly subjective and highly personalised experienced within its overall framework. It is not just *la rue* (the street) but *ma rue* (my street). This is a vital injection of the local and personal into what otherwise threatens to be the anonymous and mass-produced streets of suburban planning. Not only do all *banlieues* (suburbs) look the same, but in their portrayal in the French media in the last decade or so, they would appear to be suffering from the same litany of social problems: high crime rates, problems of drug abuse and prostitution, high rates of

11. H. Bazin, *La Culture hip-hop*, Paris, Desclée de Brouwer, 1995, pp39–44.

unemployment and educational drop-out, and higher propor-
tions of ethnic minority groups among their inhabitants. In contrast to this universalised picture of general undifferentiated
misery, many French rap artists and groups proudly assert and
identify their local and specific origins (e.g., 93 NTM, from Seine-
Saint-Denis). Indeed, tracking the origins of many of the better
known Parisian rap and hip-hop artists begins to resemble the
route map of the RER. Doc Gyneco (from the *18e arrondissement*
in Paris) encapsulates such local civic pride in his 1996 song
'Dans ma rue (On my street)' from the album *Première Consultation* (First Consultation). An ironic description of some of the
problems associated with his district (youth delinquency and
violence, inter-ethnic tensions, drugs – even the pigeons die from
scavenging from the discarded syringes of heroin users), is inter-
spersed with the chorus/reflection 'Mais qu'est-ce que tu veux,
à chacun sa banlieue. La mienne, je l'aime et elle s'appelle le dix-
huitième (But what can you do, everyone has their own version
of the suburbs. Mine is the 18th and I like it)'. It is noteworthy of
course that the *18e arrondissement* is not technically part of the
suburbs anyway, as it is strictly Paris *intra muros* (within the old
city walls). However, as Doc Gyneco highlights, all centres have
their peripheries, and even within the centre itself, there exists
the unequal relationship of inside and outside (in this case
between Paris' more glamorous areas and the less well-endowed
arrondissements in the northern part of the city). Thus, at one level
the song asserts the rapper's identification with the undifferentiated *banlieue* and its populations, even though his street is not
found in the suburb as conventionally defined. On the other
hand, to equate part of central Paris with *la banlieue* is also to
undermine the cliché as to what the latter represents, and begins
to reassert local difference, to challenge an anonymous portrayal
of social deprivation that ultimately fails to connect with the
human realities of the problem.

It is clear then that the street forms a vital focus for both the
collective memory and the personal myths that are articulated
in French hip-hop culture. More specifically though, what are
some of the various meanings that are ascribed to *la rue*, what
different roles does it play in terms of making sense of and giving permanence to the transitory and unstable? At least four distinct meanings can be identified, a list which is undoubtedly far
from exhaustive, but which will serve as a reflection on
the wider meanings of urban culture in contemporary

France.[12] These meanings are the street as danger, the street as an education, the street as a theatre, the street as an alibi, and each will be examined in turn. It is important to note however, that these meanings are underpinned and held together by a more fundamental one, namely that the street acts as a guarantor of personal and social authenticity, and thus as a yardstick against which groups or individuals and the worth of their actions can be judged. As I will finally argue, it is precisely at this point that the significance of hip-hop as a specifically French urban culture can be understood.

The street is dangerous

A recurring motif in the discourses of French hip-hop is that the street is a dangerous place. It holds many menaces and traps for the unwary: the easy thrill of hard drugs, the temptations of the quick road to material success and prosperity through crime, the threat posed by a rival seeking to usurp your own established status on the street. On the whole, there is running through French hip-hop a condemnation of those who settle for the easy option, who make a false impression through the flashy clothes they wear or the car that they drive. For those aspiring to authentic mastery of the street through adherence to hip-hop values, such markers are condemned as at best superficial, at worst potentially misleading, offering no substitute for the real education of years spent living and surviving on the street (see 'The street as education' below).[13] Increasingly, as the first and second generation of hip-

12. These four meanings (and the one that underpins them all) have been established from a wide reading of the texts of French hip-hop culture (songs, interviews with artists and practitioners, analyses of public performance), from personal contact with the scene itself (interviews/observation, DJ-ing), and from reflection on the work of French sociologists and ethnologists who have also studied hip-hop in France, particularly the work of Hugues Bazin and François Ménard.

13. This condemnation of easy material gain is not, a few exceptions aside, a manifesto for asceticism or a condemnation of materialism per se. Indeed, those very same groups and artists frequently celebrate the iconic status of certain marks and brand names in their work (e.g., Suprême NTM *'Ma Benz'* from their eponymous 1998 album, a raunchy, even priapic, celebration of the sexual potency imbued via the ownership of a Mercedes). The point is that in the eyes of the authentic hip-hop practitioner, the acquisition of particular items (brands of clothing, cars) should be seen as the deserved rewards for years of hard work spent mastering the street values and skills of hip-hop.

hop practitioners reach greater maturity, fears are expressed about the fate of younger siblings or children growing up in such a dangerous environment, without the necessary fixed points or knowledge of longer standing cultural traditions to negotiate it. Even amongst those who portray themselves as the most 'hardcore' and anti-system in their adherence to the central values of hip-hop, a certain wistful tone has developed in which the rapper casts him or herself as having gained the fruit of experience which he or she now seeks to pass on to younger successors who lack the necessary fixed points to negotiate a materialistic and corrupt world (e.g., NTM's *'Laisse pas trainer ton fils* (Don't let your son go astray)' from their 1998 album *Suprême NTM*, or Stré Strausz' *'Plus d'idéal* (No more ideals)' from the 1996 compilation *Hostile*).

In general, this theme of the dangers of the street has been articulated in two distinct ways. One is in the recurring use of the image of the *galère* (hardship/imprisonment – literally a prison ship), a theme particularly prominent in the earlier days of hip-hop in France, and picked up by the sociologist Francois Dubet[14] to characterise the experience of growing up on France's socially deprived outer-city housing estates. The *galère* has two features: firstly, it represents the fact that the individual has been condemned, sentenced by others to an almost subhuman existence of restriction and narrowed horizons, trapped in the concrete walls of the *cité* (housing estate), channelled into a future of no employment, forced to resort to illegality and criminality for the sake of survival. The result is an inevitable if unfocused rage against those held responsible for the passing of the sentence: politicians, the state, the system. However, there is a second side to the *galère*: there are those who adopt the identity of the galley slave almost willingly. From being a stigma, it becomes a badge to be worn, particularly for those who succeed in transcending the restrictions of *la galère* by the energies gained from participation in the hip-hop movement: if they have got where they are, it is all the more remarkable given where they start from. The achievement is testimony to the hard work necessary to escape the traps of one's social origins. Furthermore, the badge of *galérien* (galley slave, but more generally one who survives the experience) allows access to a kind of family, based on the shared experience of struggle in deprivation. Thus, the potentially destructive and dispersive effects of living on the street are contained, and trans-

14. F. Dubet, *La Galère: les jeunes en survie*, Paris, Seuil, 1987.

formed into the positive experience of belonging to a close-knit group or posse.[15]

The second distinct way in which the dangers of the street are articulated is in the often-repeated comparison of the street to a jungle. While reference to the asphalt or concrete jungle has perhaps become rather banal, in the context of its usage by young inhabitants of the multi-ethnic suburbs, it nonetheless retains a political charge. This is because such references deliberately and provocatively chime with the discourses of the right-wing National Front, and its allusions to the invasion of savage and uncontrollable hordes from the outside. Reference to the jungle in French hip-hop turns this discourse on its head: it adopts the stigma of savagery only to overturn it, to reinvest it with positive value and meaning. An example of this can be seen in the work of La Cliqua, a Paris group whose members originate from West Africa, France and Columbia. In the 1995 song '*Comme une sarbacane* (Like a blowpipe)' from the album *Conçu pour durer* ('designed to last'), the Columbian rapper Rocca proudly proclaims his origins:

> Né dans une jungle de sauvages et de liane, j'ai appris à manier le micro comme une sarbacane. (Born in the savage- and creeper-filled jungle, I've learnt to handle the mike like a blowpipe).

Here, the attributes of the savage are willingly adopted: if that is the identity prescribed (about which there seems to be little choice), then the rapper adopts the tools which that identity permits him or her. The tools may appear 'primitive', but they are deadly and effective nonetheless.

If the street is a jungle, the site of struggle for survival, a constantly dangerous environment, then it is above all for those for whom it is not the natural setting, that is all those who have not been decisively shaped by its testing environment. Often referred to rather indistinctly in the discourses of French hip-hop as *les bourges* (bourgeois), this 'other' would include citizens from the more affluent suburbs, officials and administrators from the distant city centre (the geographical distance symbolising an administrative and political order that is out of touch with street 'realities'), educators, journalists, transport workers, indeed any-

15. References to and acknowledgements of the peer-group recur frequently in the recorded output of rap artists. This is reinforced by long lists of personal dedications to friends and family as an obligatory part of the sleeve notes of album or single.

one whose power and authority stems from association with a space clearly (even legally) defined for its social use (office, TV studio, school, cultural and social centre, train or bus). However, the dangers posed by the street are particularly acute for those deemed to be the sole representatives of *les bourges* in the *banlieue*, the forces of the police. The controversy surrounding the Sarcelles group Ministère Amer and their 1995 song '*Sacrifice de poulet*' (Chicken-cop sacrifice) best encapsulated the manner of this threat. Released on the soundtrack album that accompanied Mathieu Kassowitz's film *La Haine* (Hatred – described by Kassowitz himself as an anti-police film in the run-up to its recognition at the 1995 Cannes festival), the film's notoriety guaranteed in turn a high exposure for the song. Its anti-police message and its apparent advocacy of violence against the forces of law and order led to the group being pursued in the courts by the National Police Federation and to criticism from the then Interior minister. However, the song is far from a simplistic anti-police rant. Like many rap songs, it conveys its rather indigestible message by the classic distancing technique of the rapper (in this case Stomy Bugsy) picturing himself as a split personality divided between the anarchic, devilish Stomy on the one hand, and the reasonable, rational Bugsy on the other. In extreme scenarios and under duress, it is the dark side of his adoptive personality that emerges. The rapper then recounts his or her reactions and diagnosis of this situation in the first person. The song picks up a similar scenario that starts the film *La Haine*, where a young man (Abdulaï) is the victim of heavy-handed policing. An angry crowd gathers, at the centre of which is the diabolical Stomy character, who is both instigator of and siphon for the crowd's growing anger. The characterisation of this central figure is such to play on all the unexpressed fears of the anonymous yet highly visible foreign outsider and stranger:

> Moi j'ai toute les caractéristiques du mauvais ethnique, antipathique, sadique, allergique aux flics, même dans la foule je porte la cagoule.
> (I have all the characteristics of the bad blackman, unpleasant, sadistic, allergic to cops, even in a crowd I wear a hood).

The crowd's anger will only be appeased by a blood sacrifice, in this case of a 'poulet', or police officer. Again, the sense of menace to *l' indigène* (the native French person) is redoubled by the obvious associations with voodoo, witch doctoring and black magic, which deliberately exploits the fear of the immigrant and their 'exotic' religious practices, fears that in the French context have been expressed in the urban myths that circulate regarding adherence to the dietary restrictions demanded by Islam, via colourful rumours of ritual sacrifice and gutters flowing with blood. As for the hip-hop practitioner, the role of the street here is to reveal the contradictory nature of the divided rapper, a division which he or she will inevitably seek to reconcile. If they can succeed in overcoming their dark side, the dangerous side of living in the streets can be seen to have a positive aspect. It can lead to a greater self-knowledge, to greater self-awareness, to a larger measure of self-control. For that to happen, the individual needs to become conscious, aware of the realities that govern life on the streets. In so doing, he or she is able to turn experience to advantage. The street becomes an education.

The street is an education

Two themes structure the manner in which the street is portrayed as an education for those forced to move in its harsh environment. If the street is dangerous, then ignorance of the dangers it throws up is fatal. However, many hip-hop artists advocate more than simple street cunning as a basis for a coherent and positive life-outlook. Instead, they call for greater knowledge, and urge their audiences to push themselves in the quest for self-improvement. Interviewed by José-Louis Bocquet and Philippe Pierre-Adolphe, the Parisian rapper Fabe explicitly outlined what he saw as the necessary link between successful living and a thirst for knowledge:

> Ton rap n'ira jamais plus loin que ton vécu, ou ce ne sera plus fiable, solide. Il faut que ton vécu avance toujours, il faut que tu t'instruises, que tu apprennes, que tu t'élèves…Moi, j'ai lu, j'ai voulu comprendre des choses, j'ai voulu m'instruire…Quand je rencontre des gens qui me demandent des conseils pour le rap, je dis: 'Lis.' Je compare souvent les livres et le rap. (Your rap will never progress further than what you live, or if it does it won't be reliable or solid. You must always progress in your life, you must instruct yourself, you must learn, you must bring yourself up…As for me, I have read, I've aimed to understand things, I've aimed to teach myself…Whenever I meet people who ask me for advice on rap, I say: 'Read'. I'm frequently drawing a link between books and rap).[16]

16. J.-L. Bocquet and P. Pierre-Adolphe, *Rap ta France,* Boulogne, La Sirène, 1996, p.195.

This intellectual strain running through French hip-hop is further exemplified by groups such as the Marseilles-based IAM, who inspired by the writings of the Africanist Cheik Anta Diop, repeatedly rehearse the origins of Western civilisation in black Africa in general and Egypt in particular. The group have elaborated a highly personalised mythology on the basis of this idea, in which references to pharaohs, pyramids and ancient religions are mixed with an anti-centralism based on Marseilles's otherness in relation to the rest of France, despite Parisian-inspired attempts to colonise it and bring it into line.[17] While evidently involving much irony and playfulness, this elaboration of an alternative history carries a political charge: in a climate where the extreme-right National Front is making advances in precisely those areas that IAM drew their initial support, the group are deliberately setting out to overturn the black-primitive couplet that underpins the racist fears on which the NF have capitalised. The battleground here is precisely that of the nature of collective memory, involving a struggle over whose interpretation of the past will prevail. According to IAM, the received ideas that they blame for maintaining the prevailing social injustices within French society, can only be combated and contradicted by a commitment to education and self-improvement.

However, in contrast to such calls for self-instruction and disciplined study, there also appears in much French hip-hop the notion that the street provides a wisdom that ultimately cannot be learnt in books. This theme occurs most frequently where there emerge issues of control over the culture's destiny. As one of the first academics in France to take a serious interest in hip-hop culture, Georges Lapassade[18] may have expected to be enthusiastically welcomed by those used to defending hip-hop against charges of encouraging vandalism, gang violence and the deculturation of the young, ethnically-mixed populations of France's suburbs. Having been introduced to hip-hop by some of his students at Université Paris VIII in Saint-Denis, in 1989 and 1990 Lapassade organised a series of festivals, workshops and courses,

17. For interviews with the group see J. Guerreiro, 'Rap like an Egyptian: Rap'n'-Marseille', *Rock & Folk*. 280, décembre 1990, pp60–5 and D. Dufresne, *Yo! Révolution rap*. Paris, Ramsay, 1991, pp149–52. The group has also published what amounts to a manifesto outlining their stances: D. Deroin, F. Guilledoux, S. Muntaner and G. Rof, *IAM, le livre*, Toulon, Plein Sud, 1996.

18. G. Lapassade and P. Rousselot, *Le Rap ou la fureur de dire*, Paris, Loris Talmart, 1990.

in which he set out to draw the links between hip-hop and other orally-based popular cultures to emerge from Africa and the black populations in America. In the process, he provoked a strong reaction from certain leaders of the Parisian hip-hop movement, not least from members of the French chapter of the Zulu Nation, who accused him of hijacking a culture he was unqualified to understand.[19] It was not only academics and sociologists who were viewed with suspicion by those who had kept the faith with hip-hop in the 'wilderness' years of the mid- to late-1980s. The second emergence of French rap in the early-1990s undoubtedly owed much to strategic advocacy within the key media outlets of television, publishing and the record industry by sympathetic individuals who were not necessarily practitioners within the culture. Figures such as Olivier Cachin, an English graduate who compered a rap music programme on the M6 channel, and subsequently founded a magazine devoted to the coverage of *les musiques nouvelles* (new music – *L'Affiche*) and wrote a history of rap for the Découvertes-Gallimard series,[20] were sometimes criticised for profiting from and even exploiting a scene which they had not invented. One of the early pioneers on the Parisian rap scene, and certainly one of France's first female rappers, Saliha, expressed this antagonism very clearly when interviewed in 1993:

> La rage que j'ai en moi et tout ce que je fais par rapport au rap, c'est impossible qu'un mec comme Cachin par exemple ait la même. Il a appris le rap dans les livres, moi je l'ai appris dans la rue. On ne devrait pas impliquer le rap à l'Université, parce que ça vient de la rue donc ça doit rester dans la rue. (The anger that I feel inside and all that I do in relation to rap, it's just impossible that a guy like Cachin can have the same thing. He learnt about rap from books, I learnt about it on the street. Rap should not get tangled up with Academia, because it comes from the street, and it should stay on the street).[21]

This attitude was far from being an isolated one. Indeed, hip-hop practitioners in France have always had a rather ambivalent attitude to institutionalisation, being glad on the one hand of the

19. For Lapassade's account of this altercation, see his 'Le Hip-Hop, "la Nation Zulu", les bandes "zoulous" et l'insertion des jeunes noirs de la deuxième génération' in Centre de Formation et d' Etudes de la Protection Judiciaire de la Jeunesse (CFREPJJ), *L'Actualité des bandes*, Vaucresson, CFRES, 1991, p.45.

20. O. Cachin, *L'Offensive rap*, Paris, Gallimard, 1996.

21. Desse and SBG (interviews). In *Freestyle*. Eds F. Massot and F. Millet, Paris, Massot & Millet, 1993, pp146–7.

recognition that it implies, but wary of recuperation. The street as theatre acts as a guard against this possibility.

The street is a theatre

While recent developments have seen the cultures of hip-hop transported to the stage, the art gallery and the museum in France, it is the street that remains the preferred theatre of expression. As the original site of impromptu gatherings, where groups of dancers or rappers would compete directly with each other for the plaudits of the audience, this theatre is also all about proving your mettle. Much of the rapper's discourse is devoted to a presentation of his or her credentials, whether that be the authenticity of one's origins, the length of time spent in mastering the power of the spoken word, or simply the sheer singularity of one's verbal prowess. Much of this discourse relies on aggressive hyperbole, an aggression no doubt enhanced by the possibility that someone in the audience may be about to emerge as more skilful.

However, the satisfaction to be gained from success in such competition is only short lived, and lasts only until the next performance. If the hip-hop practitioner is seeking a greater permanence, then the street must also allow a more indelible mark to be made. In this respect, the blank walls of metro station, subway or railway carriage have provided the perfect canvas for the tagger. Here the theatre becomes gallery. Far from marking a territory or staking a claim, the tag is much more about leaving traces, marking out the individual's itinerary across a landscape on which it is otherwise difficult to make one's mark.[22] Interviews with taggers reveal a certain pride in the ground covered in such wanderings. They proudly proclaim their hard-won knowledge of the terrain, of every twist and turn of a metro tunnel, of the shortcuts and back-ways between their various destinations, and of course of the escape routes necessary to avoid the attention of either police or agents of the RATP.[23] The high experienced in such nocturnal peregrinations is often compared to that obtained by drug-use, an association no doubt enhanced by the chemicals present in marker pen and aerosol can. In this respect the street is about freedom: freedom to move, freedom to create, freedom to express, freedom

22. A. Vulbeau, *Du Tag au tag*, Paris, Desclée de Brouwer, 1992, p.105.
23. H. Bazin, *La Culture hip-hop*, Paris, Desclée de Brouwer, 1995, pp195–7.

to compete on equal terms. It becomes the privileged arena for the expression of a creative aspiration that is central to all the practices associated with hip-hop.

The street is an alibi

There are those of course who have little time for such an interpretation of what could also be seen as gratuitous vandalism and soiling of the environment. Indeed, this has been a charge consistently levelled at the tagger or graffiti artist. Similarly, the aggressive self-promotion inherent to the rap idiom has been much criticised for producing a kind of reductive parody of the social relationships between the marginalised young and the system. It is in response to such criticisms that the street can take on a different meaning, perhaps a rather disingenuous one: that of alibi. This is perhaps best illustrated with reference to the so-called NTM affair of 1995. At an anti-racist concert at La Seyne-sur-Mer in June 1995, organised in protest at the National Front's gaining control of the nearby town hall at Toulon, the lead singer of the group NTM, Joey Starr, launched into an aggressive tirade against the police, pointing out those present in the concert hall, denouncing them as the true racist enemy, and calling for active self-defence in the housing projects and *banlieues* against police incursions. It was for these words that the Regional Police Federation later that year sued the group in the local courts. In November, they were condemned, banned from performing for a year, heavily fined and awarded a suspended prison sentence. This action of the local courts inevitably provoked a strong reaction from politicians, intellectuals and civic groups, some supportive of the judge, others condemning what was seen as an attack on the freedom of expression. What is interesting about the subsequent furore, and in particular about the defence of freedom of expression argument employed by politicians and intellectuals on the left in their condemnation of the judgement, is that this was not the line of defence employed by the group themselves. In many ways, the group seemed to acknowledge the excessive violence of Joey Starr's outburst, but claimed not a defence of freedom of expression, but rather a defence of circumstance.[24] They justified

24. For example M.-F. Etchegoin, ' "On est ce qui se passe": un entretien exclusif avec les chanteurs de NTM' in *Le Nouvel Observateur*, 1672, 21 novembre 1996, pp44–5.

their attitude on the grounds that this was what the street had made them: they were doing no more than faithfully reflecting and reporting the reality of that situation. Their crime, if crime it was, was to act as communicators of widespread feelings and attitudes shared on the ground. They were acting as '*les haut-parleurs de la banlieue* (the suburbs' loudspeakers)'. The severity of their language did no more than reflect the severity of the environment which shaped it. To an extent, this view is supported by ethnographic studies of language use amongst young populations of the *banlieue*. In particular, David Lepoutre[25] has shown the importance of the *joute verbale* (word game), a ritualised exchange of hyperbolic insults, usually targeted at the addressee's mother. In its transfer to the stage, Joey Starr's use of such ritualised hyperbolic language doubtless lost something in translation. It goes some way to explaining the three-way dialogue of the deaf that constituted the NTM affair, with representatives of left and right, and the group themselves, all talking at cross-purposes. It confirms the existence of what Jean-Pierre Goudaillier has defined in his analysis of suburban slang in general and *verlan* (backslang) in particular, as a linguistic *fracture sociale* (social division).[26] This gap at the very least poses a particular challenge for those educators charged by the state with the communication of the national memory to future generations, some of whom now appear to speak a different language all together. It perhaps even raises the question of what the linguistic base of that memory should be.

Conclusion: the street is a guarantor of authenticity

Whatever the wider consequences of the social discontinuities that are revealed by the development of linguistic subcultures, with regard to hip-hop practitioners in France, NTM's defence of their extreme verbal violence, reveals the fundamental role played by the street in the articulation of hip-hop's values. Underpinning NTM's self-justification, indeed underpinning all the meanings of 'the street' developed by French hip-hop, is the fundamental notion that the street acts as the ultimate guarantee of authenticity, the mark of both personal and collective integrity. Within French

25. D. Lepoutre, *Cœur de banlieue. Codes, rites et langages*, Paris, Editions Odile Jacob, 1997.
26. See J.-P. Goudailler, *Comment tu tchatches. Dictionnaire du français contemporain des cités*, Paris, Maisonneuve et Larose, 1997.

hip-hop then, the successful negotiation of the street as jungle is regarded as testimony to the genuine skill of the individual. Similarly, the experience and wisdom gained from the street as education are seen as providing the vital means for negotiating a world coming adrift from its moorings (*la galère*). Progress made by the collective or individual in this respect is measured only in terms of the recognition and respect accorded by fellow practitioners: this status must be repeatedly tested in the competition of the street as theatre, where only continued success can testify to genuine mastery of the terrain. The pursuit of this success frequently brings the hip-hop practitioner into confrontation with authorities, groups or individuals who seek to occupy the same terrain on different terms and with different purposes. In such cases, the street acts as an alibi for excess, violence or conflict. In all of these different contexts and confrontations, the ultimate role of the street for the hip-hop practitioner is to provide a reference point or yardstick, to sort out the false from the real, the opportunist from the committed, the mediocre from the talented. Most importantly, street values are used to assess the veracity of the group or individual's discourse, its faithfulness to the realities it describes. In the shifting and transitory urban landscape, dominated by the promotional (and therefore suspect) discourses of advertising and media, or by the *langue de bois* (newspeak) of institutions and politicians, it is at this point that French hip-hop makes its contribution to contemporary urban culture. In its articulation of street values, it responds dynamically to the necessarily shifting and in-between nature of the contemporary urban context. However, it also seeks to contain the uncertainties of such constant shifting. In promoting street values, hip-hop culture in France is also striving to construct a more solid set of markers, is aiming to leave more indelible traces on the permanently mutating cityscape. Ultimately, it is struggling to reinstate the permanence of social and personal memory in the most transitional and impermanent of contemporary contexts.

BIBLIOGRAPHY

General Bibliography

Anderson, B., *Imagined Communities*, 2nd edn, Verso, London, 1991.

Andrieux, J.-Y., *Patrimoine et histoire*, Paris, Belin, 1997.

Association française des musées d'agriculture, *Le guide du patrimoine rural*, La Manufacture, 1988.

Benhamou, F., *L'économie de la culture*, Paris, La Découverte, 1997.

Bianchini, F. and Parkinson, M., eds, *Cultural Policy and Urban Regeneration. The West European Experience*, Manchester, Manchester University Press, 1993.

Borne, D., *Histoire de la société française depuis 1945*, Paris, Armand Colin, 3rd ed., 1993.

Braudel, F., *L'identité de la France*, Paris, Fayard, 1986.

Cardona, J.and Lacroix, C., *Statistiques de la culture, chiffres clés 1998*, La Documentation française, 1999.

Choay, F., *L'allégorie du patrimoine*, Paris, Le Seuil, 1992.

Connerton, P., *How societies remember the past?* Cambridge, Cambridge University Press, 1989.

Corbin, A., *Le territoire du vide. L'Occident ou le désir de rivage, 1750–1840*, Paris, Aubier, 1988.

Debray, R., *L'abus monumental*, ed., Actes des entretiens du patrimoine, Paris, Fayard, 1999.

Donnat, O., *Les Français face à la culture: de l'exclusion à l'éclectisme*, Paris, la Découverte, 1994.

Donnat, O., *Les pratiques culturelles des français, enquête de 1997*, Paris, La Documentation française, 1998.

Donzelot, J. and Estebe, P., *L'Etat animateur*, Paris, Editions Esprit, 1995.

Ecole nationale du patrimoine, *Patrimoine culturel, patrimoine naturel*, Colloque 12, 13 December 1994, La Documentation française, 1995.

Fumaroli, M., *L'Etat culturel. Essai sur une religion moderne*, Paris, Editions de Fallois, 1991.

Furet, F., ed., *Patrimoine, Temps, Espace. Patrimoine en place, patrimoine déplacé*, Paris, Fayard,1997.

Gathercole, P. and Lowenthal, D., eds, *The Politics of the past*, London, Macmillan, 1990.

Gildea, R., *The Past in French History*, Yale, Yale University Press, 1994.

Grange, D-J.and Poulot, D., eds, *L'Esprit des Lieux. Le patrimoine et la cité*, Grenoble, Presses Universitaires de Grenoble, 1997.

Guillaume, M., *La politique du patrimoine*, Paris, Plon, 1980.

Halbwachs, M., *Les cadres sociaux de la mémoire*, Paris, Albin Michel, 1994.

Hazeerasingh, S., *Political Traditions in Modern France*, Oxford, Oxford University Press, 1994.

Jenkins, B., *Nationalism in France: Class and Nation since 1789*, London, Routledge, 1990.

Jeudy, H.-P., *Mémoires du social*, Paris, Presses Universitaires de France, 1986.

Jeudy, H.-P., ed., *Patrimoines en folie*, Paris, Ethnologie de la France, Cahier 5, Maison des Sciences de l'Homme, 1988.

Koselleck, R., *Futures past: on the semantics of historical time*, trans. Keith Tribe, Cambridge, Massachussets, Harvard University Press, 1985.

Le Goff, J., ed., *Patrimoine et passions identitaires*, Actes des Entretiens du Patrimoine, Paris, Fayard, 1998.

Leniaud, J. M., *L'utopie française. Essai sur le patrimoine*, Paris, Mengès, 1982.

Looseley, D., *The Politics of Fun. Cultural Policy and Debate in Contemporary France*, Oxford, Berg, 1995.

Lowenthal, D., *The Heritage crusade and the spoils of history*, Cambridge, Cambridge University Press, 1998.

McGuigan, J., *Culture and the Public Sphere*, London, Routledge, 1996.

'Mémoires comparées' in *Le Débat*, Paris, 78, 1994.

Métral, J., ed., *Les aléas du lien social. Constructions identitaires et culturelles dans la ville*, Paris, Ministère de la culture et de la communication, 1997.

Moulinier, P., *Politique culturelle et décentralisation*, Paris, Editions du CNFPT, 1995.

Nora, P., ed., *Les Lieux de mémoire*, 7 vols, Paris, Gallimard, 1984–93.

Nora, P., 'On ne peut faire de la France le musée de la France', interview, *Le Monde*, 29 November 1994, p.2.

Nora, P., ed., *Science et conscience du patrimoine*, Paris, Fayard,1997.

Patrimoine et société contemporaine, actes du colloque de la Direction du Patrimoine, Paris, Cité des sciences et de l'industrie, October 1987, Paris.

Poirrier, P., *Histoire des politiques culturelles de la France contemporaine*, Paris, Bibliest, 1996.

Poirrier, P., *Société et culture en France depuis 1945*, Paris, Seuil, 1997.

Poirrier, P., 'L'histoire des politiques culturelles des villes', *Vingtième Siècle*, 53, 1997.

Poulot, D., 'Le sens du patrimoine : hier et aujourd'hui', in *Mondes de l'art, annales, économies, sociétés, civilisations*, Paris, Vol. 48, 6, 1993.

Poulot, D., *Le patrimoine et la nation*, Paris, Gallimard, 1996.

Poulot, D., ed., *Patrimoine et Modernité*, Paris, L'Harmattan, 1998.

Renard, J., *L'élan culturel. La France en mouvement*, Paris, Presses Universitaires de France, 1987.

Rioux, J.-P. and Sirinelli J.-F., *Histoire culturelle de la France. Le temps des masses, le vingtième siècle*, Paris, Seuil, 1998.

Samuel, R., *Theatres of Memory. Volume 1: Past and Present in Contemporary Culture*, London, Verso, 1994.

Shaw, C. and Chase, M., eds, *The imagined past: history and nostalgia*, Manchester, Manchester University Press, 1989.

Silverman, M., *Deconstructing the Nation: Immigration, Racism and Citizenship in Modern France*, London, Routledge, 1992.

Sire, M.-A ., *La France du Patrimoine. Les choix de la mémoire*, Paris, Gallimard-CNMHS, 1996.

Urry, J., *Consuming places*, London, Routledge, 1995.

Wright, S., 'The politicisation of culture', *Anthropology Today*, vol. 14, February 1998.

Memories of War

Barcellini, S., 'Mémoire et mémoires de Verdun 1916–1996', in *Guerres mondiales et conflits contemporains*, n° 182, 1996.

Boursier, J.-Y., 'Les enjeux politiques des musées de la Résistance: multiplicité des lieux', in Grange, D. and Poulot, D. ed., *L'esprit des lieux, le patrimoine et la cité. Actes du colloque d'Annecy de septembre 1995*, Grenoble, Presses Universitaires de Grenoble, 1997.

Burke, P., 'History and social memory', in Butler, T., ed., *Memory, history, culture, and mind*, Oxford, Blackwell, 1989.

Compère-Morel, T. and Joly, M.-H., eds, *Des musées d'histoire pour l'avenir*, Paris, Editions Noêsis, 1998.

Darian-Smith, K. and Hamilton, P., eds, *Memory and history in twentieth-century Australia*, Melbourne, Melbourne University Press, 1994.

Duclos, J.-C., 'Les résistants, les historiens et le muséographe: histoire d'une transaction et de ses enseignements', in Boursier, J.-Y., ed., *Résistants et Résistance. Actes du colloque de Saint-Denis de janvier 1996*, Paris, 1997.

François, E., *Les musées de la Seconde Guerre mondiale. Rapport au ministère de la Culture, Direction des Musées de France*, 1996 (unpublished).

Gervereau, L., ed., *Musées d'histoire et histoire dans les musées*, Actes du séminaire du 17 juin 1992. Association Internationale des Musées d'Histoire/Ministère de l'Education nationale et de la culture, Paris, 1992 (French-English edition).

Gillis, J. R., ed., *Commemorations: the politics of national identity*, Princeton, Princeton University Press, 1994.

Huyssen, A., 'Monument and memory in a postmodern age', *Yale Journal of Criticism*, 6, 1993.

Joly, M.-H., 'Des musées de la Résistance', in Boursier, J.-Y., ed. *Résistants et Résistance. Actes du colloque de Saint-Denis de janvier 1996*, Paris, 1997.

Karp, I. and Lavine, S. D., *Exhibiting cultures: the poetics and politics of museum display*, Washington, Smithsonian Institution, 1991.

Marcot, F., 'Des étoiles et des croix', in *Mélanges en l'honneur du Professeur Guy Pedroncini*, Paris, Economica, 1995.

Marcot, F., 'Musées d'histoire: enjeu de mémoire, enjeu d'histoire, enjeu social', in *Des musées d'histoire pour l'avenir, Colloque de Péronne de novembre 1996*, Paris, Noêsis, 1998.

Martin, M., *Etude de l'évolution des musées de la Résistance et déportation en région Rhône-Alpes*, unpublished Master's thesis under the supervision of Max Sanier, Lyon II, 1993.

Maubant, C., 'Aider à reconstruire l'enfant citoyen: un nouvel enjeu pour les musées d'histoire' in *Des musées d'histoire pour l'avenir, Colloque de Péronne de novembre 1996*, Paris, Noêsis, 1998.

Ministère de l'Enseignement Supérieur, *Musées et Recherche*. Actes de colloque, novembre–décembre 1993, Dijon, OCIM, 1995.

Musée d'archéologie et d'histoire de Montréal, *La société et le musée, l'une change, l'autre aussi*, Montreal, Pointe-à-Callière, 1997.

Schaer, R., *L' invention des musées*, Paris, Gallimard/RMN, 1993.

Winter, J., *Sites of memory, sites of mourning*, Cambridge, Cambridge University Press, 1995.

Maritime Heritage

Cabantous, A., *Les citoyens du large. Les identités maritimes en France XVII-XIXème siècle*, Paris, Aubier, 1995.

Cabantous, A., *Le ciel dans la mer*, Paris, Fayard, 1995.

Cadoret, B., Duviard, D., Guillet and J., Kérisit, H. *Ar Vag. Voiles au travail en Bretagne Atlantique*, vols 1 & 2, Grenoble, Editions des 4 seigneurs, 2 vol., 1978–1979, vol. 3, Douarnenez, Editions Estran, 1985.

Chappé, F., *L'épopée islandaise (1880–1914). Paimpol, la République et la mer*, Thonon-les-Bains, Editions de l'Albaron, 1990.

Couliou, J.-R., *La pêche bretonne. Les ports de Bretagne-Sud face à leur avenir*, Rennes, Presses Universitaires de Rennes, 1997.

Cousquer, J.-Y. and Picard, J., *Brittany*. Bristol, Bristol Classical Press, 1996.

Duviard, D., *Groix, l'île des thoniers. Chronique maritime d'une île bretonne*, Grenoble, Editions des 4 seigneurs, 1978.

Estuaire 92, le patrimoine maritime et fluvial, Paris–Nantes, Ministère de la Culture, Direction du Patrimoine, 1993.

Kerlévéo, J., *Paimpol au temps de l'Islande*, Paris, Slatkine, 1980.

'Le port de commerce de Port-Rhu, 1850–1970' in *Mémoire de la ville, Le Pays de Douarnenez de la fin du Moyen-Age à nos jours*, no 21, Centre de recherche bretonne et celtique (CRBC), Brest.

Lespagnol, A., *Messieurs de St Malo*, Rennes, Presses Universitaires de Rennes, 1997.

Neill, P. and Ehrenwald, B., eds, *Great Maritime Museums of the World*, New-York, Balsam Press Inc. & Harry N. Abrams Inc., 1991.

Péron, F., 'Pour une définition sociale et culturelle du patrimoine maritime' in *Le Patrimoine maritime et fluvial, Estuaires 92*, Paris – Nantes, Ministère de la Culture, Direction du Patrimoine, 1993.

Péron, F., 'Fonctions sociales et dimensions subjectives du littoral' in "Littoraux en perspectives", *Etudes Rurales*, Ecole des Hautes Etudes en Sciences Sociales, No 133–134, Paris, 1995.

Péron, F., *La maritimité aujourd'hui*. Conference organised with Jean Rieucau. 'Géographie et Cultures' collection, L'Harmattan, 1996.

Péron, F., *Ouessant, l'île sentinelle. Vie et tradition d'une île bretonne*, Douarnenez, Le Chasse-Marée/Ar Men, 1997.

Picard, J., 'Gallic revival', *Maritime Heritage*, Volume 2.2, April 1998.

Roux, M., *L'imaginaire marin des Français. Mythe et géographie de la mer*, Paris, L'Harmattan, 1997.

Culinary Heritage

Agriturist, *I magnifici cento sconosciuti*, Milano, Angeli, 1991.

Amirou, R., *Imaginaire touristique et sociabilités du voyage*, Paris, Presses Universitaires de France, 1995.

Barjolle, D. and Bussy, C., 'PDO Products impact of agricultural and rural development', in *The Regional dimension in agricultural economics and policies*, European Association of Agricultural Economists, proceedings of the 40th seminar, 1996.

Bérard, L., 'La reconnaissance juridique des productions "de terroir": comment traiter le culturel?' in *La qualité dans l'agro-alimentaire. Emergence d'un champ de recherches*, AIP Construction sociale de la qualité. Paris, INRA, 1996.

Bérard, L., Froc, J., Hyman, P. and Marchenay, P., *Inventaire des produits régionaux de la France*, Paris, Albin Michel, (already published: Nord-Pas-de-Calais, 1992; Ile-de-France, 1993; Bourgogne, 1993; Franche-Comté, 1993; Pays de la Loire, 1993; Poitou-Charentes, 1994; Bretagne, 1994; Rhône-Alpes, 1995, Provence-Alpes-Côte d'Azur, Midi-Pyrénées, Corse, 1996).

Bérard, L. and Marchenay, P., 'Fruits locaux ou anciens: un fait social d'actualité' in Meiller, D. and Vannier, P., eds., *Le grand livre des fruits et légumes. Histoire, culture et usage*, Besançon, La Manufacture, 1991.

Bérard, L. and Marchenay, P., 'Lieux, temps et preuves: la construction sociale des produits de terroir', *Terrain*, 24, 1995.

Bérard, L. and Marchenay, P., 'Patrimoine et modernité: les produits de terroir sous les feux de la rampe', *Journal des anthropologues*, 74, 1998.

Bérard, L. and Marchenay, P., 'Terroirs, produits et enracinement' in *Pour une anthropologie impliquée. Argumentations face aux extrémismes*, Association Rhône-Alpes d'anthropologie. Special Number, 43, 1998.

Bérard, L. and Marchenay, P., eds, *Les produits de terroir en Europe du Sud: caractérisation ethnologique, sensorielle et socio-économique de leur typicité; stratégies de valorisation*, Final Report, Brussels, European Commission, Direction générale de l'Agriculture.

Bessière, J., 'Local development and heritage: traditional food and cuisine as tourist attractions in rural areas', *European Society for Rural Sociology*, vol 38, no 1, 1998.

Boidron, V., Guenin, A.-M. and Laligant, S., 'Le cassis de Dijon: délocalisation et atomisation d'une production emblématique', in *Cassis, Oignons, Cerises, Cornichons: quatre produits des terroirs bourguignons*, Ecomusée de la Bresse Bourguignonne, Pierre-de-Bresse, 1992.

Bonnain, R. and Chevallier, D., *Une politique pour le patrimoine culturel rural*, Report presented to the Minister of Culture, Paris, 1994.

Bucaille, R. and Levi-Strauss, L., *L'architecture rurale française: la Bourgogne*, Paris, Editions Berger-Levrault, 1980.

Chiva, I., 'Le patrimoine ethnologique: l'exemple de la France', *Encyclopaedia Universalis*, Paris, Symposium, 1990.

Csergo, J., 'L'émergence des cuisines régionales', *Histoire de l'alimentation*, eds J-L. Flandrin and M. Montanari, Paris, Fayard, 1996.

Csergo, J., 'La construction de la spécialité gastronomique comme objet patrimonial en France, fin XVIIIe-XX siecle', *L'esprit des lieux: le patrimoine et la cité*, in Grange, D. J. and Poulot, D., eds, Grenoble, Presses Universitaires de Grenoble, 1997.

Delfosse, C., *Recherche sur l'antérité, la notoriété et le caractère traditionnel du fromage de chèvre du Charolais*, Etude, Segesa, Paris, 1994.

Delfosse, C. and Lestablier, M.-T., *Relances fromagères, réinventer une tradition, construire une identité*, Ministère de la Culture, Paris, 1993.

Delfosse, C. and Lestablier, M.-T., *Le transport des savoirs traditionnels dans l'univers industriel*, report, Centre d'Etudes de l'Emploi, Noisy le Grand, 1994.

Demossier, M., *Le cru, la cuvée, le vigneron et le village, la transmission des pratiques et savoir-faire en côte bourguignonne*, doctoral thesis, EHESS Thesis, Paris 1995.

Demossier, M., *Hommes et Vins, une anthropologie du vignoble bourguignon*, Dijon, Editions universitaires de Dijon, 1999.

Denis, D., *Appellation d'origine et indication de provenance*, Paris, Dalloz, Coll. 'Connaissance du droit', 1995.

Faure, M., 'Un produit agricole "affiné" en objet culturel, le fromage de Beaufort dans les Alpes du Nord', *Terrain*, 33, September 1999.

Fischler, C., *L'homnivore*, Paris, Editions Odile Jacob, 1990.

Frossard-Urbano, S., *La Volaille de Bresse. L'évolution d' un savoir-faire*, Ecomusée de la Bresse Bourguignonne, Pierre de Bresse, 1992.

Guenin, A.-M., 'Aux marges de la monoculture viticole: l'évolution des associations de productions agricoles', in Demossier, M., Portet, F., eds, *Vignerons, propriétaires et négociants en Bourgogne*, Die, Editions Die, 1994.

Insor and Ministero agricoltura e foreste. *L'Italia dei formaggi Doc.* Milano, Angeli, 1992.

Laferté, G., *Le renouveau contemporain des confréries culinaires: production et usage de traditions*, rapport de thèse, EHESS, 1999.

Lizet, B., 'L'herbe violente, enquête botanique en pays Brionnais', *Etudes rurales*, vol. 129, 1993.

Masson, G. and Moscovici, P., *Programme de recherche R94/25 Aliment demain*, Ministère de l'agriculture et de la recherche, Consommateur et Marché, 1993.

Ministère de la culture et de la communication, *L'ethnologie de la France, besoins et projet*, Paris, 1979.

Ministère de la culture et de la communication, *Le patrimoine: une politique 1974–1981*, Paris, 1981.

Muxel, A., *Individu et mémoire famililiale*, Paris, Nathan, 1996.

Pellegrini, P., 'La Volaille de Bresse, un terroir et des hommes', Musée des pays de l'Ain, Bourg-en-Bresse, 1992.

Pitte, J.-R., *Gastronomie française. Histoire et géographie d'une passion*, Paris, Fayard, 1991.

Portet, F., 'Les communautés viti-vinicoles', in Demossier, M., Portet, F., eds, *Vignerons, propriétaires et négociants en Bourgogne*, Die, Editions Die, 1994.

Poulain, J.-P., 'Goût du terroir et tourisme vert à l'heure de l'Europe', *Ethnologie française*, 26 (1), 1997.

Rautenberg, M., *Evaluation et mise en valeur des patrimoines de l'agriculture dans les projets de développement: quels patrimoines pour quel développement? A propos du patrimoine agri-culturel rhônalpin*. Actes des rencontres régionales des 13–14 novembre 1997, Ardèche, Le Pradel, 1997.

Verdier, Y., *Façons de dire, façons de faire. La laveuse, la couturière, la cuisinière*, Gallimard, Paris, 1979.

Vialles, N., 'De l'animal à la viande', in *Du sauvage, du vivant et du cru, cahiers du stage ethnologie de l'alimentation*, Dijon, Editions universitaires de Dijon, 1989.

Urban Cultures and New Expressions

Bachmann, C., *Violences urbaines: ascension et déclin des classes moyennes à travers 50 ans de politiques de la ville*, Paris, Fayard, 1996.

Barreyre, J.-Y. and Vulbeau, A., eds, *La jeunesse et la rue*, Paris, Desclée de Brouwer, 1994.

Baudelot, C. and Mauger, G., eds, *Jeunesses populaires: les générations de la crise*, Paris, L'Harmattan, 1994.

Bazin, H., *La culture hip-hop*, Paris, Desclée de Brouwer, 1995.

Bocquet, J.-L. and Pierre-Adolphe, P., *Rap ta France*, Boulogne, La Sirène, 1996.

Bonduelle, B., *Nord et Pas-de-Calais. L'impossible tête-à-tête*, Lille, La Voix du Nord, 1998

Boucher, M., *Rap, expression des lascars: signification et enjeux dans la société française*, Paris, L'Harmattan, 1999.

Boyer, R. and Coridian, C., eds, *Jeunesses d' en France*, Condé-sur-Noireau, Panoramiques-Corlet, 1994.

Cachin, O., *L' offensive rap*, Paris, Gallimard, 1996.

Cannon, S., 'Paname City Rapping: B-boys in the banlieues and beyond' in Hargreaves, A. G. and McKinney, M., eds, *Post-Colonial Cultures in France*, London and New York, Routledge, 1997.

Castells, M., *The Rise of the Network Society*, Vol. I: The Information Age: Economy, Society and Culture, Oxford, Blackwell, 1996

Cathus, O., 'La vibration de la rue' in Barreyre, J.-Y. and Vulbeau A., eds, *La jeunesse et la rue*, Paris, Desclée de Brouwer, 1994.

Chamboredon, J.-C., 'Adolescence et post-adolescence: la "juvénisation". Remarques sur les transformations récentes des limites de la définition sociale de la jeunesse' in Alléon, A.-M., Morvan, O. and Lebovici S., eds, *Adolescence terminée, adolescence interminable*, Paris, Presses Universitaires de France, 1985.

Chenoune, F. and Poirier, J.-F., 'Rap et tag: l'esthétique des banlieues sur la place publique' in Encyclopaedia Universalis, *Universalia 1993*, Paris, Encyclopaedia Universalis, 1993.

Chevalier, L., *Laboring classes and dangerous classes in Paris in the first half of the nineteenth century*, Princeton, New Jersey, Princeton University Press, 1981 (2nd edition).

Corbel, M., *Vénissieux la rebelle*, Paris, Cercles d'Art, 1998

Damette, F., *La France en villes*, Paris, La Documentation Française, 1994.

Delarue, J.-M., *Banlieues en difficulté: La relégation*, Paris, Styros, 1991.

Deroin, D., Guilledoux, F., Muntaner, S. and Rof, G., *IAM, le livre*, Toulon, Plein Sud, 1996.

Dubet, F., *La galère: les jeunes en survie'*, Paris, Le Seuil, 1987.

Dubet, F., 'Jeunesses et marginalités', *Regards sur l'actualité*, 172, July 1991.

Dubet, F. and Lapeyronnies, D., *Quartiers d'exil*, Paris, Le Seuil, 1992.

Dubois, V., 'Action culturelle/action sociale: les limites d'une frontière' in *Revue Française des Affaires Sociales*, no.2 (48th year) April-June 1994.

Dufresne, D., *Yo! Révolution rap*, Paris, Ramsay, 1991.

Etchegoin, M.-F., '"On est ce qui se passe": un entretien exclusif avec les chanteurs de NTM', *Le Nouvel Observateur*, 1672, 21 November 1996.

Fox-Przeworski, J., Goddard, J. and de Long, M., *Urban regeneration in a changing economy: an international prerspective*, Oxford, Clarendon Press, 1991.

Galland, O., 'Un nouvel âge de la vie', *Devenir adulte, Revue française de sociologie*, XXXI, 4, October-December 1990.

Galland, O., *Sociologie de la jeunesse: l'entrée dans la vie*, Paris, Armand Colin, 1991.

Galland, O., 'La jeunesse en France, un nouvel âge de la vie' in Cavalli, A. and Galland, O., eds, *L'allongement de la jeunesse*, Poitiers, Actes Sud, 1993.

Gerin, A. *Minguettes. Challenge pour une ville*, Paris, Messidor/Editions Sociales, 1988.

Goudaillier, J.-P., *Comment tu tchatches. Dictionnaire du français contemporain des cités*, Paris, Maisonneuve et Larose, 1997.

INSEE, *Données Sociales*, Paris, INSEE, 1999.

Jazouli, A., *Une saison en banlieue–Courants et perspectives dans les quartiers populaires*, Paris, Editions Plon, 1995.

Lapassade, G., 'Le Hip-Hop, "la Nation Zulu", les bandes "zoulous" et l'insertion des jeunes noirs de la deuxième génération' in Centre de Formation et d' Etudes de la Protection Judiciaire de la Jeunesse (CFREPJJ), *L'Actualité des bandes*, Vaucresson, CFRES, 1991.

Lapassade, G. and Rousselot, P., *Le Rap ou la fureur de dire*, Paris, Editions Loris Talmart, 1990.

Lephay-Merlin, C. 'Les dépenses culturelles des communes en 1993', in Pumain, D. and Godard, F., *Données Urbaines*, Paris, Economica, 1996.

Lepoutre, D., *Cœur de banlieue. Codes, rites et langages*, Paris, Editions Odile Jacob, 1997.

Menanteau, J., *Les banlieues*, Paris, Le Monde Editions/Marabout, 1994.

Ménard, F., 'L'histoire du logement à travers la revue Informations Sociales de 45 à 90', *Informations Sociales*, 53, 1996.

Reid, P.J., 'Calais, the Red City: its position in economic development in Nord Pas-de-Calais', *Modern and Contemporary France* NS1/4, 1993.

Rizzardo, R., 'Action culturelle et réseau de villes en Rhône-Alpes', *Cadmos*, 56, 1991.

Roulleau-Berger, L., 'Des microcultures et des jeunesses au centre et à la périphérie de l'espace urbain', in *La culture des jeunes de banlieues*, *Document de l'INJ*, 4, October 1989.

Roulleau-Berger, L., *La ville intervalle: jeunes entre centre et banlieue*, Paris, Méridiens-Klincksieck, 1991.

Roulleau-Berger, L., 'Cultures et danses urbaines', *Danse ville danse*, Vénissieux, Préfecture de la Région Rhône-Alpes, Editions Paroles d'Aube, 1992.

Sabot, E., 'Traitement d'espaces, traitement d'image; de la difficulté d'être et d'avoir été: le cas de Saint-Étienne', *Modern and Contemporary France*, NS5/4, 1997.

Saez, G., 'Villes et culture: un gouvernement par la coopération', *Pouvoirs*, 73, 1995.

Segalen, M., *Nanterriens. Les familles dans la ville: une ethnologie de l'identité*, Toulouse, Presses Universitaires du Mirail, 1990.

Sueur, J.-P., *Demain, la ville. Rapport présenté au ministre de l'emploi et de la solidarité*, Vol.I, Paris, La Documentation Française, 1998.

Vulbeau, A., *Du tag au tag*, Paris, Desclée de Brouwer, 1992.

Warne, C., 'Articulating identity from the margins: le Mouv' and the rise of hip-hop and ragga in France' in Perry, S. and Cross, M., eds, *Voices of France: social, political and cultural identity*. London, Cassell, 1997.

NOTES ON CONTRIBUTORS

Laurence Bérard and **Philippe Marchenay** are the directors of the Research Centre *Ressources des terroirs*, Apsonat, *Centre National de la Recherche Scientifique* (CNRS). They are working on anthropological aspects of local agricultural products. They have published extensively on the savoir-faire, practices, conservation, use and diffusion of these resources with an emphasis on their geographical protection at national and European level.

Sarah Blowen is Lecturer in French Studies at the University of the West of England, Bristol. Her Ph.D studies museum policy and its implementation in contemporary France. She has written on various aspects of museum and cultural policy in France and Britain, and is active in the development of collaborative projects between cultural institutions in the two countries.

François Chappé is a Senior Lecturer in Contemporary History at Université de Bretagne Sud, Lorient (UBS). His doctoral thesis on 'Paimpol, the Republic and the Sea–1880–1914' was about cod fishing in Iceland. He was a member of the ministerial team of J. Y. Le Drian and C. Josselin (when the latter was Secretary of State for maritime affairs), with special responsibility for heritage.

Marion Demossier is a Lecturer in French and European Studies at the University of Bath. She is the author of *Hommes et vins, une anthropologie du vignoble bourguignon* (Editions Universitaires de Dijon, 1999) and is currently working on the culture of wine and its consumption in France. She has written several articles on French culture, politics and society.

Brian Jenkins is Professor of French Area Studies at the University of Portsmouth. He has published widely on French history and politics, and on the theory and history of nationalism. He is editor of the *Journal of European Area Studies*.

Marie-Hélène Joly is Senior Curator at the *Inspection Générale des Musées*, part of the Museums Directorate of the French Ministry of Culture. Between 1993 and 1997, she was responsible for overseeing the opening and management of history museums. Author of *Musées et collections d'histoire en France*, with Laurent Gervereau in 1996, she is now Assistant Head of the *Inspection Générale des Musées*.

François Ménard is a sociologist working for *FORS Recherche Sociale*, a non profit-making organisation which carries out social projects and evaluations of public policy. As project leader, he has worked on youth integration in urban centres, focusing on initiatives linked to the workplace and cultural participation. He has also worked on the evolution of the voluntary sector in France in response to changing lifestyles and public policy priorities.

Susan Milner is Reader in European Studies at the University of Bath. She has been involved in comparative research on the impact of socio-economic change on local political cultures in France and Italy, and is currently investigating the relationship between local voluntary associations and municipal authorities in the field of cultural policy in Lille.

Françoise Péron is Professor of Geography at Université de Bretagne Occidentale, Brest (UBO). She is a member of the CNRS reseach unit *Géolittomer* at the Institut Universitaire Européen de la Mer (Brest). She is the author of various works on the culture of island-dwelling communities on the French West coast.

Jeanine Picard is a Senior Lecturer at the University of the West of England, Bristol. She has produced several articles concerning a range of issues related to Brittany and is the co-author of *Brittany*, published in 1996. She has recently written a monograph on the Breton author Pierre-Jakes Hélias.

François Portet has been an advisor for ethnology at the *Direction Régionale aux affaires culturelles*, DRAC (Regional Management of

Cultural Affairs) in Burgundy since 1985 where he has supervised a number of studies on food and local productions. He is currently working on a research project with Bernadette Lizet on the revival of the carthorse in France. He has published extensively on rural France, wine communities and the culture of the motorbike in France.

Siân Reynolds is Professor of French at the University of Stirling. She works on French history of the nineteenth and twentieth centuries, and is the author of *France between the wars: gender and politics* (Routledge, 1996)

Chris Warne is a Lecturer in French at the University of Sussex. Forthcoming publications include a book on youth and society in post-war France, and an edited volume on the relationship between stardom and modernisation of French culture during the 1950s and 1960s.

Jay Winter is Reader in Modern History in the University of Cambridge and Fellow of Pembroke College, Cambridge. He is the author of many books on the First World War, including *Sites of memory, sites of mourning: the place of the Great War in European cultural history* (1995). He is a founder and a director of the *Historial de la grande guerre*, Péronne, Somme, the first European museum of the Great War. Winter was chief historian and co-producer of the award winning series 'The Great War and the shaping of the twentieth century', screened on PBS and the BBC in 1996.

INDEX

Resistance (the) 20, 26–27, 35, 68–88
  entrée en résistance 80, 83, 84
  valeurs de la résistance 43, 83
Reynaud, F. 118
Ricoeur, P. 77, 114
Rieucau, G. 133
Rigaud, Jacques 194
Rispal, Adeline 60
Roncière, J. 114
Rougeron, Gérard 58–61, 62
Roulleau-Berger, L. 229
Roux, M. 120
rural France 7, 51, 75, 98
rural life and society 7, 51, 75, 98,
  142, 147, 149, 150, 151, 176, 180,
  227
  neo-rural 148
ruralité 1

S
Saez, G. 194
sailing crafts 99, 103, 113
  boats 2, 101, 102–103, 105, 107,
  117, 123–137
Saint-Etienne 190
Samuel, R. 28
savoir-faire 146, 152, 154, 155, 156,
  160–161, 164, 181
Segalen, M. 188
Serres, M. 220
Seton-Watson, H. 109
Service Historique de la Marine 102
Sites Remarquables du Goût 142, 156
social
  capital 205
  exclusion 20, 191, 195, 207
  integration 216, 218, 219, 222, 223
  movements 20
society 136
  cohesion of 205, 206
  fragmentation of 3, 105, 149, 207
socio-culturel (le) 214
SOS Racisme 217
Spain 157, 161
street (*la rue*) 211, 218, 221, 226, 233,
  234, 235–245

T
Tavernier, Bernard 205
terroir 147, 150, 178, 181

tradition 7, 144, 147, 149, 150, 151,
  152, 158, 159, 163, 200, 236
tourism 6–7, 37, 47, 106, 119, 122, 124,
  142, 145, 148, 149, 151, 203
tourist industry 104, 123, 126–127,
  204

U
UNESCO 29, 117
urban culture 8, 207, 209–225,
  226–245
  definition of 209–210
Urban Development Fund (*Fonds
  social urbain*) 201
urban governance 198, 208
urban identity 187–208
  definition of 188
urban life and society 75, 98, 104,
  148, 150, 151, 176, 180
  neo-urban 92
  regeneration of 187
urbanisation 7, 54, 145, 150

V
vagabondage alimentaire 7
Venissieux 187, 190, 193, 216
Verdier, Y. 172–174, 184
Verdun 40, 47, 49, 57
verlan (backslang) 244
Veyne, P. 114, 115
Vichy regime 35, 49, 83–84
vie associative 19, 20
Vieville, D. 79
voluntary sector 4

W
war memorials 32, 35, 40, 41, 62
war veterans 2, 5, 33–41, 58, 68–88
  Ministry for 43–46
Wright, S. 2, 200

Y
young and youth 97, 214, 215, 216,
  217, 220, 220, 226–245
youth culture *see* culture youth